# ALASKA
*and the*
## U.S. REVENUE CUTTER SERVICE
## 1867–1915

# ALASKA
## *and the*
# U.S. REVENUE CUTTER SERVICE
## 1867–1915

Truman R. Strobridge
*and* Dennis L. Noble

Naval Institute Press / Annapolis, Maryland

Library of Congress Cataloging-in-Publication Data

Strobridge, Truman R.

Alaska and the U.S. Revenue Cutter Service, 1867–1915 / Truman R. Strobridge and Dennis L. Noble.

p.  cm.

Includes bibliographical references and index.

ISBN 1-55750-845-3 (alk. paper)

1. United States. Revenue-Cutter Service—History.  I. Noble, Dennis L.  II. Title.  III. Title: Alaska and the US Revenue Cutter Service, 1867–1915.

HJ6645.S77    1999

973.9'7'0973—dc21        98-53366

Printed in the United States of America on acid-free paper ∞

99  00  01  02  03  04  05  06    9  8  7  6  5  4  3  2

First printing

Portions of chapter 2 appeared in a different form in *Pacific Northwest Quarterly* 78, no. 3 (July 1987): 74–82. Portions of chapter 4 appeared in a different form in *Arctic: Journal of the Arctic Institute of North America* 30, no. 1 (March 1977): 2–12. Unless otherwise noted, all photographs are from the U.S. Coast Guard.

In memory of my son Lance J. Strobridge, who had a short, but full and happy, life
—Truman R. Strobridge

To Loren A. Noble
—Dennis L. Noble

# Contents

# Preface

For many decades, the U.S. Coast Guard has laid claim to being a multimission service. Public affairs offices have pointed out the many tasks that can be traced to an organization claiming five maritime predecessors: the U.S. Revenue Cutter Service, the U.S. Life-Saving Service, the U.S. Lighthouse Service, the Steamboat Inspection Service, and the Bureau of Navigation. Nowhere is the history of this diversity more evident than in Alaskan waters, especially in the Bering Sea and Arctic regions. From the time of the first reconnaissance of the new territory, small cutters of the U.S. Revenue Cutter Service, and then the U.S. Coast Guard, have sailed into the remote waters of the forty-ninth state. Indeed, cutters and cuttermen have even ventured into interior portions of the state. Interestingly enough, up until the early part of the twentieth century, the U.S. Revenue Cutter Service made many visits to Siberia, and cuttermen even claimed Wrangel Island, above northern Siberia, for the United States. Some landmarks in western Alaska carry the names of early cuttermen. Hooper Bay, northwest of Norton Sound, for example, is named after Capt. Calvin L. Hooper, the first official commander of the Bering Sea Patrol. The cuttermen of the early Bering Sea Patrol explored, assisted those in distress, protected wildlife, enforced federal laws, instituted "floating courts," and gave medical help to remote villages—to name only a few of the contributions the sailors of that small organization performed.

Some of the best officers of the service sailed in Alaskan waters. Two officers who became most important to the history of the U.S. Coast Guard operated in Alaska and the Bering Sea Patrol as young men. Capt.-Cmdt. Ellsworth P. Bertholf, who led the service in its transition from the U.S. Revenue Cutter Service into the U.S. Coast Guard, also participated in the Overland Relief Expedition. Adm. Russell R. Waesche, Sr., who sailed the Bering Sea, became commandant of the U.S. Coast Guard in 1936, a post he held until 1945, a tenure longer than that of any other officer in the history of the organization. Admiral Waesche guided the Coast Guard from its nadir, at the time of the large cutbacks in personnel after the rum war at sea during Prohibition, through its rapid expansion during World War II, and he set plans for its future after that conflict.

For all the duties and contributions of these men, however, the work in Alaska, especially in the Bering Sea and the Arctic, has, with three exceptions, been largely overlooked by historians. One exception concerns the cutter *Bear.* This 198-foot steam barkentine, launched in 1874, spent her first decade as a sealer off Newfoundland. Purchased by the U.S. Navy in 1884, she played an important role as part of the relief force that rescued the survivors of the ill-fated Greely Arctic Expedition. From the time of her transfer the following year until her decommissioning in 1929, she served in the U.S. Revenue Cutter Service and the U.S. Coast Guard, sailing each year to Alaskan waters. After her sale, she served as a museum ship in Oakland, California. Adm. Richard E. Byrd, the noted polar explorer, bought her in 1932 for his second Antarctic expedition. She served again in World War II in the Greenland Patrol as the *Bear* (AG-29). Returned to decommissioned status, the cutter then deteriorated until bought by a private individual for use as a floating restaurant in Philadelphia. Unfortunately for all who cherished her memory, she sank on 19 March 1963 during a storm in the North Atlantic while under tow. Many old salts felt this a more fitting end to such a gallant ship. The cutter *Bear* has had more books written about it than any other cutter in the history of the Coast Guard.

The *Bear* also plays a part in the other two historical subjects that have brought the cuttermen of Alaska publicity. Capt. Michael A. Healy began to receive some of the credit due him after authors in the late 1960s and early 1970s "discovered" and began to write about his African-American heritage. Since then Healy has received continued attention, and in 1998 a new polar icebreaker was named after him. Although little remembered until the sixties, in his own time, however, Captain Healy was the best known Arctic navigator in the Western Arctic. The cutter he was most associated with was the *Bear.*

One of the things Captain Healy is noted for is the importation of reindeer into Alaska to help the natives. The cutter transporting the deer was the *Bear*. Those reindeer are an important feature of the third subject that has brought the cuttermen of Alaska publicity. In 1897 the early arrival of winter cold trapped an entire whaling fleet in heavy ice near Point Barrow. When the owners of the whalers expressed their concern over the fate of those on board, the Revenue Cutter Service launched a rescue operation, known as the Overland Relief Expedition, to bring food to the sailors. Three officers, among them 2d Lt. Ellsworth P. Bertholf, drove a herd of reindeer an incredible fifteen hundred miles in the dead of the Arctic winter to ensure a food source that would last until the breakup of the ice. For their work, the three officers received Gold Medals from the U.S. Congress. The cutter from which the officers departed to undertake their mission was the *Bear*.

After well over a century of neglect, it is time that the cuttermen who accomplished so much be brought into the light of history. The purpose of this book is to paint a broad picture of the major duties performed primarily in the Bering Sea and Arctic Ocean. Cutters and cuttermen served throughout Alaskan waters, but it is the Bering Sea where the greatest efforts took place. It is impossible to detail every duty, as each patrol had different missions assigned to it, with some being only one-time efforts. We have chosen to recount the missions that received constant attention throughout the period of the U.S. Revenue Cutter Service and well into the years of the U.S. Coast Guard: search and rescue, exploration, assistance to other agencies, medical care, and law enforcement. Readers will note that there is no chapter on the *Bear*, as we feel that it has been covered more than adequately in other places. As might be expected, however, the cutter appears throughout the narrative. The Overland Relief Expedition receives only short mention, as it too has been adequately covered elsewhere, and we wanted readers to have an understanding of other cases of search and rescue undertaken by the cuttermen of the north.

Capt. Michael A. Healy is the dominant personality throughout this book, and rightfully so. For many years Healy and the *Bear* were the Bering Sea Patrol. His service in Alaskan waters spanned the most important years of the patrol, and his contributions were enormous. His life is so controversial and so full of unanswered (and in many cases unanswerable) questions that any historian attempting to write on the man enters into hazardous waters. All too often in the past Captain Healy has received what we call the "public affairs" treatment of his life. That is, only his accomplishments are featured, and his shortcomings, which, because he was human, were many, are overlooked—or they are given such passing mention that no one can assess his faults. Captain Healy, with both his good and bad traits, is important to this story, and consequently he receives two chapters.

We have chosen to cover the years from 1867 to 1915, and the end of the U.S. Revenue Cutter Service, for two reasons: The end of the Revenue Cutter Service in Alaska makes for a logical stopping point. The story of the U.S. Coast Guard in Alaska, also important, must wait for another time. Those (including the junior author of this book) who served in Alaska and on the Bering Sea Patrol, now called the Alaskan Patrol, also deserve to have their exploits chronicled. The second reason to stop the narrative at 1914 is that all of the work accomplished in Alaska, and especially on the Bering Sea Patrol, had been established, tested, and proven during the U.S. Revenue Cutter Service era.

If this narrative brings the cuttermen who served for so long and faithfully in a hazardous environment back from behind the veil of time, it will have served its purpose.

# Acknowledgments

The U.S. Coast Guard employs only two historians in their historical office: Dr. Robert M. Browning, Jr., and Mr. Scott Price. We were continually amazed at the amount of work these two men produce and how rapidly they responded to requests for information. We could not have completed this book without their help.

The archival work for this book spanned many years. We wish to thank the archivists who helped us, both those who have retired, or moved to other locations, and those still working on U.S. Coast Guard records. William Sherman has retired, and Terry Matchett is in another division of the National Archives. Angie VanDereedt, archivist in Archives I, Reference Branch, now assists those working in the records of the service.

Peggy Norris did her normal, outstanding reading of the manuscript to locate inconsistencies and misspellings. She also did the difficult task of indexing the book. Susan Browning did excellent maps for the book.

Dr. Mark D. Mandeles of the J. De Bloch Group and Stephen J. Walsh of the U.S. Army National Guard Bureau served as indispensable computer gurus in northern Virginia. Mark learned more about Unalaska than he ever wanted to know while rescuing chapters 5 and 6, and Stephen kept both the computer and printer operating during the roughest times.

Chief Boatswain's Mate (BMC) Richard M. Belisle, serving in the U.S. Coast Guard Cutter *Storis* (WMEC-38), quickly answered a request to provide information on the cutter's activities to keep alive the traditions of the old Bering Sea Patrol.

Capt. LeRoy Reinberg, Jr., U.S. Coast Guard (Ret.), graciously gave us permission to use photographs that his father, Rear Adm. LeRoy Reinberg, U.S. Coast Guard (Ret.), took in Alaska as a young officer in the U.S. Revenue Cutter Service. Admiral Reinberg's photographs are an excellent example of why people of the armed forces should keep diaries and make an effort to record and preserve what they see while on active duty.

Cindee Herrick, curator of the U.S. Coast Guard Museum at the U.S. Coast Guard Academy, helped with manuscripts and photographs.

At the Naval Institute Press, we wish to thank those people who guided the manuscript on its voyage to becoming a book, including Scott E. Belliveau, acquisitions editor; J. Randall Baldini, managing editor; and Martin Hanft, freelance copy editor.

# ONE

# Alaska and the U.S. Revenue Cutter Service

W hen the United States purchased Alaska from Russia in 1867, many Americans decried the folly of the transaction. Newspapers were quick to coin terms such as "Seward's Wallrussia" to express their displeasure. Indeed, looking at the state of geographic knowledge in the mid-nineteenth century, one can understand why there was opposition to this expenditure. Most, if not all, Americans had very little understanding of this vast and largely unexplored land far to the north. Surely, they thought, it must be covered with ice and snow throughout most of the year. What could such an icebox contribute to the nation? The government needed information on the land and turned to a small federal seagoing force to undertake the initial survey of Alaska's coastal region. The U.S. Revenue Cutter Service cutter *Lincoln* set sail in 1867 from San Francisco to undertake the inspection, the first of many such scientific investigations of these mysterious northern latitudes.

The small cutters of the U.S. Revenue Cutter Service worked throughout Alaskan waters, but the importance of the fur seal dictated that most of the service's interest center on the Bering Sea. The landmark 1880 cruise of the cutter *Corwin* in the Bering Sea initiated what would prove to be the yearly patrols that became formalized in 1895 as the Bering Sea Patrol.[1] The cutters eventually became the only semblance of government known to the inhabitants of Alaska's western and northern coastlines. They helped protect both the fur seals and the fishing industry, and they provided a search and rescue service. As the years passed, they served as explorers, floating medical centers, and maritime courtrooms; they also provided a taxi, postal, and rescue service to natives, destitute seamen, and scientists. One historian has noted that "without the transport made available by the Revenue Service, the islands and mainland of the Bering Sea would have been virtually inaccessible to scientists . . . and the progress of knowledge would have been considerably slower."[2] The *New York Sun* described one of the service's officers as "a good deal more distinguished [a] person in the waters of the far Northwest than any president of the United States."[3] All of these duties were performed by an organization that in 1878 could boast of a national force of fewer than 204 officers and 36 cutters, with no cutter over two hundred feet in length.

Despite its many contributions to the maritime history of the United States and Alaska, the U.S. Revenue Cutter Service has slipped behind the veil of history. Very few people today have ever heard of this unique service, which existed for 125 years and evolved into the U.S. Coast Guard. What was the U.S. Revenue Cutter Service?

The revenue cutters that sailed in Alaskan waters could trace their lineage to the earliest days of the American republic. One of the first acts of the newly created U.S. Congress, in 1789, was to impose a tariff on imported goods. The tariff would provide the fledgling nation with much-needed revenue and also serve to protect local industries that had sprung up during the years of the revolution.

One of the rallying cries for the break from England had been "no taxation without representation," and many citizens could see little difference between the tariff instituted by the U.S. Congress and taxation by England. Even before the struggle for independence, some Americans had become skillful smugglers. The war not only made this illegal activity fashionable but also wrapped it in patriotic trappings. Independence caused many of these bootleggers to look upon the revenue tariffs as just another challenge to overcome.

Alexander Hamilton, the first secretary of the treasury, quickly realized the necessity for a seagoing police force to enforce the custom laws. He sought funds to construct ten boats to prevent smugglers from landing contraband cargo.[4] The boats would patrol the Atlantic seaboard from New England to Georgia. Hamilton specified that each vessel be "armed with swivels," small cannons on revolving bases that could be turned in any direction.[5] Congress authorized the request on 4 August 1790.

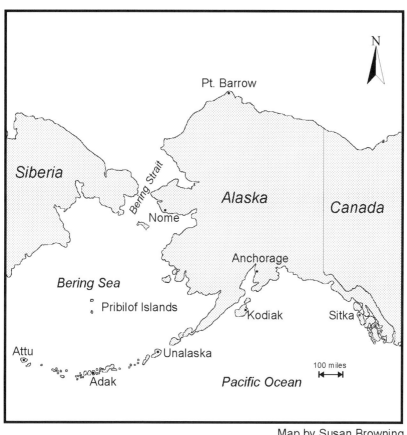

N

Pt. Barrow

Siberia

Bering Strait

Alaska

Canada

Nome

Anchorage

Bering Sea

Pribilof Islands

Kodiak

Sitka

Attu

Unalaska

Adak

Pacific Ocean

100 miles

Map by Susan Browning

Hamilton took a proprietary interest in the newly formed service. He personally ensured that the crews of the small boats, or cutters, were of "respectable character." Unbeknownst to many, in 1785, after independence, the United States had disbanded its navy and would not have one again until 1798; thus Hamilton could not give the revenue cutter officers naval commissions. The officers were, however, granted commissions as "officers of the customs," signed by President George Washington, an action that achieved Hamilton's desire of inducing "fit men the more readily to engage" as well as "attach[ing] them to their duty by a nicer sense of honor."[6]

There are no complete personnel records on the crews of the first ten cutters. We can surmise, however, that the service drew sailors from the former colonial merchant marine, privateers, or warships from the disbanded Continental and state navies. It is not unreasonable to presume that some may have even had first-hand experience as patriotic smugglers in sneaking contraband past British customs officers. Each revenue cutter had a master, three mates (first, second, and third), four men, and two boys authorized, but, in the interest of economy, Hamilton urged the use of a smaller crew. As the passing years would illustrate, those appointed to the new service would be skillful not only in seamanship and laying cannon but also in handling cutlasses and pistols.[7]

Very early in its history, the new service began to acquire missions, duties, responsibilities, and tasks that Hamilton had not imagined. Two of the more unusual early tasks dealt with pirates and human "contraband."

In the early nineteenth century, pirates operated throughout the Gulf of Mexico. The notorious Jean LaFitte, for example, operated out of New Orleans. The Florida Keys were another favorite area for buccaneers. Pirates, of course, interfered with U.S. trade and revenue, so it was natural that the U.S. Revenue Cutter Service should be given the job of combating them. In 1819 the service gained two new cutters to use against the freebooters, the *Alabama* and the *Louisiana,* each being fifty-seven feet in length, seventeen feet in beam, and with a shallow draft of six feet. Upon commissioning, they had orders to take station in New Orleans.

On 31 August 1819 the *Alabama* and *Louisiana* fought it out with the pirate ship *Bravo,* commanded by one of Jean LaFitte's lieutenants. After a volley of musketry wounded his first officer and three of his men, Capt. Jarvis Loomis of the *Louisiana* ordered boarders to take the *Bravo.* The battle was decided when the cuttermen overcame the pirates in a hand-to-hand struggle. The following year the same two revenue cutters destroyed a major pirate den in Patterson's Town on Brenton Island. The *Louisiana* captured five pirate vessels in 1822; the *Alabama* brought three slave ships to justice.[8]

As early as 1794, the revenue cutters had been instructed to prevent the importation of new slaves ("contraband" in revenue terminology) from Africa to the United States. The further prohibition against the foreign slave trade in 1807 enlarged this effort. Before the Civil War ended, the cutters had captured numerous slave ships and freed almost five hundred slaves.

Other duties followed. In 1799 came the responsibility for aiding in the administration of quarantine regulations and laws. After President Thomas Jefferson declared a highly unpopular total embargo of imports in 1808, the revenue cutters had to close all the nation's ports. In 1822, only the shallow-draft revenue cutters proved equal to the task of preventing the illegal cutting of live oaks growing in the timber reserves on public lands in Florida. These trees had been set aside for the naval fleet created by Congress.

The enforcement of navigation laws, and later, ship safety, along with assistance to keepers of lighthouses and lifesaving stations, fell in part upon the revenue cutters and their officers as a logical result of their location in the Treasury Department.[9] Until the acquisition of the first lighthouse tender in the mid-1800s, the cutters performed such vital functions as setting buoys, carrying lighthouse keepers and their supplies to lighthouses, and transporting lighthouse inspectors. The cutters had always obeyed the unwritten law of the sea—rendering assistance whenever possible to mariners and ships in distress—and, as early as 1831, they had been ordered to "winter cruise" along the Atlantic Coast during the months of worst weather in order to seek out and aid seafarers and ships in danger. A cutter officer, Capt. Douglas Ottinger, supervised the building of the first lifesaving stations on the New Jersey coast in 1848–49 and also invented the lifecar, for the carrying to shore of persons rescued from a wreck.[10] Cutter officers subsequently transported keepers, crews, and supplies to remote lifesaving stations and served as inspectors of the stations or in other administrative capacities.

The coming of America's first international conflict, the Quasi-War with France (1790–1800), marked the beginning of the service's long military service to the United States. On 2 March 1799 Congress gave the president, whenever he so desired, the power to order the revenue cutters to cooperate with the U.S. Navy. At those special times the cutters took their direction from the secretary of the navy. Congress also changed the merchant marine titles of a cutter's master and mates to the military ranks of captain and lieutenant.

In 1799 eight revenue cutters sailed with the fleets of the newly organized navy in hostile operations against the French. In all, the American vessels captured twenty ships flying the French flag. Of these, the revenue cutters captured sixteen unaided, and assisted in the seizure of two more.

The spirit of these early revenue cutters was demonstrated by the performance of the outgunned and outmanned *Pickering* (with fourteen four-pounder guns and seventy men) against the French privateer *L'Egype Conquise* (with fourteen nine-pounders, four six-pounders, and 250 men) on 18 October 1799. For nine long and desperate hours the two ships sought to blow each other out of the water. Then the French privateer struck its colors. American seamanship and bravery had won a notable victory, and a revenue cutter proved to be the instrument by which it had been accomplished.

During the War of 1812, nine revenue cutters, averaging 125 tons, armed with six to ten light guns, and manned by crews of fifteen to thirty men, captured fourteen British ships. Two cutters particularly distinguished themselves. The stubborn resistance of the greatly outnumbered crew of the *Surveyor* so impressed the British commander who captured them that he returned the revenue captain's sword in recognition of his gallant defense. To avoid capture by a British brig and its accompanying sloop, cuttermen ran their outclassed and outgunned revenue cutter *Eagle* aground and dragged its guns up a high bluff to continue the fight. After expending all their large shot and fixed ammunition, they tore up the ship's log book to use for wadding and fired back the enemy's shot that had lodged in the hill. Daring crew members three times raced down the bluff to refly the revenue cutter's flag that had been shot away. When their six-hour-long bombardment failed to achieve results, the British sailed away. The cuttermen then returned to the *Eagle,* replaced the cannons, and floated her off.

After the Seminole War of 1836–39 broke out, nine revenue cutters eventually participated with the U.S. Army and Navy in this struggle. Because of their shallow draft, they could work closer inshore than any navy frigate and could operate effectively in the riverine environment. In the main, the cutters transported supplies and troops, carried dispatches, blockaded rivers to prevent the passage of Seminole war parties, rescued the survivors of battles, and landed its cannon- and musket-armed cuttermen to defend menaced settlements. Some of the cuttermen, in addition to ferrying soldiers and marines in small boats over the inland waters of Florida, ran a real risk of death when they found themselves trailing on foot an elusive foe through the sandburs and palmettos into the Everglades.

During the Mexican War (1845–48), ten revenue cutters engaged in naval operations, providing valuable service in the successful attacks on the ports of Frontera and Tabasco. Besides accurate gunfire support for amphibious landings, the cutters also performed excellently in the blockading fleet off the Mexican coast. In short, they performed "scout, convoy, towing, and blockade duty, transported troops and supplies, carried mail and dispatches, and even put down a mutiny of troops on the ship *Middlesex* (26 July 1846)."[11] The revenue cutters *Ewing* and *Legare* landed one thousand muskets at Point Isabel just in time for Gen. Zachary Taylor to use them in the battles of Monterey and Buena Vista.

The service again fought an elusive but deadly foe during the Yakima Indian War in the Pacific Northwest.[12] By 1854 the inevitable clash between the American settlers and the Indians living on the shores of Puget Sound in Washington Territory had erupted into bloodshed. The revenue cutter *Jefferson Davis,* commanded by Capt. William C. Pease, sailed into Puget Sound in the fall to reinforce the army regulars and volunteers and to provide them with a means of transportation other than canoes. Within two months of her arrival, the revenue cutter, rigged as a topsail schooner and armed with six twelve-pounder cannons, found herself loaded with soldiers and in pursuit of escaped Indian prisoners from Fort Steilacoom. When a camp of Clallam Indians refused to give them up, Captain Pease had his cuttermen land the soldiers from their small boats. The riflemen stormed inland, only to find the Native Americans fading away to safety in the dense forest. The schooner covered the soldiers' withdrawal by raking the woods surrounding the village with cannon fire, killing five Indians. Only the capture and holding of a Clallam chief as hostage forced the surrender of the escapees, who were imprisoned again.

Almost a year later, the ever-increasing number of Native Americans at war resulted in the revenue cutter's being sent from Seattle to anchor off Fort Steilacoom and unload arms and ammunition for use by recently called up volunteers. Captain Pease held back only enough muskets and cutlasses to arm twenty of his crew. He intended to use these cuttermen at a moment's notice as reinforcements for the fort or, if the fort seemed in danger of falling, as a landing party to provide a safe retreat route ashore by which women and children could reach the schooner.

On 20 October 1855, the Regular Army commander requested, and received, ten cuttermen for the fort. He then mentioned that Company C, U.S. 4th Infantry, was ready to take the field but lacked a commissioned officer as second in command. Second Lt. James E. Harrison of the *Jefferson Davis* promptly offered his services; Captain Pease approved, and the Regular Army commander accepted. This revenue officer-turned-infantryman encountered fierce combat as a member of Company C. While pursuing the main body of hostiles, the regulars, accompanied by fifty volunteers, ran into an ambush at the White River on 2 November. Unable to cross, they engaged in a six-hour firefight that killed more than thirty Yakimas and wounded many others, at the cost of only one soldier slightly wounded. As this mixed regular-volunteer force attempted to cross the Puyallup River on the sixth, the Yakima warriors struck again, this time killing three soldiers and wounding another three.

Most of the white inhabitants of the territory were crowded into blockhouses or in towns defended by home guard units. This was not tolerable to the whites, and there was a call for offensive action to force the bulk of the Native Americans back to the reservations, thus isolating the hard-core hostiles for subsequent retaliation. The strategy called for a four-prong movement converging upon one geographical area. Each of the attacking forces would operate independently. Company C, one of the prongs, moved out as scheduled on 24 November, reaching a prairie about a mile from the Puyallup River just before the Yakimas attacked under the cover of darkness. The infantry company quickly dug in. The warriors remained hidden during the next two days but used the night fogs to creep in close enough to snipe at the troops and make the nights hideous with their war cries. After being reinforced by twenty-five regular soldiers from Fort Steilacoom, Company C resumed its march on the twenty-sixth. The Yakima warriors kept a safe distance in the heavy forest, but a chilling rain made life miserable for the infantrymen. Not until the third day of December did they reach their objective, the forks of the White and Green rivers.

That night, a Yakima warrior, using the flickering flames of a camp fire to locate the soldiers, crept close enough to use his rifle. He shot and immediately killed the army commander of Company C. Revenue officer Second Lieutenant Harrison immediately assumed command. Under Harrison's direction the soldiers returned fire. By dawn, their losses totaled four dead and five wounded.

The overall military commander of the four-pronged expedition now became alarmed by the numerous reports of sick soldiers and exhausted packhorses. Concluding that caution was the better part of valor, he dispatched orders recalling his troops from the field. Second Lieutenant Harrison successfully led his infantrymen back to safety within the walls of Fort Steilacoom on 21 December 1855. Released from his brief career as an infantry company commander, Harrison resumed his duties aboard the revenue cutter. Within two months the *Jefferson Davis* sailed for San Francisco, thus ending for all practical purposes its role in the Indian Wars of the Pacific Northwest.

Not all of the service's combat was limited to declared wars or America's own shores. When the Paraguayans objected in 1858 to an American ship making scientific explorations of their waters, they retaliated by slamming two cannon holes into the vessel's hull and killing the sailor at the wheel. Congress protested, and soon a naval armada of fifteen small warships headed south.

Within the armada was the revenue steamer *Harriet Lane*. This steam-propelled cutter carried eighty-two men, twenty-two marines, two nine-inch guns, and one twelve-pound and four twenty-four-pound howitzers, making her the heaviest-armed vessel in the American naval squadron. Confronted with such a show of force, the Paraguayans proved amiable. An American diplomat quickly negotiated a treaty resolving all the difficulties between the two countries.

The Civil War was the next major conflict in which the U.S. Revenue Cutter Service gained battle honors. The cutters performed "incalculable service" on blockade duty by preventing men, mail, supplies, and money from reaching the South.[13] The cuttermen also chased Confederate privateers and provided naval support for Union military ventures. Three cutters have received a special place in Civil War history.

The side-wheeler *Harriet Lane* won fame for firing "the first shot of the Civil War from a vessel" in April 1861 during the bombardment of Fort Sumter.[14] She participated that summer in the first joint amphibious operation of the war—the capture of the strategic Confederate forts at Hatteras Inlet, North Carolina, the gateway for rebel privateers and blockade runners. The navy then permanently transferred to its fleet the revenue steamer that had proved so useful in combat.

The revenue cutter *Miami,* a converted steam yacht, accommodated many high-ranking dignitaries at various times during the Civil War. In May 1862 she ran unescorted from Washington to Fortress Monroe, where Gen. George B. McClellan was directing the Peninsular Campaign, bringing President Abraham Lincoln to his first visit to a battlefield.

The *Naugatuck,* however, was without doubt the oddest looking revenue cutter of the conflict. A unique vessel, she was a semisubmersible ironclad,

The U.S. Revenue Cutter Service cutter *Lincoln,* the first cutter to survey some of the coastal areas of the newly purchased Alaska in 1867.

needing only fifteen minutes to take on enough water ballast to sink almost three feet. Thus she could enter battle with only her impenetrable turret mounting a Parrot gun above water. Afterward, she could pump the water overboard again in just eight minutes.[15] In early 1862 the revenue ironclad served as bait for the Confederate *Merrimack.* The two-part plan of deception called for the *Naugatuck* to steam to within a quarter-mile of the rebel battery at Sewell's Point. The cutter would then open fire, hoping to draw out the *Merrimack.* Just as planned, the Confederate ironclad ventured forth. The second part of the plan called for the *Naugatuck* to retire slowly toward a squadron of navy steamers. Hidden among the squadron was the *Monitor.* This was the heart of the deception: luring the enemy ironclad into combat with the Union's ironclad. The skipper of the *Merrimack,* however, sensed danger, refused the bait, and withdrew.

The revenue ironclad next led a naval assault flotilla up the James River to try to shell the Confederate capital into submission. During a four-hour-long duel between this flotilla and a strong rebel battery on Drewry's Bluff, the *Naugatuck*'s Parrott gun exploded, but she "continued in her position during the entire action, firing her broadside guns."[16] After being repaired, the revenue ironclad passed the remainder of the war guarding the approaches to New York City.

The coming of peace in 1865 shifted the emphasis placed on the service's various traditional missions, as well as its newly acquired ones. It no longer had to intercept slave ships, but it did have to try to stop the smuggling of aliens into the country, as required by the 1862 congressional ban on the importation of Chinese workers.

Capt. Charles M. Scammon, commanding the revenue steamer *Shubrick,* visited Russian Alaska in 1865 and is the first U.S. Revenue Cutter Service commander to have sailed in Alaska's waters. Two years before the purchase of Alaska, the side-wheel *Shubrick* was the flagship of a six-ship expedition that the Western Union Company had hoped to use in its attempt to lay an underwater cable across the Bering Strait to Siberia. The cable was to have connected an overland telegraph line running to the Bering Sea with another running overland to St. Petersburg.[17] The telegraph company, however, abandoned the project after the laying of the Atlantic cable to Europe proved successful. This failed plan, however, became a good example of the service's contributions to science. Captain Scammon had been a whaling officer before becoming a revenue officer, and he possessed a passion for scientific observation. In the 1850s he discovered the haunts of the gray whale in a bay on the California coast, subsequently named Scammon Lagoon in his honor. From his observations on the voyage of the *Shubrick* to Russian Alaska and his later cruises in other cutters, he collected the scientific data that served as the basis for his study of whales, *Marine Mammals of the North Western Coast* (1874). Scammon illustrated the work with his own detailed drawings. The book remained the standard text for decades.

Interestingly enough, this failed effort, spearheaded by the revenue steamer *Shubrick,* played a pivotal role in removing the Russian czar's foothold in the Western Hemisphere. One of the expedition's members, Henry M. Bannister, arrived in Washington, D.C., just in time to serve as the only authoritative source on the existing conditions in Russian America to both Secretary of State Seward and Senator Charles Sumner, chairman of the Senate Committee on Foreign Relations, which was then considering the treaty to purchase this territory. Bannister, who went on to become a museum curator, medical doctor, and author, proudly stated years later that the attempt to lay a telegraphic cable "across the Bering Straits to Europe was a failure, but its greatest result was the annexation of Alaska."[18]

When confronted in 1867 with the immediate need to implement the purchase of Alaska, government officials naturally turned once again to the most appropriate federal vehicle to perform this task. Not only had the revenue cutters already proven invaluable in accomplishing numerous unusual and complex missions but in addition their captains carried out their assignments at the most economical cost. Their service had a long and distinguished history, one rich with traditions, gallant skippers, combat honors, dramatic rescues, and a high sense of duty.

Once Alaska became America's northernmost possession, a special relationship quickly developed with the U.S. Revenue Cutter Service, which remained virtually the sole U.S. representative in this new territory—especially in the Bering Sea and Arctic regions. Since the uniformed cuttermen dispensed both law and humanitarian aid, many observers began referring to them as American Northwest Mounties.[19]

The unique and demanding requirements upon both the revenue cutters and their crews had an unforeseen effect upon the U.S. Revenue Cutter Service. News coverage of a wild and little-known area was avidly devoured by a curious public, and this focused the attention of Congress as well as many others upon the need for a reorganization of the service to make it more efficient, economical, and effective. Bowing to political pressure, the Treasury Department centralized the entire U.S. Revenue Cutter Service administration in a new division.[20] Thereafter, this new Washington headquarters could alone promulgate regulations and authorize expenditures, the inspection of cutters, and the selection and promotion of personnel—now solely on the basis of merit instead of the spoils system. It greatly improved the quality of the officer corps in 1877 by establishing a School of Instruction, the forerunner of the service academy, aboard an old schooner, to educate the young officers and provide practical training. The rejuvenated U.S. Revenue Cutter Service also began replacing the obsolete sailing cutters with newer ones specifically designed for its unique needs, with emphasis on steam power, ease of maneuverability, and operation by smaller crews. These new policies resulted in a 50 percent increase between 1870 and 1886 in the number of miles cruised annually by cutters, bringing that number to more than three hundred thousand, as well as an increase in the number of vessels in distress assisted (more than three hundred).

Congress continued tasking the U.S. Revenue Cutter Service with additional missions. In 1880 came the requirement to cooperate with the Bureau of Fisheries to promote the increase of food fish. Planning and enforcing anchorage regulations began in 1898. Other law enforcement responsibilities followed: overseeing regattas and marine parades (1896); water pollution control (1899); oversight of the landing, delivery, curing, and sale of sponges in the Gulf of Mexico and Straits of Florida (1906); and the regulation of motor boats (1910).

During the last twenty years of the nineteenth century, the removal of floating dangers to navigation—primarily by destroying derelicts by exploding and sinking them—became a significant safety function of revenue cutters, with legal tasking coming in 1906. The interdiction of smuggled illegal narcotics also rose in importance. The tragic 1912 collision of the luxury liner *Titanic* with an iceberg and the resulting heavy loss of life led to the formation of the International Ice Patrol under U.S. Revenue Cutter Service direction. The cutters of the U.S. Revenue Cutter Service on International Ice Patrol kept an eye on floating ice hazards in the North Atlantic. The same year, a federal law instructed the service to extend medical and surgical aid to American ships engaged in deep-sea fisheries.

During the Spanish-American War (1898), eighteen revenue cutters saw action.[21] The feats of two particularly stand out. The *McCulloch* not only fought with Admiral Dewey's fleet in the Battle of Manila Bay but also then

U.S. Revenue Cutter
BEAR
1885-1927

Line drawing of the cutter *Bear,* the most famous ship of the U.S. Revenue Cutter Service and U.S. Coast Guard. *Drawing by John Tilley, courtesy of the U.S. Coast Guard*

raced to the nearest telegraph at Hong Kong to alert the world of the American victory. The *Hudson* braved deadly fire from Spanish guns at Cardenas, Cuba, to tow the crippled navy torpedo boat *Winslow* out of range of enemy shore batteries and certain destruction. Such courage so impressed the members of Congress that they ordered special medals minted and presented to the officers and men of this cutter.

With their return to peacetime duties, the cuttermen faced a real uncertainty as to their future. Previously, many recommendations had been made to save money by having some other federal agency perform the functions of the Revenue Cutter Service. The service had survived earlier such threats, but the first years of the twentieth century proved to be dangerously unsettled and characterized by many changes. Certain powerful congressmen now believed that, since the U.S. Revenue Cutter Service "could be defined basically as nothing more than a military force afloat—a small-bore counterpart of the Navy, so to speak—it should be incorporated with the Navy."[22] The beginning of the service's demise proved to be the recommendation of a commission appointed by President William Howard Taft to divide functions of the Revenue Cutter Service among the navy and several civilian agencies, thereby supposedly saving a million dollars a year.

The commandant of the U.S. Revenue Cutter Service, Capt. Ellsworth P. Bertholf, disputed the projected savings, arguing that those agencies absorbing the functions of his service would still need the same amount of money and number of men to carry them out. Abolishing the service, he added, would result in needless duplication and would cost more, rather than less. The many friends of the U.S. Revenue Cutter Service, both among the public and in Congress, supported Captain Bertholf's stand, as did Secretary of the Treasury Franklin MacVeagh, who advocated instead that the U.S. Revenue Cutter Service absorb the U.S. Life-Saving Service as a more efficient means of increasing the effectiveness of their joint efforts.

At just this time, a heroic rescue of the crew from the burning deck of the SS *Ontario* by cuttermen and lifesavers, working closely together, provided a dramatic example of the desired cooperation. The operation won national praise, as did the U.S. Revenue Cutter Service for its organization and operation of the International Ice Patrol. The outbreak of World War I in Europe highlighted the potential military value of the federal civilian agency's possession of armed cutters. Congress now passed a bill to create a new agency—the U.S. Coast Guard. President Woodrow Wilson signed the bill on 28 January 1915, and the merger of the U.S. Revenue Cutter Service with the U.S.

Life-Saving Service took place two days later. This act of Congress also made the new U.S. Coast Guard an armed military force at all times, operating as an integral part of the navy in wartime or whenever the president so directed.

These, then, are the origins of the organization that sent the small revenue cutters north to face the hazards of Alaskan waters. Even though the U.S. Revenue Cutter Service had faced many unusual duties and hazards in the past, the northern latitudes would provide missions that no one could have conceived of. From 1867 to 1915 the cuttermen of the U.S. Revenue Cutter Service would have their mettle tested. The service recognized the special dangers of Alaskan waters: In the register of officers there was a special notation for the amount of duty an officer had spent in northern waters, thus indicating that a seagoing officer had been tested in a truly hostile and hazardous environment.

Despite all its myriad duties in the far north, the primary reason for the presence of Revenue Cutter Service cutters in the Bering Sea was a marine mammal: *Callohinus alascanus,* the Alaska fur seal. The thick pelt of this sleek mammal made it an economic bonanza. The seal industry, according to historian Gary O. Williams, "was recognized in 1869 as perhaps the greatest single economic benefit accruing to the United States by reason of its purchase of Alaska. It was the source of the only revenue income." Recognizing this, Congress set aside the Pribilof Islands, the breeding grounds of the animal, as a special government preserve. The Treasury Department granted a twenty-year lease to the Alaska Commercial Company on 1 April 1870 with authorization to kill seals on the Pribilofs. In return for the lease, the company paid the government an annual rent and tax on each skin taken. During the period of the lease the Alaska Commercial Company took 1,977,277 skins, with the Treasury Department realizing an income of $6,020,153. This is only slightly less than the purchase price of the huge territory. Obviously, any danger to such a productive source of national income would receive immediate attention. The chance that such a danger would arise soon became apparent.[23]

The sealing industry in the Bering Sea can trace its origins back as far as 1706 under the Russians. By the mid-1840s the Russians, who began the leasing method, were using a herd control method of harvesting only surplus males. At the time, the lessee could kill the mammals on land only. This produced a twofold benefit: Only extra animals were taken, and the government could control the killing.

The Alaskan fur seal is the largest of the pelagic fur seals. The noted diplomatic historian Samuel Flagg Bemis wrote: "Amphibious is the fur seal, ubiquitous and carnivorous, uniparous, gregarious and withal polygamous."[24] From December to May the seals dwell entirely at sea, ranging as far south as the latitude of southern California. The mammal is indeed both highly gregarious and polygamous, with a limited intelligence and possessed by instinct that allows nothing to stand in its way. One observer maintained that the "fur seal exhibits no . . . ability to learn from its experience." This inflexibility would play a part in the forthcoming dispute and almost cause the animal's extinction.[25]

Around the first of May the great bull seals begin to come ashore in the Pribilof Islands. The bulls stake out their territories in the rookeries. These huge animals, weighing more than a quarter ton, take possession of an area of from six to twelve square feet and defend it fiercely. The choicest locations are close to the water's edge; those are the most advantageous for attracting the cows, who usually arrive in the first week of June.

The cows arrive pregnant and must give birth to their pups on land. Before the cows depart the island for their long stay at sea, the bulls begin to entice cows into their harems and mate with them. They continue their sequence of enticing, mating, and defending for more than six weeks, all without consuming any food or water. Cows, however, usually leave the rookery to feed.

The male animals who are not yet strong enough to have a harem—those called bachelor bulls—are driven to an area of their own. Bachelorhood usually lasts for about six years. Bachelor seals, like cows, will also leave the island seeking food at sea. Because the bachelors are young, it is difficult to distinguish a male from a female at sea. In the land killing method, the bachelor bulls are the seals herded to a killing ground and dispatched by natives with clubs. Thus there is no real danger to the herd under the land system, if properly controlled.[26]

Because no one knew anything about the fur seals, the secretary of the treasury appointed a young artist-naturalist, Henry Wood Elliott of the Smithsonian Institution, as a special agent to conduct a study of the animals. Elliott, no stranger to the far north, had participated in the Russian-American Telegraph Expedition in 1865. He began his studies by trying to obtain an estimate of the seal population, and, during his first six weeks at St. Paul Island in the Pribilofs, he somehow also found time to marry the daughter of a former Russian official.

The *Bear* sails through the Bering Sea.

Elliott left the islands in the fall of 1873 and returned again in 1874 and 1876. In 1874, while en route to the Pribilofs aboard the Revenue Cutter Service cutter *Reliance,* he observed the fur seals in migration and began to think more about their yearly travel. He would eventually spend at least fifty years studying the mammals, and he became one of the main reasons that the animals did not go the way of the dodo bird or the passenger pigeon. Elliott became the first to map the migration route of the fur seal. When he published his findings, his mentor, Spencer F. Baird of the Smithsonian Institution, convinced him not to include his map of the route, which might endanger the marine mammal. The artist-naturalist estimated the fur seal population at three million breeding seals. Elliott felt that the "highly polygamous nature of the breeding bulls would allow the fur company to take one hundred thousand bachelor seals each year without injury to the natural increase of the herd, '*provided no abnormal cause of destruction occurred.*'" The "abnormal cause of destruction" proved to be the result of pelagic hunting, government malfeasance, and shady practices by the fur companies in charge of harvesting the seals.[27]

In 1881 the price of fur seal pelts more than trebled, from three to ten dollars per pelt. This proved too much for many to resist, and pelagic sealing—the taking of the animals at sea—began. Native Americans along the Pacific Northwest coast had previously taken seals that came in close to the shoreline with spears or from sealing craft run by whites who used natives as spearmen. Now the sealers began working along the northern California and Oregon coasts and followed the animals into the Bering Sea. As the sealing fleet increased, there were fewer native hunters, so white men resorted to firearms and sometimes even used explosives. But when they were not killed with spears and lines, many of the seals would sink and be lost. More important, however, females were being killed; the sealers were interested mostly in the size of their catch, and the instructions to the crews were to "kill everything." Females eventually became the predominant catch. When a female was taken in the Bering Sea at breeding time, its pup left on land would not be fed by another female, and thus pelagic hunters would, in effect, be killing three seals every time they harvested a female: the female, the pup on land, and the pup inside the female.[28]

It is quite natural that the U.S. Revenue Cutter Service would find itself in the role of protecting a valuable source of revenue. In 1868 the cutter *Wayanda* steamed northward with orders to protect the interests of the United States, and "for the purpose of preventing the killing of fur-bearing animals."[29] Early in 1869 the service assigned Lts. Robert Henderson and Winslow B. Barnes to the Pribilofs "to prevent illicit traffic and the violation of the revenue laws, with particular reference to . . . the killing of fur seals."[30]

From 1868 to 1911 the one standard operating order for the small cutters centered on the protection of the seals. In 1884 the cutter *Corwin*, under the command of 1st Lt. Michael A. Healy, seized the schooner *Adele* of Hamburg, and in 1886 the *Corwin*, under the command of 1st Lt. Charles A. Abby, seized one American and three Canadian ships for illegal sealing activities. This precipitated the lengthy controversy between the United States and Great Britain known as the Bering Sea Controversy and nearly led to armed conflict between the two nations.[31]

The act of seizing the three ships more than three miles from land caused angry outcries from both Ottawa and London. President Grover Cleveland approved of the arrests, but his secretary of state, Thomas F. Baynard, did not believe they were justifiable. Baynard managed to have the cutters stopped from seizing ships in 1888 and asked for a closed season. He failed to obtain a closure with Great Britain or Russia, however, the only countries with major sealing interests in the Bering Sea. In the closing days of his administration, President Cleveland signed an act directing the president to issue an annual warning stating that anyone who entered "all the dominion of the United States in the waters of Behring's Sea" would be arrested if engaged in pelagic sealing. The new Republican administration of President Benjamin Harrison issued the warning on 22 March 1889 and authorized the arrest of several British sealers. These actions indicated to Great Britain that the conciliatory actions of Baynard were at an end, and they brought forth a not unexpected storm of words. Great Britain, which at that time managed Canada's foreign policy, took a firm stand, and negotiations between the United States, Russia, and Great Britain took place.[32]

The British minister, Sir Julian Pauncefote, and Secretary of State James G. Blaine sparred back and forth, and eventually the British asked for a closed season on land and sea for two years while a joint commission of experts examined the seal herds and reported back on needed regulations. Sealing vessels would not be permitted to approach within ten miles of the rookeries from July through September. This was basically the proposal Blaine had sought, but then another factor entered into the equation.

On 12 March 1890 a new twenty-year lease of sealing rights on the Pribilofs was awarded to the North American Commercial Company. The Alaska Commercial Company had held those rights since the United States had purchased the new territory, and it had seemed a foregone conclusion that the lease would be renewed. It appeared on the surface that the North American Commercial Company had simply outbid its rival, but there was another reason for the change in lessees, one that would shape the course of the Bering Sea Controversy.

The North American Commercial Company had on its board two men who had strong political connections: Darius Ogden Mills, "one of the wealthiest men in the country" and strong supporter of both President Harrison and Secretary Blaine, and Stephen B. Elkins, Blaine's financial adviser and "intimate associate over the years," who would also become President Harrison's secretary of war. One student of the controversy, James Thomas Gay, notes that there is no evidence of the two men using their influence to obtain the lease, but there is "good reason to look to Elkins and his associates for the major explanation of Blaine's termination of the negotiations . . . and for the decision to send American revenue cutters to the Bering Sea on the provocative mission." It is natural that the North American Commercial Company would view with alarm any agreement stopping sealing on land.[33]

In London, Lord Salisbury, the prime minister, consulted the queen and cabinet and then telegraphed Pauncefote to warn Blaine that a formal protest would soon be delivered. Next he secretly ordered four warships to be held in readiness, two in Yokohama and two in Esquimalt, British Columbia; they were to proceed to the Bering Sea if word came that the revenue cutters were seizing British sealers.

From a "secret source," Pauncefote learned that the revenue cutters *Rush* and *Corwin* would sail about the middle of June to the Bering Sea. He therefore issued the formal warning—the *New York World* called it an "ultimatum." At the same time, the American government learned of the preparation of the four British warships. The British sealers, probably thinking that they would be safe, began moving into the Bering Sea. Pauncefote had also received secret information to the effect that the revenue cutters were to be held in Seattle. The British diplomat continued to press Blaine about the revenue cutters. The United States decided to back down, and no Canadian sealing vessels were seized in 1890—although Lt. Francis Tuttle of the *Rush* did board the *Ariel* and issue a verbal warning.

Avoided in 1890, armed intervention still looked possible in 1891. Things also did not bode well for the United States concerning the seals on land. Agents on the Pribilof Islands all noted the decrease in the number of seals, and three of the four treasury officials on the islands put the blame on the land management as well as pelagic sealing. Charles J. Goff, the chief agent, advised that only a complete suspension of all killing, at sea and on land, for an undetermined time could save the marine mammals. At this time Elliott again entered the picture.

Elliott came back to the Pribilofs when he heard the unbelievable report from Goff that the "seals are about gone." Elliott persuaded Goff to order the North American Commercial Company to discontinue the killings. Elliott returned to Washington, D.C., and filed a report that stated that the killing on land and sea was threatening the seals. He recommended that commercial killing on the islands be halted for seven years, that an Anglo-American commission of experts be appointed to advise on regulations, and, in the meanwhile, that pelagic sealing be banned. If Elliott's report were to become known to the British, it would enforce their request for the regulation of sealing on land, as well as at sea. Elliott thus agreed to suppress his report, but only on Blaine's promise to prohibit land sealing if Britain would suppress pelagic sealing.[34]

In 1891, a representative of the North American Commercial Company, perhaps Mills, told Secretary Blaine that the British were preparing to send a number of sealers into the Bering Sea. The United States must not be seen to be running away from the British, he said, or the Republicans would surely face defeat in the next election.[35]

The United States first offered a modus vivendi sponsored by Blaine, and then, three weeks later, another sponsored by President Harrison. Pauncefote eventually received a modus that prohibited all killing on land and sea pending arbitration. This offer, unknown to the British, came from President Harrison. Pauncefote advised Lord Salisbury that this could not be a serious offer, as it went against what the Americans had previously negotiated and, coming during a political campaign, might be highly suspect.

Mills learned that the North American Commercial Company might have to stop their sealing operations. Eventually pressure was brought upon Blaine not to include the modus on the cessation of killing. The Treasury Department removed Goff as chief agent, and President Harrison issued the annual warning—while in secret issuing a permit for the fur company to kill sixty thousand seals in 1891.

Lord Salisbury favored the *modus* prohibiting all killing. This put the U.S. government in a quandary. It could not say that it would ban killing and then issue a permit to kill seals. It could also not withdraw the offer, or else President Harrison would look foolish. President Harrison then put forth a condition: that the North American Commercial Company could kill enough seals to compensate it for the cost of supporting the natives who did the killing. Blaine also added a condition of his own: The modus should not become effective until agreement was reached on the terms of arbitration.

Elliott, in the meanwhile, suspecting trickery by the Harrison administration, took a highly unusual step, especially as he was an employee of the Treasury Department. He went to Pauncefote inquiring as to the British position. Elliott then wrote a letter to the *New York Post* revealing the secret permit. The letter came out on 24 April, and Elliott was dismissed the next day. Undaunted, Elliott continued to release material, including his secret report advising the government to stop the killing for at least seven years. Harrison now found himself in a very bad position, and he eventually ordered Blaine to negotiate with the British and canceled the secret permit.

Great Britain did eventually relent and allow seventy-five hundred seals to be killed on land, but none at sea. The British, however, insisted that a joint commission be formed to determine what arrangements could be made to safeguard the seals. The United States did not care to have its land operations revealed; it allowed only observers, but not a commission, to visit the islands, and stated that a full-scale joint commission would be appointed on conclusion of an arbitration treaty. The North American Commercial Company and the Canadians were both furious. The company, for obvious reasons, sent wrathful letters to Washington, while the Canadians, who wanted payment for damages, blasted Lord Salisbury.

The arbitration went against the United States. The British demanded that the arbitrators see Elliott's full report. They paid attention to the material on land sealing but ignored pelagic sealing. Between 1893 and 1896 pelagic sealers took at least five hundred thousand animals. Elliott, conscious-stricken, worked furiously trying to save the seals, but to no avail.[36] He grew disillusioned, and his spirit broke—nothing seemed to work. After 1905 the Japanese began to make forays into the Bering Sea. Now completely overcome, Elliott dropped out of the fray, but before leaving he wrote to Dr. William T. Hornaday, director of the New York Zoological Garden: "Do something to save those seals."[37]

Hornaday eventually uncovered shady government dealings and wrote to Elliott to "get into the fight any way you see fit." Elliott returned with renewed vigor. He charged the Department of Commerce and Labor, which now oversaw the leases, with misconduct. He demanded and obtained a congressional investigation into the Bureau of Fisheries, which oversaw the fur seal industry. The hearing began in 1911 and lasted three years. Elliott proved tireless. Eventually, in July 1911, Japan, Great Britain, Russia, and the United States passed a treaty concerning the seals. It was not until 1913, however, that the land killing finally ceased. From that date forward, the seal harvesting was to be under government control, with no leases to private companies. The herds slowly began to recover. Elliott died in 1930. As one author noted: "He left a unique bequest to the world: the fur-seal species, *Callorhinus alascanus*." Just as important as Elliott's long fight to save the animals is the fact that fashion no longer dictated the wearing of the pelts of seals, thus there was no longer the high demand for the animals' hides.[38]

For many years, the U.S. Coast Guard's public affairs offices have put forth information that the U.S. Revenue Cutter Service and U.S. Coast Guard in Alaska saved the fur seal. That is not strictly true. Both services, however, did provide the platforms for enforcing the laws to save the seals. Without Elliott's dedicated efforts, nothing could have taken place—but without a means to enforce the actions, Elliott's works would have been for naught. Interestingly enough, many of the humanitarian deeds accomplished by the U.S. Revenue Cutter Service came about because their cutters were patrolling the Bering Sea to enforce the seal laws. For example, medical care for the natives began when the cutters pulled into a village from a patrol and saw people in need. The captains of the cutters were not ordered to do this, nor were they funded for such work. Yet they did it. Strangely enough, U.S. Coast Guard public affairs offices have failed to give credit to the cuttermen for this large humanitarian effort. The use of the U.S. Revenue Cutter Service's cutters to protect the fur seals can truly be said to have been the foundation of all aspects of the old Bering Sea Patrol.

# TWO

# Cuttermen of the North

W ho were the men who manned the U.S. Revenue Cutter Service vessels that plowed Alaska's waters and were the heart of the Bering Sea Patrol? Although some of the cutters' names may be familiar to students of maritime history, virtually nothing is known about the commanders and crews. All too often merely the names and ranks of the officers have survived the passage of the years; those of the crew members, rarely.

Prior to 1915, when it merged with the U.S. Life-Saving Service to form the U.S. Coast Guard, the U.S. Revenue Cutter Service did not maintain personnel or service records as the army and navy did. Instead, its records for commissioned officers consisted solely of brief, handwritten notations—for the most part about changes in duty stations. Since crew members signed on for one-year terms, usually aboard a particular cutter, a practice similar to that in the merchant marine, no service records exist for enlisted men. Only cuttermen who became U.S. Coast Guardsmen after 1915 accumulated the traditional detailed personnel files—which, unfortunately, are still closed to researchers. The discovery of some forgotten letters in the National Archives, however, has made it possible to piece together partial histories of the early U.S. Revenue Cutter Service officers about whom so little is known.

The majority of the early officer cuttermen claimed prior merchant marine experience, and most of the remainder had served in the U.S. Navy. Administered by the Treasury Department, the old U.S. Revenue Cutter Service was a civilian agency, but its crews performed in many respects as if they served in a military capacity. This dual nature of the service persisted for close to two centuries, being present today in the U.S. Coast Guard. The collectors of the customs had the responsibility of seeking out suitable candidates—maritime officers or young men with potential—and recommending them to the secretary of the treasury. He, in turn, passed their names on to the president of the United States for official appointment as commissioned officers. The captain of each cutter had the privilege of selecting and enrolling his own crew. These practices existed from 1790, when the service was founded, until 1915.

Once in the service, the officers spent a great deal of time at sea, with very little rotation to shore duty. In most cases the prolonged sea duty, coupled with their prior experience, produced excellent officers for sea commands. Young men with no previous sea service were commissioned as junior officers

nt Officers, Bering Sea Fleet, 1909

The grizzled warrant officers of the 1909 Bering Sea Patrol pose in front of the small boat of the cutter *Perry.* The man sitting in the center has tentatively been identified as Boatswain-Gunner William Hallberg. In the great San Francisco earthquake, Boatswain Hallberg, as a part of a landing party, disarmed a drunken deputy sheriff. *Courtesy Capt. LeRoy Reinburg Jr., USCG (Ret.)*

and served many years in cutters, acquiring their on-the-job training in seamanship and cutter handling before being given a command.

One serious defect, however, existed in this method of selecting commissioned officers. The collectors of the customs were political appointees, as was the secretary of the treasury. The president, in turn, was the nominal head of his political party, the victor in the last presidential election. Hence at every step of the officer selection process existed the possibility of political dealing and influence peddling.[1]

This flaw is amply demonstrated by the career of Capt. William A. Howard, who entered the U.S. Navy as a midshipman on 1 January 1825. He had attained the rank of acting lieutenant by 31 December 1829, when he received a furlough to accept a revenue officer's commission and promotion to captain. Four days later the secretary of the treasury ordered him to proceed to Portland, Maine, and assume command of the *Detector* under the supervision of the local collector of the customs. His crew, the secretary informed him, consisted of six warrant officers, four able-bodied seamen, a cook, a steward, and four boys. He was cautioned not to pay the seamen more than fifteen dollars a month, and they were to be shipped for one year. The cruising waters of Captain Howard's first cutter stretched from Cape Elizabeth to Penobscot Bay. In January 1832, when the secretary decided to end the practice of employing naval officers on the revenue cutters, Howard decided to resign his naval commission. At that time the service consisted of ninety-two officers and eighteen cutters, and Howard commanded the *Swiftsure,* stationed at Passamaquoddy, Maine. Five years later Captain Howard suddenly found himself placed on "waiting orders" status, a nineteenth-century military method of, in effect, suspending an officer without pay; he promptly tendered his resignation.[2]

The reason for his abrupt removal from command probably stemmed from the spoils system then rampant in the federal government. Each newly elected president, his cabinet members, and his political appointees promptly dismissed incumbent office-holders and replaced them with members of their own party.

The Seminole War (1835–42), meanwhile, had created a critical need for small ships, commanded by naval officers skilled in working close to shore, to support the army troops pursuing the elusive Indians through the swamps and forest trails of Florida. Since the navy lacked both the vessels and the officers, the U.S. Revenue Cutter Service had to provide them. As a result of this wartime demand, Captain Howard accepted temporary command

Any type of diversion was welcomed in the long patrols to the north. *Courtesy Capt. LeRoy Reinburg Jr., USCG (Ret.)*

Cuttermen could also be used as a landing party and had to train accordingly. The landing party from the cutter *Manning*.

of the *Madison,* cruising the waters off the Florida coast from 2 November 1837 until 30 October 1838.[3]

His separation from the U.S. Revenue Cutter Service lasted until the political party in the White House had changed once again. President John Tyler restored his commission as "Captain of a Cutter in the service of the United States, for the protection of the revenue," on 19 December 1842. The following year Howard was designated superintendent of construction for seven new cutters.[4]

According to an anonymous writer, whose veracity must be suspect, the cutters built under Howard's supervision "proved to be entire failures" and prohibitively expensive. Capt. Alex V. Frazier, whom the U.S. Revenue Cutter Service considers its first commandant, was brought in to take over from Captain Howard in April 1843; he built one iron cutter that proved to be "a perfect success," according to the anonymous letter. The revolutionary shift from wooden ships and sails to iron ships and steam, like all radical changes, was accompanied by initial difficulties. In that day, the challenges of building with iron and powering with steam made every new ship an engineering adventure. Early Revenue Cutter Service efforts were not notably successful, and Howard's "failures" should be viewed in that context.[5]

During the Mexican War (1846–48), the need again arose for skilled commanders of small ships to transport troops, supplies, and dispatches and to perform other functions, such as providing naval gunfire support for the soldiers ashore. Captain Howard helped out by commanding the cutter *McLane* in support of the army from 20 January 1846 until 10 September 1847.[6]

In 1848, upon General Zachary Taylor's becoming president, Howard found himself dismissed from the U.S. Revenue Cutter Service once more. He reentered again under the Lincoln administration, but only for a short period. With the outbreak of the Civil War, the Union needed experienced officers, especially ones skilled in gunnery. In 1861, after organizing and equipping the First New York Marine Artillery Regiment "while still on active duty," Howard resigned from the U.S. Revenue Cutter Service to assume command of the newly formed regiment. He was "especially commended in official dispatches for highly meritorious services and successful operations" during the 1862 amphibious assault of Fort Fisher in North Carolina, as well as "for conspicuous gallantry in action" and "coolness and bravery in command of the artillery." In March 1863 he was commissioned a colonel in the 13th New York Heavy Artillery, and he was mustered out with his regiment on 4 July 1865.[7]

One of the hardest and dirtiest jobs aboard a steam cutter was coaling, as evidenced by these cuttermen in Unalaska.

William A. Howard was again restored to the U.S. Revenue Cutter Service with the grade of captain in 1865. In this, the anonymous writer claimed, an "arrangement" had been made to make it appear as if Howard had been on continuous duty in the service since 1829. Ever since his reappointment Howard had spent "pretty much of his time in and about the Treasury Department, only excepting about two or three months when he made a visit to the Territory of Alaska and back to the Department at Washington."[8]

The trip that took Howard away from Washington was in fact a voyage aboard the *Lincoln,* which, under his command, carried the flag and U.S. officials to Alaska immediately following ratification of the purchase treaty with Russia. It earned him the distinction of being the first commander of a cutter in Alaskan waters after the purchase (see chapter 5 for further details of this cruise). Howard never ventured north again. A few years later he was placed on permanent waiting orders, an arrangement by which the U.S. Revenue Cutter Service, which had no pension plan, permitted retired officers to draw partial salary. He died on 17 November 1871.[9]

Every Fourth of July when cutters were in Unalaska there were celebrations, including a massed rifle salute.

William Howard was probably typical not only of the type of officer produced by the spoils system but also of the early commanders of the cutters in Alaska. Calvin L. Hooper, on the other hand, probably was representative of the next generation of cutter officers serving on the Bering Sea Patrol.

In 1864, during the waning years of Howard's career, Calvin L. Hooper obtained his first appointment as a third lieutenant in California, after serving in the merchant marine. For the next seventeen years he sailed on cutters that operated from Astoria, Oregon, and Port Townsend, Washington, rising to second lieutenant in 1868, to first lieutenant in 1870, and finally receiving his first command of a cutter—the *Lincoln*—in 1871. During this time he made three cruises to Alaska. A succession of other assignments took him to the Midwest and the East Coast. In January 1878 he was promoted to captain and transferred to the command of the *Wolcott* at Port Townsend.

His next assignment, to the cutter *Corwin* in 1880, earned him the distinction of being the first captain of the service to begin regular cruising in the Arctic Ocean. A newspaper report of that year described him as being "thirty-eight years old, quiet, unpretentious, studious, calm and resolute in the moment of danger—in brief 'every inch a sailor.'" Subsequent events aboard the *Corwin* bore out this characterization. His primary mission during the 1880 and 1881 season was to find the exploring steamer *Jeannette* and two whalers, *Mount Wollaston* and *Vigilant,* which had been unreported for many months. Hooper even dispatched officers by dogsled in order to save precious time while waiting for the ice to break up. Throughout both navigation seasons, the cutter continued her search through Arctic waters, although partially disabled by a damaged rudder. Hooper's persistence demonstrated his skills in seamanship and the desire to help those in distress. (Further details of this cruise are given in chapters 5 and 8.)[10]

During the Bering Sea controversy of the 1890s, Hooper's skill brought praise from the U.S. Navy. The commander of the navy's Bering Sea force, Robley D. Evans, ordered the capture of a steamer that was receiving illegal seal skins. When "Fighting Bob" Evans found that the USS *Mohican*'s inept captain had bumbled the job, he turned to Hooper and the *Corwin*. Hooper was to stop near an island where illicit traders were apt to be conducting business, "send down his topmasts and [cover] his lower masts with bushes, so that he would be well hidden." When illegal activities began, the cutter would steam out and catch the traders with the furs. Evans, who noted that Hooper was "an able, fearless man . . . [who] would carry out . . . orders," recorded that in spite of dense fog the *Corwin* apprehended the British steamer *Coquitlan* in Port Etches. The steamer was towed to Sitka as a prize and bonded for $600,000, which Evans thought "paid most of the expenses of our summer's work."[11]

His skills in Alaskan waters ensured that Hooper would be appointed the U.S. Revenue Cutter Service's first commander of the Bering Sea Patrol, an appointment that occurred on 9 April 1895. He was also named superintendent of construction and repair, and he performed these duties whenever he was not at sea. He held these two important positions for close to four years. On 16 July 1898, Captain Hooper took command of the cutter *McCulloch*, which had played a small but significant role in the Battle of Manila Bay, including bringing out the first word of Admiral Dewey's victory. In late 1899 the service detached Hooper from sea duty and made him superintendent of construction for the Pacific Coast. On 29 April 1900, while still on active duty, Captain Hooper died at the age of fifty-eight in Oakland, California. He had served continuously for thirty-six years, and a good part of that time in Alaskan waters. At his death only six U.S. Revenue Cutter Service officers outranked him.[12]

As early as 1877 the U.S. Revenue Cutter Service had established its School of Instruction in Maryland; the school later evolved into the U.S. Coast Guard Academy, now located in New London, Connecticut, whose purpose was to train young men of merit as professional officers. Sumner I. Kimball, the first civilian head of the service, had opposed officers' obtaining promotions through political influence. In an effort to curb the practice he developed a cadet system and training school. Moreover, unlike its predecessor, the new system could keep pace with the growing need for sea commanders skilled in the technology used to construct and operate sophisticated modern cutters.[13]

Capt. John Cassion Cantwell is an example of the new type of officer trained at the School of Instruction. Cantwell was born in Raleigh, North Carolina, on 9 January 1859. He entered the U.S. Revenue Cutter Service as an enlisted man on 1 July 1879, and, as a boatswain the following June, he passed the examination for cadet. He served aboard the school ship *Chase* and attended classes at the School of Instruction. On 5 July 1882, Cantwell was commissioned a third lieutenant and ordered to his cutter, the *Bibb*, in Detroit. Next he served on the *Woodbury*, then the *Boutwell*, and, finally, on 26 March 1884, while still a third lieutenant, he reported to the *Corwin* for his first duty in Alaskan waters.[14]

Cantwell thus came under the tutelage of Capt. Michael A. Healy, who is considered one of the great Arctic navigators of the service (Healy is covered in detail in chapters 3 and 11). There is no evidence of friction between the two men; indeed, fifty years later, Cantwell wrote that Healy's "decisions in all matters [had] been so marked with justice that he had won the confidence and respect of all concerned." Healy apparently "played a major role in the formulation of Cantwell's attitude towards the Arctic."[15]

Cantwell was placed in command of two major expeditions while aboard the *Corwin* (see chapter 5). The officer remained aboard the *Corwin* until 1887, when he was transferred to the School of Instruction as an instructor of gunnery and navigation. One year later, on 25 July 1888, Cantwell was promoted to second lieutenant, and on 16 April 1889 he reported aboard the *Bear* in San Francisco for duty as navigator in Alaskan waters. In 1890 another transfer brought Cantwell aboard the *Rush*, which also sailed northern seas. Four years later he shipped aboard the *Colfax* on the East Coast and, in 1895, received shore duty with the U.S. Life-Saving Service in North Carolina. At the outbreak of the Spanish-American War, Cantwell was executive officer aboard the *Morrill*. During the war, the *Morrill* patrolled off Havana, and for their capture of two schooners the officers and men of the cutter received bronze medals.

On 4 March 1899, Cantwell requested duty aboard the *Bear* as executive officer, a request immediately approved. John F. Murphy, Cantwell's biographer, notes that perhaps "the normal duties of the COLFAX lacked the excitement of dueling with Spanish batteries or possibly the news from Alaska

Unlike the enlisted cuttermen, officers had the opportunity to entertain guests in the wardroom. Inasmuch as they were sailors on a long patrol, there is little doubt whom they would invite, if possible. Probably taken in Unalaska.

proved too attractive for Cantwell to resist."[16] He hoped to take command of the *Nunivak,* a stern-wheeler built to bring order to the lawless Yukon River valley during the gold rush days. The revenue officer had heard that one of the duties of the commanding officer would be to explore the region. Cantwell, "playing the role of experienced Alaska explorer to the hilt," addressed a long letter to Capt.-Cmdt. Charles F. Shoemaker requesting assignment as commanding officer to the *Nunivak.*[17] By April Cantwell was back in northern waters, awarded his first command.

The *Nunivak* under Cantwell was to enforce customs and navigation laws from the mouth of the Yukon to a thousand miles upriver. The new commander was to cooperate with military organizations in law enforcement, aid customs officers, arrest any outlaws and turn them over to civil authorities, make hydrographic surveys, collect specimens of the flora and fauna, gather meteorological data, and assist anyone in distress. Because the *Nunivak* would be frozen in during the winter, her crew would remain aboard from July 1889 until the summer of 1900.

One of the more notable missions of that first tour was the quarantining of St. Michael. On the last day of June 1900, Cantwell learned that a small-pox epidemic was raging at Nome. Fearing that the epidemic would spread up the Yukon Valley once ships from Nome began touching at St. Michael,

One activity while in Unalaska was climbing a nearby mountain. *Left,* Lt. R. R. Waesche, completes the rite of passage. Waesche would become commandant of the U.S. Coast Guard from 1936 to 1945, the longest tenure in the history of the service.

he urged the U.S. Army commander at St. Michael to declare a quarantine. Although it took three days to convince the commander, Cantwell succeeded, and the *Nunivak* enforced the quarantine for three weeks. The cutter anchored in the outer harbor, and its crew boarded and checked all vessels. Ships from Nome were sent to an island some ten miles distant. One writer has noted that smallpox along the Yukon was made "practically impossible by the work of the *Nunivak*."[18]

On 16 September 1901, Cantwell was relieved of his command and returned to San Francisco, where he was detailed to write the report of the *Nunivak*'s work. The remainder of his career may be quickly summed up: He was promoted to captain, 11 October 1904; named commanding officer of the *McCulloch* and *Hartley* at San Francisco to 1909; assigned to various shore duties with the U.S. Life-Saving Service and U.S. Coast Guard to 1917; promoted to senior captain, U.S. Coast Guard, 3 October 1917; designated commanding officer, Naval Reserve Camp, San Diego, during World War I; appointed commander, Northern Division, Seattle, 9 September 1919; and placed on the retired list on 10 May 1920, after more than forty years of service. Senior Captain John C. Cantwell died at Sausalito, California, on 8 October 1940, being buried at sea two days later.[19]

Despite a search for information on the enlisted men who sailed Alaska's waters for the U.S. Revenue Cutter Service, only one small snippet could be found in the records of the National Archives. Capt. J. W. White, of the *Wayanda,* wrote: "Last night Henry Miller (seaman) returned on board from liberty, and somewhat intoxicated, got into a fight . . . on the Berth Deck with Alexander Gorman (seaman) and . . . Miller had nearly one half of his left ear bitten off. . . . Considering the circumstances, I prefer taking no further action in the case. . . ."[20] But one man, who had served aboard the *Bear* in 1917, just after the formation of the U.S. Coast Guard, came forward in 1977 to share his recollections. F. S. Sandel entered the service under the old enlistment system whereby a man joined for one year, usually for a particular ship. No depression or unfortunate love affair prompted him to enlist; he had dreamed of it ever since his first sight of a cutter. His observations and those recorded in official logbooks and in the few written accounts by U.S. Revenue Cutter Service enlisted men show that Sandel's recollections accurately reflect an enlisted man's life aboard a Revenue Cutter Service cutter.[21]

The routine day for enlisted men assigned deck duty aboard a Bering Sea Patrol cutter consisted of four hours on watch and four hours off, day and night. Besides the normal work of keeping a ship running, cuttermen had to

A young cutterman serving on the cutter *Rush* must have
looked impossibly young to someone like . . .

John Hall, in 1909 a thirty-six-year veteran of the U.S. Revenue Cutter Service. *Courtesy Capt. LeRoy Reinburg Jr., USCG (Ret.)*

stand wheel watches and lookout duty. When least expected each day, they had to drop everything and perform a drill, such as general quarters, collision, or fire. The thing Sandel hated most during the daily routine was putting on or taking in sail. Since the *Bear* also used coal as fuel, the soot would cause those going aloft to "go up clean and come down looking like a miner after a day's work." On their four hours off, some sailors relaxed by tying knot belts, reading, writing letters, or gambling. For Sandel, however, "recreation was trying to get some sleep" before the next watch.

Only the occasional stop, such as at patrol headquarters at Unalaska, broke the routine. But even in port, cuttermen spent much time in formal inspections, filling the coal bunkers, and doing the maintenance work not possible at sea. Some shore liberty was always granted, though not necessarily in a town. Frequently the men used time off the ship to hike, pick blueberries, fish, hunt, collect curios, or just relax.

The common complaint aboard the Bering Sea Patrol cutters was the food. Because of the lack of refrigeration, fresh meat quickly disappeared from the menu once the cruise began. From time to time the larder improved; bagging reindeer, duck, or fish was not a difficult feat for those skilled in hunting and fishing, and fish and game provided a welcome respite from preserved rations. Even so, enlisted men found living conditions at sea far from comfortable. Sleeping forward in cramped quarters derogatorily referred to as the "glory hole," they never had any privacy nor could they escape the noise of others engaged in off-duty activities. Always present was the reek of sweat, damp clothes, and, in heavy weather, vomit.

These cuttermen led a lonely, rough, and thankless existence, one extremely isolated and forlorn even by a sailor's standards. Typically, they worked, played, and drank hard. But always these enlisted men were—or quickly became—skilled practitioners of their craft.

Life aboard ship was not only difficult but also occasionally hazardous. Just how dangerous it could be is illustrated by this 1896 report from the cutter *Perry* in the Bering Sea: "While making evening colors, the pennant became fouled and would neither break out nor lower. Seaman C. C. Mauethrop, who was assigned as acting quartermaster and had the watch, went aloft to clear the pennant. He reached the trunk and endeavored, for the space of a minute, to break out the pennant, when for some unaccountable reason, he fell to the deck and was instantly killed."[22]

Cuttermen in northern waters were lost to freak accidents less often than to the environment they operated within. The cold sea that the cutters

Aboard the *Rush* in 1886. The officer in first row, center, has been identified as Capt. Calvin L. Hooper, the first official commander of the Bering Sea Patrol. The boy in the second row, second from left, has been identified as Fred Healy, Capt. Michael A. Healy's son.

patrolled is fickle. The Bering Sea, in general, is relatively shallow and small in area. But it lies in the seasonal path of low-pressure weather systems that traverse the North Pacific Ocean, and its shallow waters can be quickly whipped into mountainous seas by intense lows that sweep the Aleutian Islands. The air is always cool, even in the summer, and it is a rare week in which there is no rain, drizzle, or fog.

Then there is the Arctic cold. Even in summer the chill can penetrate heavy clothing when the wind comes up. The noted naturalist John Muir, who in 1881 accompanied the cutter *Corwin* as it searched the Siberian coastline for the exploring ship *Jeannette,* described in a letter the weather in May: "How cold it is this morning! How it blows and snows! It is not 'the wolf's long howl on Unalaska's shore,' as Campbell has it, but the wind's long howl. A more sustained, prolonged, screeching, raving howl I have never heard."[23]

The cold can numb the senses, causing one to make mistakes in an environment that does not forgive. The "raving howl" of the wind causes surf to build along the shores of the islands of the Bering Sea and the coastline of Alaska. Most of the locations the cuttermen visited required the landing of small boats on an open beach, one of the most difficult of small craft maneuvers. Capt. David Evans, commanding the *Lincoln,* wrote about an incident at St. Paul Island, one of the Pribilofs, in 1869. Captain Evans had come ashore to examine the seal herd. Upon learning of a whaler nearby he sent his boat, with four enlisted men and an officer, out to board the ship while he continued to work with officials ashore. Shortly thereafter some natives rushed up to him and told him that the boat had capsized in heavy surf and that cuttermen were clinging to the keel. Captain Evans, with a crew of natives, launched a boat into the raging surf, but after "about half an hour, of hard maneuvering with the furious surf, we rescued two out of the five of the boat's crew." The remaining three cuttermen were lost. One of the men drowned, Lewis Garlip, twenty-three, of Hamburg, Germany, "had been capsized, in a boat, in the very spot, fourteen months" previously, at which time "all were lost except himself. The poor fellow was telling it to his shipmates at the time they left the ship." Today, the bodies of cuttermen lie buried and forgotten throughout Alaska, far from the bustling and technologically oriented modern world. The remains of Seaman C. C. Mauethrop, along with those of other cuttermen, lie in the little graveyard at Unalaska. Lewis Garlip and his shipmates, according to Captain Evans, were buried on St. Paul's Island.[24]

Despite all its discomforts, loneliness, and danger, the life of a cutterman in Alaskan waters had a distinct and beguiling appeal. More often than not its attraction proved lasting. Sandel, for example, even after sixty years, could still say: "If I wasn't so damned old, I'd sure like to do it again."

# THREE

# "Hell Roaring Mike"

Historians little remember those who sailed on the Bering Sea Patrol. This includes even the man who became the personification of the patrol during the years of the U.S. Revenue Cutter Service, Capt. Michael A. Healy. Captain Healy's biography portrays everything good—and bad—about the patrol. From 1874 until 1895 and again, briefly, from 1900 to 1904, he sailed annually to the Bering Sea and the Arctic. Healy became, in the words of the *New York Sun,* "the ideal commander of the old school, bluff, prompt, fearless, just. He knows [the] Bering Sea, the Straits, and even the Arctic as no other man knows them." Furthermore, the *Sun* described Healy as "a good deal more distinguished [a] person in the waters of the far Northwest than any president of the United States."[1]

Healy received his captaincy in 1884 and took command of the seemingly immortal *Bear* two years later. The captain, the *Bear,* and the Bering Sea Patrol became almost one. During this time Healy earned a well-deserved reputation as possibly the best Arctic navigator in the United States. The maritime historian John Bockstoce wrote that the "cogency of . . . [Healy's] views was such that they were reprinted in the *United States Coast Pilot for Alaska* for fifty years."[2] During all the years of command in the dangerous Bering Sea and Arctic, he never lost a ship. Stories are still told of Captain Healy and the *Bear* even today in some isolated villages in western and Arctic Alaska. Apart from his renown as a seaman, the U.S. Revenue Cutter captain also rescued countless mariners in distress and gained a reputation for his humane treatment of the natives of Alaska. And he was the author of an unusual experiment in social engineering.

The public remained enthralled by the strange land to the north many decades after its purchase by Seward. Thus it is understandable why San Francisco reporters eagerly sought out the famous captain at the dock when the *Bear* returned from one of her patrols; nor did Healy shrink from the limelight. Helping to secure his reputation, but little noted by the few biographers who have written on Captain Healy, is the fact that he was a better writer than most sailors. For example, the following passage makes the dangerous Arctic ice pack equally vivid to both those who have been there to see it and those who have explored only from the comfort of their armchairs: "There is in this [icepack] that which man can never conquer. Inside its solid front no vessel can penetrate and once caught within its grasp it is almost a miracle that she ever escapes. No ship can be built that will stand its crushing force, and no ram can be made so powerful as to break its way through it. It is only when the elements combine against it that man can evade its domain."[3] By the 1890s Captain Healy ranked number ten in seniority among all U.S. Revenue Cutter Service captains, thereby possessing a position and reputation that many other officers would envy.

Amazingly enough, the captain managed to accomplish another major feat: He concealed an important fact about his family. That fact, as Healy knew only too well, if revealed would ruin everything he had worked so hard to obtain.[4] Almost as if an ancient Greek had scripted the story of Capt. Michael A. Healy, just as the U.S. Revenue Cutter Service skipper was reaching the zenith of his career, a crowd of demonstrators worked their way through the streets of San Francisco with a banner proclaiming the injustice of "monster Healy." Five years later, Captain Healy stood stripped of his command, lowered to the bottom of the list of captains, and placed on waiting orders status for four years. Then, again as if he were a character in a play by Sophocles, Healy was restored to command four years later, only to have headlines in the Pacific Northwest scream "Healy insane!" Shortly thereafter the aging skipper was confined to a mental hospital. Again restored to command, he retired in 1903 a broken man. Less than a year later he died. (This stage of Captain Healy's life is related in further detail in chapter 11.) After his death his accomplishments were quickly forgotten. If it were not for the efforts of a few researchers, his name would today have been completely lost. As it is, very few people know of the tragedy of Capt. Michael A. Healy.[5]

Capt. Michael A. "Hell Roaring" Healy.

Healy's father, Michael Morris Healy, a native of Ireland and a devout Catholic, had enlisted in the British Army during the War of 1812. He arrived in North America too late to take part in the fighting and soon found himself assigned to garrison duty in Nova Scotia, from where he quickly deserted to the United States.

The elder Healy settled in western Georgia. He either won by lottery or purchased thirteen hundred acres of farmland when former Creek Indian lands were thrown open to white settlers in 1823. Within only seven years his holdings had increased to sixteen hundred acres and seventeen slaves. Two years later he had doubled the size of the plantation. At some point during this time Healy entered into a union with a slave named Mary Eliza. She remained his consort throughout their lives, and the two of them were buried together in a spot overlooking the Ocmulgee River in Jones County. The origins of Mary Eliza are unknown, but it is certain that she was a mulatto slave girl not more than a few months over sixteen years of age when Healy for all practical purposes took her for his wife. Under the prevailing laws of the time, Healy could neither legally marry nor grant freedom to Mary Eliza, and all his children remained property. Upon his death the state of Georgia could dispose of Mary Eliza and all ten of their children as it might any other slaves.[6]

In 1837, Michael Morris Healy took his oldest son, James, to New York City. There were two reasons for this. The Southern states did not permit slaves to learn to read or write, and thus James could obtain an education only in the North; also, he would find it easier to conceal his African-American heritage there. Eventually two other of the Healy boys received an education from the Quakers at Flushing, Long Island. Michael A. Healy came into the world on 22 September 1839. The laws of Georgia, beyond prohibiting slaves from being educated or being freed upon their master's death—even if their emancipation were stipulated in a will—also prohibited money or property from being passed to a slave through inheritance. Nonetheless, Michael Morris Healy took great care, through a carefully worded will and with the help of friends, to provide for the care and education of his children in the North.[7]

Even in the North, the Healy children bore the brunt of the prevailing prejudices of the time. Not only did their swarthiness attract hateful comments but they also heard all the anti-Irish and anti-Catholic epitaphs common during that period. Michael Morris visited his children yearly. In 1844 he transferred the boys to Worcester, Massachusetts, and enrolled them in the College of the Holy Cross, a Jesuit institution.[8]

Five years later the boys' father informed them by letter that their mother had died. The seven children now living in the North planned a family reunion in 1850 in New York. But before that meeting could take place, they learned that Michael Morris Healy had died of cholera on 29 August 1850. His sudden death left three of the youngest children stranded in Georgia. Hugh Healy took a calculated risk and traveled to Georgia to take custody of the younger children; he transported them to New York and placed them in a foster home. Since Michael Morris had planned well, enough money came to the family in the North to finance the education of the younger children.[9]

Michael A. Healy, unfortunately, never settled into the role of scholar. Instead he continually ran away, wanting to become a sailor. Finally, James, the eldest and the head of the family, gave up and let Michael, at the age of fifteen, go off to sea. Michael became the only member of the family not to enter the church. Some of his brothers later became very well placed in the Catholic hierarchy and played an important part in Michael's career.

The little-known facts of Healy's first years at sea come solely from an autobiographical letter that he wrote in 1865 when applying for admission to the U.S. Revenue Cutter Service. Briefly, Healy began his career in the forecastle and worked his way "up through the hawsepipe" to become an officer. According to his application, he sailed to China and the East and West Indies before settling into the Mediterranean fruit trade. He then spent the majority of his time at sea in that business, eventually becoming a first mate on a fruit freighter. He noted that his life had "been comparatively easy[,] having never yet suffered actual shipwreck, although I have at different times lost spars, sails, etc."[10]

Michael's oldest brother, James, a Catholic priest and personal secretary of the bishop of Boston, urged him to apply for an officer's commission in a government seagoing service. Since his chances of being accepted as an officer by the U.S. Navy after the Civil War seemed practically nil, Healy hit upon the U.S. Revenue Cutter Service. This urging by James brings us the first indication that perhaps Michael did not hesitate to use political influence to achieve his goals. As one student of Healy notes, James remained "relatively well placed to muster a degree of political influence, and aid [to] his young seaman brother in obtaining a federal commission." The letters of recommendation written in behalf of Michael hint of some type of political backing. The bishop of Boston and Representatives Alexander H. Rice and George F. Emery of the Massachusetts congressional delegation all wrote favorable endorsements. Later, when his career seemed in jeopardy, there would be other hints of political influence by brothers who had attained high rank in the Catholic church. In any event, in 1865 Michael began his career as a third lieutenant in the U.S. Revenue Cutter Service.[11]

In the early years of his life Michael considered Boston his home, and he occasionally returned there during times ashore. It was there in the 1860s that he met Mary Jane Roach. The two were married on 31 January 1865, shortly after Michael's appointment to the Revenue Cutter Service. Mary Healy proved to be an amazing woman. She followed Michael from one home port to another throughout his career. Mary also accompanied him on some of his voyages to the Bering Sea and Arctic regions, making her one of the few American women to travel into this isolated region of the world during the last century. She experienced eighteen pregnancies, only one of which resulted in a live birth, that of Frederick Healy in 1870. Mary proved to be her husband's most loyal supporter when Michael began his fall from grace. Only once did she seem to falter, and then only for a short period.[12]

In 1868, Third Lieutenant Healy found himself serving in the cutter

*Reliance,* a 110-foot topsail schooner of 228 tons. The cutter, built in Baltimore in 1867, sailed around the Horn and arrived in Sitka on 24 November 1868. The ship then spent most of the intervening time anchored in the harbor before returning south the following year. Healy moved upward to second lieutenant and received orders to the cutter *Lincoln* in San Francisco. Then, on 8 January 1872, he received orders to report as a first lieutenant to the cutter *Active* in New Bedford, Massachusetts. This port, still important for whaling, gave Healy his introduction to the masters of whaling ships, who would play a critical part in his career. According to one researcher of his life, the Revenue Cutter Service officer "would later come to be highly regarded by these tough mariners for his seamanship, as well as his life saving activities in the North, and was accepted into their tight fraternity as one of their own."[13]

In 1875 the cutter *Richard Rush* dropped her hook in San Francisco's harbor. The newly appointed 1st Lt. Michael A. Healy had received orders to this cutter, and he now began his long career in northern waters. In 1880, Capt. Calvin L. Hooper requested—and obtained—Healy as his executive officer in the *Corwin* during its first cruise to the Arctic Ocean. After serving and learning more of his trade from that excellent seaman, First Lieutenant Healy received his first command in August 1881: his old cutter the *Richard Rush.* By this time, Healy, forty-two years old, had served fifteen years as an officer of the U.S. Revenue Cutter Service and eleven in the merchant marine. Five years of his sea time had involved cruising on the West Coast or Alaskan waters, and his reputation as a seaman and navigator continued to grow. Throughout his career he gained a reputation for getting the most out of the vessels he commanded.

Healy's next assignment, in 1882, took him to his former cutter, the *Corwin,* this time as the commanding officer. At Angoon, in southeast Alaska, Healy ordered the shelling of an Indian village. His actions seem completely out of line with his policies concerning the native people of the Bering Sea and Arctic regions. The alleged aggressiveness of the Tlingits does not explain the act. This is only the first contradiction that makes up the enigma of Michael A. Healy.

One of the most striking contradictions of Healy's life, however, centers on alcohol. Healy spent a great deal of his time battling the smuggling of illegal whiskey, better known as hootch, to the natives of Alaska.[14] Part of the reason for this constant war against alcohol was simply that it was among the duties of all revenue officers to enforce the law prohibiting the trading

Capt. Michael A. Healy, at Unalaska, date unknown. The woman to Healy's right has been tentatively identified as his wife, Mary. Compare Healy's condition in this photograph with his appearance in the one taken in 1896 (chapter 11).

of liquor to natives. A large part of the effort, however, was Healy's concern for the welfare of the natives of Alaska. He undertook these efforts to stop the smuggling of liquor with vigor. In 1892, for example, when Captain Healy found that Capt. Joseph Whitesides, of the whaler *Belvedere,* had traded whiskey to the St. Lawrence Island Eskimos in exchange for whalebone, he pursued the whaler all the way to the Siberian coast. In his report Healy wrote, "Even though the amount traded was under the statutory limit of $400 and would not authorize the seizure of the vessel . . . I hoped to be able to recover and confiscate the whalebone and as a Justice of the Peace for the Territory to impose a fine on the master." Healy missed the whaler but confiscated the keg as evidence.[15] Healy spent so much time fighting liquor smuggling, according to one account, that he ran into trouble for neglecting his other duties.

Thus perhaps the greatest irony in Captain Healy's life was the revenue captain's long war with John Barleycorn, a war he would eventually lose. Liquor clearly played the leading role in Healy's eventual disgrace. Although most who knew Healy commented favorably upon the captain's seamanship, when pressed they usually remarked that he was a hard drinker. One can explain this away by saying that most captains of the time, especially those who had made the difficult (almost impossible) passage from forecastle to wardroom, were hard drinkers. Healy was aware of his problem, but, like many before and after him, he could not master it. In 1883, Michael's brother, Father Patrick, "toyed with the idea of advising Mary . . . to leave her husband, as a means of bringing him to his senses." Mary did in fact leave him, but only for a short period. Father Patrick wrote that he "never saw a man whose wits and tongue sharpen so under liquor of which he was redolent, yet could walk like a grenadier and bow like a dancing master." When Mary and Frederick accompanied Michael on a patrol, the captain seemed able to keep his drinking under control. Mary could not make every voyage, however, and as time went on Captain Healy began to earn a reputation for being a difficult man to serve under. He seemed to allow some leeway for enlisted men, perhaps because of his own beginnings, but junior officers learned to their regret why their captain had earned the sobriquet of "Hell Roaring Mike." Eventually he lost the ability to "walk like a grenadier and bow like a dancing master" when under the influence. He also began to lay the blame for his misfortunes on others.

The revenue cutters that plied the waters of the Bering Sea usually carried medical doctors who, whenever possible, treated the sick in isolated villages and settlements. From this humane act evolved the duty of caring for the sick, whether native, miner, settler, or whaler (see chapter 9). Captain Healy and the *Bear* provided the only available assistance for the natives and settlers, as well as at least two thousand whalers, in the Arctic.[16] Crews from whaling ships invariably required care for broken bones or other injuries, and the more seriously injured often had to endure the difficult passage over to the cutter for surgery. The doctors not only treated the natives and settlers on shore but also helped those caught in periodic epidemics. In 1893, for example, the doctor aboard the *Bear* treated those at Unalaska struck down by influenza. Healy recorded that, "but for the presence of this vessel and aid of the surgeon, many deaths would have occurred."[17]

Both the masters and crews of the whaling ships in the north came to respect the captain for his ceaseless efforts to help them in times of distress.

Healy often criticized the boldness of the whaling skippers who risked ships and crews in pursuit of profits, but he would search both the Alaskan and Siberian coastlines if any of them went missing. In 1885, Congress officially recognized Captain Healy's life-saving work in the Arctic. Three years later the masters and crews of four whalers wrecked near Point Barrow, all of whom had been rescued by Healy, wrote a testimonial to him in the *San Francisco Chronicle*. In December 1889, fifty masters and owners presented another testimonial in a ceremony at San Francisco's Occidental Hotel.[18]

The very next month, Captain Healy went from being feted to being labeled a torturer. In "a strange, but effective alliance," the California Woman's Christian Temperance Union (WCTU) and the Seaman's Union caused a board of investigation to be held to consider charges of drunkenness and cruelty against the revenue captain.[19] Mrs. M. B. Eden, WCTU superintendent for Work among Sailors, wrote to the secretary of the treasury accusing Healy of being "an inebriate," of remaining in a drunken state for days while in command of the *Bear,* and of being "guilty of great cruelty towards the men on board the whalers and some of the merchant vessels."[20]

The whaleship skippers, whom Captain Healy had always supported, now rose to his defense with depositions, causing the drunkenness charges to be quickly dismissed. The remaining cruelty indictment centered on incidents aboard the whaler *Estrella* in 1889, when Captain Healy, responding to a request by a master for aid and protection, used a punishment known as "tricing up" to restore order. Tricing up entailed handcuffing a seaman's hands behind his back, running a short length of line through the irons, and then passing the line through a ringbolt high on a bulkhead or mast. The offending seaman would then be hoisted up until his toes barely touched the deck.[21]

Captain Healy defended his actions by saying that the punishment was justified by the conditions at hand: "[Tricing up] is not a customary treatment except on frontier places. We are empowered by Congress to suppress mutinies. . . . If a mutiny occurred at San Francisco, . . . we would go and arrest the man, and turn him over to the police. But, up there, where there is no jail to bring men to, that is the last resort, to trice men up."[22] Captain Healy managed to escape conviction, but the case proved to be a watershed in his life and, to a great extent, that of the U.S. Revenue Cutter Service—although neither the captain nor his service recognized the fact at the time.

Evidence of how close Captain Healy came to losing command of the *Bear* in July 1889 lies buried in the records of the U.S. Revenue Cutter

Service; the incident proved to be a harbinger of the future. Capt. Leonard Shepard first learned of Healy's drinking problem while commanding the *Rush* at Unalaska. The captain of the *Bear* committed a serious breach of naval etiquette by appearing intoxicated during a courtesy call to the *Rush*. Shortly thereafter Shepard became the captain-commandant of the service, and not long afterward he wrote to Healy, apparently to warn him that if he did not control his drinking he would face loss of command. Healy responded: "I take your advice in everything. I honor your frankness, and admire your friendship and pledge to you by all I hold most sacred that while I live never to touch intoxicants of any kind or description. It is a duty I owe myself, my friends and the service, and you personally. Rest assured that nothing will alter the determination that out of this trouble good will come to me. One thing I will hate and that is to give up my command of the BEAR. I love the ship, tho [it is] hard work."[23] Six years later, in a manner reminiscent of Greek tragedy, events would close in upon the skipper of the *Bear*.

Hard on the heels of the Board of Investigation and just prior to his downfall, Capt. Michael A. Healy took part in an unusual experiment in social engineering, one that illuminates his concern for the natives of the North. Captain Healy, like many others in the U.S. Revenue Cutter Service and other walks of life, had became concerned over the fate of the Eskimo. Captain Hooper, captain of the cutter *Corwin,* for example, had noted in 1881 that "not one step has been taken looking towards the improvement of their condition. On the contrary, they are sinking each year lower and lower . . . at the mercy of the whiskey-seller. This is a great wrong, and unless remedied will prove a lasting disgrace to our country."[24] Entire villages were reported decimated from starvation, with much of the blame being laid at the doorstep of the whalers and sealers. As the whales began to disappear in the north, so did a large supply of food for the natives. Whalers also indiscriminately killed walrus for their ivory tusks, depleting yet another major source of food. The numbers of seals and sea lions also diminished. Sheldon Jackson, missionary and superintendent of education for Alaska, noted that the lack of animals had started "the process of slow starvation and extermination . . . along the whole Arctic coast of Alaska."[25] In sharp contrast, the Siberian natives, much like the Lapps of Finland, herded reindeer, which supplied a reliable source of food, clothing, and shelter. These small animals could mean the difference between starvation and salvation for the North American Eskimo.

Capt. Michael A. Healy making ready to harpoon something. Healy was not young when commanding the *Bear*, and this illustration gives an idea of the toughness of the man. Note the *Bear*'s figurehead, now in the Mariner's Museum, Newport News, Virginia.

Who first looked toward the Asian continent for a solution to this problem still remains a mystery. Transforming the Alaskan Eskimo into herders of reindeer certainly would free them from both their dependency on the hunt and possible starvation. Some authors give Sheldon Jackson the credit for the importation of reindeer to North America. Others might also deserve this honor. Dr. Charles H. Townsend, while aboard the cutter *Corwin* on her 1885 cruise, wrote that reindeer could be used to help the Alaskan natives. John F. Murphy, the biographer of Lt. John C. Cantwell, gives Cantwell the credit for suggesting the idea. Cantwell, according to Murphy, first discussed the idea with Townsend, who then made his contribution, investigating whether the vegetation on the North American continent would sustain the animals. Afterward, he brought the plan to Capt. Michael A. Healy, and the three men—Cantwell, Townsend, and Healy—according to Murphy, can claim credit for the introduction of the reindeer into Alaska. However, historian Gerald O. Williams points out that Captain Hooper also suggested the idea, in 1880.[26]

In the final analysis, it is probably best to say that the idea came from many sources. What is not in question about the project is the importance of Captain Healy and Sheldon Jackson. Jackson would later write: "It was my good fortune to make my visit to the Eskimo in the United States Revenue steamer BEAR, commanded by Capt. Michael A. Healy. Having seen much of the native population and taken a great interest in their welfare, he has probably a better knowledge of their condition than any other person. His attention was early called to the advantage that the introduction of domesticated reindeer would be to the inhabitants of Northern Alaska, and he has given the subject considerable thought."[27]

Both individuals contributed their unique skills to furthering the cause of the reindeer project. Dr. Jackson used his considerable skills among the halls of Congress and the press to advance the project and obtain the necessary funding. Captain Healy, meanwhile, aided by his brothers, tried to convince both the Treasury Department and the U.S. Revenue Cutter Service to undertake the project, urging the use of the *Bear* to transport the animals. His reputation among the natives of Siberia, he stressed, would be a crucial factor in successfully completing the work. He also spoke freely to the *San Francisco Chronicle* about the project, hoping to enlist the power of the press. Even the captain's fight to clear himself of the charge of being a heartless torturer did not sidetrack him. He continued laying the foundation for a lasting humanitarian solution to the starvation facing the natives of the north, and so did Jackson. Their efforts at persuasion began in earnest after the patrol of 1890. Despite their most strenuous lobbying, however, Congress did not authorize money for the project until June 1892.

Dr. Jackson, meanwhile, took his project to the American people. He appealed for donations that would enable him to begin the project as soon as possible, as the need was "urgent and so many lives are at stake." All those who contributed ten dollars, Jackson emphasized, would have the "satisfaction of feeling that they have furnished one reindeer to the herd, and have a share in the creation of an industry that will ultimately save thousands of people from starvation." By the spring of 1891 the campaign had raised more than two thousand dollars. Captain Healy used these funds to purchase trade goods for barter with the Siberian natives. The Treasury Department approved the procurement and transportation of the reindeer on 5 March 1891. Captain Healy, in turn, received orders to investigate the procurement of the animals and their transportation, as well as to provide transportation for Dr. Jackson on the 1891 patrol.

The first attempt at purchasing reindeer came on 8 July 1891, when the *Bear* came to anchor off the village of Indian Point, Siberia. Healy and Jackson had selected Indian Point because it provided a quick journey for the reindeer to the proposed test location on St. Lawrence Island. Unfortunately, however, their attempts at obtaining an interpreter failed, which put them at a very great disadvantage. In addition, the village proved to be a poor one for the test, as the natives had only a small herd. The chief very correctly pointed out that he did not "like to starve any more than American Indians." Jackson and Healy, furthermore, found that the chief had a surplus of trade goods, a fact that further diminished his interest in the proposed barter.

While anchored, the cuttermen made a serendipitous discovery: Among the visitors to the *Bear* were an old Eskimo and his son, who spoke some English. The young man agreed to act as an interpreter, and here the importance of Captain Healy to this project again came to the fore: The father told Jackson that he would never trust his son to go aboard a whaler, for he would probably never see him again or be ill treated, but he knew that Captain Healy would look after the boy.

When ice prevented the *Bear* from visiting villages farther north, Captain Healy decided to visit Holy Cross Bay on the northwest side of the Gulf of Anadyr. This meant that any reindeer purchased would be afloat for thirty to forty-eight hours if transported to St. Lawrence Island, and their food supply would be critical. Only now did Healy and Jackson learn the disturbing news that Siberians had tried to place reindeer on St. Lawrence Island sometime in the past but had been unsuccessful.

Arriving for the first time at Holy Cross Bay, Captain Healy cautiously navigated the poorly charted waters. Fog set in soon after the ship anchored, and two days were wasted waiting for the murk to lift. This delay, and the knowledge that St. Lawrence Island was likely unsuitable for reindeer, caused Dr. Jackson and Captain Healy to reevaluate their plans. They finally settled for the promise of purchasing reindeer the next year. On 27 August 1891 their native interpreter negotiated the purchase of four deer at the village of Enchowan near Cape Serdze. Jackson entered in his diary, "Paid 1 Rifle and 200 cartridges for 4 deer."[28] The next day, Lt. David H. Jarvis supervised the loading of the first reindeer aboard the *Bear*. The cutter then proceeded on course. The deer seemed to thrive on the oats they were fed on board the cutter.[29] They did so well in fact that Jackson and Healy decided to return to Indian Point to obtain more. They managed to purchase twelve more animals and put them ashore at Unalaska before the *Bear* proceeded southward to her home port. The project, although not as successful as they had wished, did seem to Jackson and Healy to be off to a good start. They had proven that reindeer could be purchased in Siberia and transported to a suitable location in Alaska. Captain Healy, according to the missionary's later praise, "is well known for thousands of miles on both sides of the coast and natives have confidence in him. With a stranger in command I am confident that but little could have been accomplished this season."[30] Jackson next turned to finding people to manage the herd and teach the Eskimos reindeer husbandry. Teller, Alaska, eventually became the main location for the reindeer, and William Lopp became the manager of the experimental station.

From this small beginning, the reindeer project grew. Each year until the imperial Russian government withdrew its support in 1906, a revenue cutter appeared off various villages in Siberia to barter for reindeer and then transport the animals to Alaska. The herd eventually grew to number over a million by the outbreak of World War II. Many writers stop the story of the reindeer experiment there, implying a successful project. Stephen H. Evans, the author of the standard history of the U.S. Revenue Cutter Service, simply concluded that "Healy and Jackson hoped that with Uncle Sam's benevolent guidance the Innuits could clamber up the grade [from hunters to herders] within a generation. By 1930, domesticated deer herds in Alaska had multiplied to 600,000 (estimated) head and 13,000 drew on them for their life's essentials."[31] In a sense, Evans and others are correct: The animals were successfully imported, and they did thrive on the North American continent. Furthermore, William Lopp and later managers of the reindeer station did teach some Eskimos the skills of reindeer husbandry. All of this is as Jackson and Healy had planned. In the final analysis, however, the project did not do what the missionary and the revenue officer had wished. The Eskimos did not take to herding: The cultural change proved too much to overcome—that in spite of the fact that Dr. Jackson even brought in Lapp herders from Finland when Alaskan Eskimos proved unsatisfactory managers for the herd.[32]

This failure in social engineering does not however detract from the real concern Captain Healy felt for the natives of the north. In fact, the effort and work that Healy put into the project speaks volumes for his feelings about the perceived dangers to the natives and the pains that he took to alleviate their plight. In yet another ironic twist in Healy's strange life, one of the most amazing rescues in the annals of the U.S. Revenue Cutter Service—the Overland Rescue Mission—propelled the service into the national spotlight, and reindeer played a major role in that rescue. Unfortunately, Captain Healy could not point out to the public and his superiors that the plaudits resulting from that rescue were solely the result of his efforts, for the rescue came one year after his fall from grace.

In a remarkable bit of understatement, Gerald O. Williams, the only person to do a detailed study of the life of Michael A. Healy, notes that the revenue cutter officer "was a strong and complex character."[33] Healy was the sort of man who, when encountering starvation on King Island in 1891, appealed to his officers to contribute to the purchase of food: "I know," he wrote to the wardroom of the *Bear,* "all of you have too deep an interest in the natives of this section to leave them to what seems now a most probable fate. . . . I shall therefore be obliged to test the proverbial generosity of the sailor and the amount of interest each may take in life or death of these natives."[34] When Healy's profound interest in helping the natives is contrasted with his shelling of natives in Angoon, a contradictory and complex picture of the man results. A political cartoonist might very well have portrayed a senior revenue cutter captain with one hand smashing bottles of whiskey while with the other he drinks to intoxication. Michael A. Healy was indeed a complex man and one who is still not well understood. Perhaps, after his exoneration in 1890 and his involvement in the reindeer project, he felt his life in order; from that time forward, because of this perfect balance, he and the *Bear* would continue their journeys north each spring. Six years later, however, the final acts in the tragedy of Michael A. Healy would begin.

# FOUR

# The Indomitable *Thetis*

In 1881 a 250-ton, wooden-hulled steam whaler measuring 188 ½ feet in length, 29 feet in beam, with a draft of 17 feet 10 inches, and displacing 1,250 tons slipped down the ways of Alexander Stephen and Sons of Dundee, Scotland. The builder had placed solid six-inch-thick Scottish oak planking on her ribs, fastened with the best Swedish iron and sheathed with Australian ironwood. Her builders named her *Thetis*, after a sea goddess in classical literature. Once christened, the new ship was intended to spend her days pushing through sea ice with the Newfoundland sealing fleet. Instead, her career took unpredicted directions, and the *Thetis* spent many years in service far removed from sealing.[1]

The first major change in the *Thetis*'s career came about because the Western world had become obsessed by a "polar passion." Many of the North Atlantic nations sought the glory of being the first to place their explorers at the North Pole. In 1881 the U.S. Army sent what was described as a scientific expedition to establish a base camp at Lady Franklin Bay, in Greenland. Resentment over the U.S. Navy's successful exploitation of the publicity-rich polar regions probably had more to do with the army's expedition than did science. In any event, the leader of the army expedition, Lt. Adolphus W. Greely, was encouraged to push as far north as possible.[2] No sooner had a camp been established than Lieutenant Greely dispatched advance depot parties to facilitate a drive northward. One of his sorties even won the record to that time for latitude: eighty-three degrees and twenty-four minutes north, at Lockwood Island, north of Greenland.

The cutter *Thetis* hove to in a lead in the ice.

Despite this success, the ill-starred expedition began experiencing a series of fateful mishaps. The failure of the 1882 supply ship to penetrate the ice-choked Smith Sound and reach the base proved to be a major setback. The crowning one came on 23 July 1883, with the sinking of the long-awaited relief ship and the sailing away of her naval escort without caching any provisions. These misfortunes doomed the Americans to first deprivation, then starvation, and eventually cannibalism.

Lieutenant Greely had a fallback plan in the event his supply line was cut. Using a steam-driven launch left by the ship that had transported the expedition, the craft would tow three whaleboats, also left by the ship, to safety. The leader of the expedition had his steam-driven launch tow three whaleboats in an attempt to reach safety. Misfortune again struck the expedition when a storm sank all but one whaleboat, and the survivors just managed to reach Cape Sabine with only a few provisions. Greely decided to wait there, with dwindling supplies and strength, while searching despondently for any sign of rescue.

Unbeknownst to Lieutenant Greely, the failed 1883 relief effort had not landed a strong rescue party, as Greely's plan had envisioned. In the camp of the huddled expedition members, an outbreak of scurvy further reduced the party's chances of survival. Even Lieutenant Greely's execution of a man accused of stealing food failed to control the hunger-crazed survivors, who continued to die amid an atmosphere of mistrust, hatred, and even cannibalism.

Greely's "disappearance" caused the United States to form the Greely Relief Expedition. One of its first acts involved the purchase of the steam whaler *Thetis* for the navy, since only ships specially constructed to enter the ice pack stood any chance of reaching the Greely party. The American government also accepted the donation of the ice-reinforced *Alert* from Great Britain.

The navy selected Cdr. Winfield S. Schley as expedition leader and insisted that each ship carry its own experienced ice pilot and a steam-powered launch. Commander Schley assumed command of his squadron on 8 February 1884. At his disposal were the newly commissioned USS *Thetis*, which the commander selected as his flagship, the Arctic steamer *Bear*, the *Alert*, and the collier *Loch Garry* to carry the huge amount of coal needed to fuel the ships as they forced their way through the ice pack. The *Alert*, being the slowest and least fitted for ice work, became the standby vessel.

Commander Schley steamed northward, driving his officers, crews, and

Lt. LeRoy Reinburg in the Arctic while serving aboard the *Thetis* during the 1907–8 patrols. Lieutenant Reinburg took many photographs with an inexpensive camera and preserved them for his family. They are an invaluable source for learning about life in the U.S. Revenue Cutter Service in the early twentieth century. Lieutenant Reinburg retired as a rear admiral. *Courtesy Capt. LeRoy Reinburg Jr., USCG (Ret.)*

ships to make the best possible speed. He put into Greenland only long enough to load dog teams, sleds, and native drivers. On 29 May, at the jumping-off point for Melville Bay, considered the most dangerous portion of the journey north, Schley left the *Alert* and *Loch Garry* to follow at a slower but safer pace. He ordered the *Thetis* and the *Bear,* however, to maintain their rapid speed. The two ships forced their way up the coast, pausing only at likely points long enough to land search parties to seek out signs of the Greely party or to question the Eskimos.

The relief expedition knew that time was vital, and the *Thetis* continued to work northward through Arctic gales and the sea ice. Another frustrating month slipped by without a sign of the Greely party. At last, in late June, the relentless searching of Commander Schley and his men paid off. Lieutenant Greely later recalled: "By the morning of the 22nd we were all exhausted, and . . . about noon, [we obtained] some water. That and a few square inches of soaked seal-skin was all the nutriment which passed our lips for forty-two hours prior to our rescue. . . . Near midnight of the 22nd I heard the sound of the whistles of the *Thetis*, blown by Captain Schley's orders to recall his parties. I could not distrust my ears, and yet I could hardly believe that ships would venture along that coast in such a gale."[3]

Schley's relief expedition found Greely's remaining party in terrible shape. Only seven emaciated men remained out of the original twenty-six-man expedition. None, according to a doctor in the rescue squadron who examined them, could have lasted more than a few days longer, a judgment readily accepted later by Lieutenant Greely.

News of the *Thetis* forcing her way through more than thirteen hundred miles of ice pack to effect the rescue electrified the American public, which had been waiting to learn the fate of Greely. The rescue ships and crews returned to tumultuous welcomes. On 1 August 1884 the relief expedition came to anchor at Portsmouth, Virginia, where the U.S. Atlantic fleet greeted them by "having dressed ship with every available flag and pennant."[4]

The *Thetis*'s fame was short lived, and the ships of the rescue squadron were soon on the auction block. Only the personal intervention of the secretary of the navy stopped the sale of the *Thetis*. She remained a navy vessel, but out of commission in the New York Navy Yard. Then, in 1887, the navy fitted out the former whaler as a gunboat before reactivating and assigning her to duty in Pacific waters. Departing New York on 27 March, the *Thetis* spent 207 days, 102 of them in various ports, reaching her new station of San Francisco.

The *Thetis* began her first mission in the Pacific Ocean almost immediately. Her first cruise would take her to Sitka, Alaska, stopping only briefly at Port Townsend, Washington, before dropping her hook in southeastern Alaska on 4 December 1887. She remained for eight days at this navy station, which had a detachment of marines ashore and the gunboat *Pinta* offshore. Then the *Thetis* took the territorial governor, A. P. Swineford, and his wife aboard for a visit to various Alaska villages in the region. The governor and his party departed the ship at Juneau and the gunboat headed south to

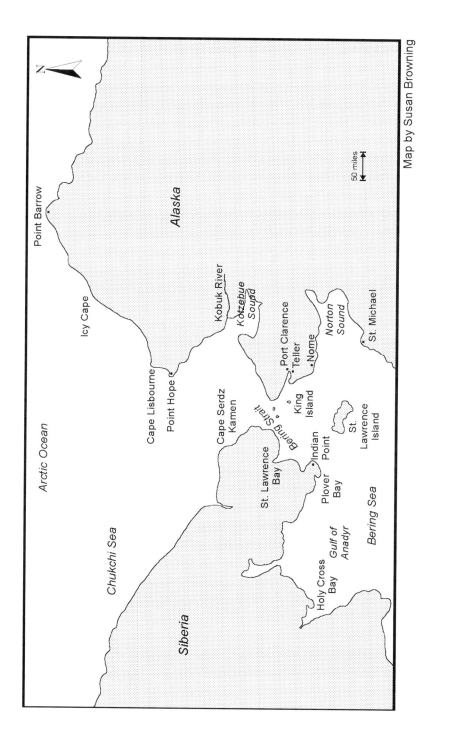

Map by Susan Browning

the San Francisco Bay area, where she spent the winter.

The *Thetis* returned to Sitka on 19 May 1888. Her commanding officer, Lt. Cdr. William H. Emory, had orders to "extend to the governor every facility to visit the outlying ports of the Territory."[5] Governor Swineford became the first governor to gain an understanding of the vastness of the land he governed. Departing Sitka on 27 May, the *Thetis* and the governor and his party began a cruise that would last for four months and five days. The official party would view almost the entire coast between Sitka and Point Barrow, except for the far Aleutian Islands. Near Point Barrow they met the *Bear*, now under the U.S. Revenue Cutter Service, and joined her in an unsuccessful search for a missing whaling-trader, the *Jane Grey*, which had been abandoned by her crew. Southbound, the *Thetis* called at Saint Michael and embarked seventy-one stranded and destitute miners from the Yukon River, giving them passage to San Francisco.

Although fitted out as a naval gunboat, the *Thetis* primarily performed survey work. For eleven years she cruised or surveyed from Central America to as far north as Alaska. During 1891 and 1892, she surveyed proposed cable routes between California and Hawaii.

Cuttermen from the *Thetis* water ship in the ice by pumping the melted sea ice, which becomes fresh.

Despite being a relatively young ship, the sail-rigged, wooden-hulled *Thetis* began appearing more and more obsolete to naval eyes. Ships of the line by then had steel construction, and modern armored warships had amply demonstrated their battle effectiveness during the Spanish-American War. The navy again decommissioned the Arctic veteran and placed her at the Mare Island Navy Yard, California, in a status similar to that of the present-day "mothball fleet."

The next major change in the life of the *Thetis* began, strangely enough, in the context of a sister ship of the relief expedition, the *Bear*. As pointed out in chapter 3, the plan to import reindeer came to fruition aboard the *Bear*. In 1899 the *Bear* was unavailable to transport reindeer. The U.S. commissioner of education, W. T. Harris, being directly responsible for the importation of the animals, recommended a quick solution. In March 1899, Congress approved a Sundry Civil Bill that authorized the repairing and operating of the *Thetis* for a period of six months as a revenue cutter.

On 16 March 1899 the U.S. Revenue Cutter Service officially accepted "the *Thetis* with steam launch, quarter boats, sails, blocks, running gear, compasses, and other belongings," and authorized $7,000 for her repairs.[6] Although the Sundry Civil Bill specifically limited the ship's operation to only six months, her active duty in the service turned out to be much longer. Not until 1916, in fact, was she once again decommissioned. During those seventeen years the *Thetis* sailed regularly under the revenue ensign in Alaskan waters. There are three significant aspects to the story of the *Thetis* during her years with the U.S. Revenue Cutter Service: her first Alaskan cruise as a revenue cutter in 1899; her cruise to Point Barrow in 1906; and her "floating court" cruise of 1911.

Ready for sea by 26 May 1899, the *Thetis* sailed for Seattle from San Francisco to pick up barter goods for the Siberian natives. The commanding officer, 1st Lt. Albert Buhner, followed Dr. Jackson's advice and loaded up with "tobacco; powder; shot; steel traps; calico; duck; large case knives; a little flour; a few boxes of pilot bread; a box of tea, with the tea in small paper packages; some tin plates and cups; also cheap iron spoons."[7]

Departing Seattle on 13 June, the revenue cutter headed for Siberia via Saint Lawrence Island in the Bering Sea. While her slim wooden hull slipped through the waters of the North Pacific and Bering Sea, the crew performed the duties required of all saltwater sailors, plus the unique task of "making hobbles for reindeer."[8] The *Thetis* gained Saint Lawrence Island by the morning of 10 July. By that afternoon, the officer of the day had logged the

Hoisting reindeer aboard a cutter in Siberia for transportation to Alaska.

purchase of more trade goods: "16 bolts white drill, 24 blankets, 15 large brass kettles, and 22 small brass kettles."[9] After stowing the new cargo, the revenue cutter weighed anchor and started toward Siberia.

The *Thetis* "anchored in Lutki Harbor" at nightfall the following day.[10] The log entry recorded a position of 65 degrees 40 minutes north and 171 degrees 12 minutes west, which is probably the location of the present Zaliv Lavrentiya in Siberia. On the morning of the 12th, First Lieutenant Buhner dispatched 2d Lt. Harry G. Hamlet "on shore to purchase reindeer."[11] Hamlet proved so adept at dealing with the Siberian natives that he ended up handling all the negotiations for the cruise. The ship's carpenter, meanwhile, soon finished "building troughs and reindeer pens" for the live cargo.[12]

Once her crew had loaded "on board 14 reindeer for transportation to Alaska," the *Thetis* slipped her anchorage in the early morning hours of 15 July and arrived that afternoon at Cape Prince of Wales, Alaska.[13] She continued the next day on to Point Spencer for a meeting with Dr. Jackson. The 19 July log entry states that "Lieut. Hamlet and Dr. Jackson went ashore on land spit to determine advisability of landing reindeer there, returning . . . with information that deer could be landed and cared for . . . heaved up anchor and steamed into Port Clarence coming to at 1150 . . . 1230 lowered three boats and commenced hobbling reindeer and loading them into boats. . . . [B]oats in charge of Lieut. Hamlet and accompanied by Dr. Jackson left ship and landed deer in good condition. Scrubbed boats ashore."[14]

Taking aboard a native interpreter by the name of Chio, Lieutenant Buhner upped anchor within twenty-four hours and headed back to Siberia. What happened next proved typical of the six additional crossings made on the first U.S. Revenue Cutter Service cruise of the *Thetis*. As the revenue cutter neared the shore of Siberia, the watch began to make reindeer hobbles and gather lumber for pens. Upon anchoring, Second Lieutenant Hamlet, Dr. Jackson, and Chio would go ashore and begin bartering. Once they sealed the bargain, the watch immediately put "up reindeer pens and covered the deck with ashes" and ran out the ship's small boats to the beach where the herd had been driven by the natives.[15]

Then, in an activity reminiscent of a Wild West show, the cuttermen roped, hobbled, and manhandled the reindeer into the small boats for the trip to the revenue cutter. The small craft pulled alongside the *Thetis*, placed the deer into slings, and hoisted them by means of block and tackle onto the deck to be unhobbled and led into the pens. After a brief journey between continents, the crew reversed the whole process. They cleaned the small boats once the reindeer had been landed safely in Alaska and "took down reindeer pens and washed deck."[16]

All too often this operation did not run as smoothly as desired, as the following peculiar problems illustrate. After rowing ashore one day, the cuttermen learned to their disgust "that no reindeer could be bought from the large nearby herd because illness in the family of the owner prevented barter by native superstition."[17] On other occasions the row ashore had proved fruitless because the reindeer herds were too far inland. Even when the herds were close by, the natives often "refused to go after the deer unless furnished whiskey, which was not done."[18] To the astonishment of the cuttermen, the natives delayed the reindeer drive one day, until "after the heat of the day"; the thermometer aboard the *Thetis* read all of 68 degrees at this time.[19] To his chagrin, the officer of the day sounded the fire alarm for drill one day, only to find the "port gangway being closed for reindeer pens and deck filled with natives, interfering with manning and working of pumps."[20]

During her initial temporary six-month assignment, however, these and many other difficulties did not prevent the *Thetis* from transporting eighty-one reindeer, steaming 8,552 nautical miles in a season that "was exceptionally inclement, [with] high winds and thick fog prevail[ing]," and successfully completing her mission.[21] The *Thetis* then shaped a course for San Francisco, arriving there after many stops on 20 September 1899.[22]

In his official report of this unique first voyage of the *Thetis*, First Lieutenant Bulmer praised all his officers, but he singled out Second Lieutenant Hamlet for special praise, stating that this "officer tramped miles of Tundra," handled all the bartering, and "it is just to say that without his help the reindeer bought could not have been obtained."[23] This laudatory mention in official dispatches so early in the career of this young officer was a portent of his abilities, which would eventually be recognized when he was selected to become the commandant of the U.S. Coast Guard in 1932.

The officers of the cutter *Thetis* during the patrol of 1908. *Courtesy Capt. LeRoy Reinburg Jr., USCG (Ret.)*

The weather of the Bering Sea could take a toll on the small cutters. The *Thetis* after a storm.

The self-evident value of the seasoned Arctic veteran to the service's role in Alaskan waters, meanwhile, encouraged the U.S. Treasury and Revenue Cutter Service to try to convert the *Thetis* into the permanent property of the service. Their skillful maneuvering through the bureaucratic maze in Washington succeeded, for the former navy gunboat soon appeared on the official register of commissioned revenue cutters. Some idea of the value placed on her can be gained from the orders directing the *Thetis* to San Francisco in April 1900 for $50,000 of "necessary repairs" in preparation for northern cruises.[24]

Each year following her reconditioning until 1916, except for a brief period of out-of-commission status from July 1905 to April 1906, the *Thetis* was sent north by the U.S. Revenue Cutter Service, her primary duty being the Bering Sea Patrol. Over these years, her home port shifted between San Francisco, Port Townsend, and Honolulu.[25]

The Bering Sea Patrol required cutters to undertake a variety of duties. Normally the *Thetis* patrolled the entire length of the Aleutian Chain from Unimak Pass to Attu Island, with side cruises to the Pribilof Islands to harass fur seal poachers. Like her sister revenue cutters in these northern waters, she enforced the custom laws, performed search and rescue missions, administered justice, apprehended fugitives, arrested whiskey smugglers, towed disabled whalers to port, fed the hungry, healed the sick, and performed a myriad of other chores, such as providing a ferry service and assisting scientific expeditions in every way possible. All too often the visits of the revenue cutters provided the only contact inhabitants of western coastal Alaska had with civilization.

The extremity and caprice of the Bering Sea weather belabored the *Thetis* during every one of her seasons in the north. Patrolling in the fog-shrouded waters of the Bering Sea was dangerous, and all too often revenue cutters ran afoul of the Bering Sea's poorly charted waters and drastically changeable weather. The *Thetis*, for example, "lost her jibboom, fore-topgallant mast and yard, . . . part of the foremast, the rigging and gear of the spars, [and] a part of her radio antennas" during a heavy gale in 1912.[26]

Not until 1905 did the *Thetis* first venture through the Bering Strait and conduct a cruise into the polar regions. The revenue cutter *Bear* had traditionally made these northern cruises, but, that year, "showing her age, . . . [she] had been forced to retreat from the Arctic before performing her mission to Point Barrow. *Thetis*, a bit older, but having led an easier life, was recalled from her station in Honolulu and sent to the yards . . . in preparations for . . . [the] Arctic cruise."[27] In "working through the ice," boasted a senior officer with years of Arctic experience, "the *Thetis* has no superior afloat."[28]

Probably the most representative Arctic cruise by this revenue steamer was her voyage of 1906. Her jumping off point was the Bering Sea Patrol headquarters, located at Unalaska. One former crew member recalled that once underway, the *Thetis* encountered "nothing unusual" while feeling her way carefully along the Alaskan coast toward Nome, Alaska, with her skipper performing the normal "marriage ceremonies at various stops."[29] After stopping long enough at Nome to be sworn in as both deputy U.S. commissioner and deputy U.S. marshal, the commanding officer, Capt. Oscar C. Hamlet, began working his revenue cutter farther north.

At what is now called Cape Lisbourne, Alaska, the cutter met "both the real Arctic and the Native on his home ground . . . , the former with its restless burden of ice and the latter with his oomiak—the family boat. Navigation changed its course from point to point, turning and twisting through irregular masses as only ice can do. . . . Almost three weeks of backing and filling were required to make it to the lee of Point Barrow."[30]

Upon discovering five whaling ships trapped in the ice, Captain Hamlet dispatched his ship's doctor to check on the health of their crews, as well as

The enlisted men of the *Thetis* pose for the camera. Note the various uniforms.
*Courtesy Capt. LeRoy Reinburg Jr., USCG (Ret.)*

the sanitary conditions aboard the stranded whalers. Next he sent his executive officer to see if the Norwegian exploring ship *Gjoa,* reported to be only
twelve miles away and stuck in the ice, needed any help. None proved necessary, for she soon escaped the ice pack by sail power alone. A sharp-eyed
cutterman, meanwhile, had spotted a dead whale nearby. The *Thetis*
promptly "steamed out to get the carcass as food for the natives and returned
with it and grounded it off the village."[31]

In addition to performing more marriages, Captain Hamlet also dispensed
justice at Point Barrow. At this time, sexual relations with native women,
unless sanctioned by marriage, was illegal. Captain Hamlet fined both the
master and first mate of the *Beluga* for committing adultery under this law.
In many other "suspicious cases," the revenue officer found that he lacked
"enough evidence to convict," so he "called in" all the whalers and gave

them a stern "warning," hoping this would deter them from future illegal acts.[32]

After a two-week layover, the *Thetis* slowly retraced her course back to Nome. Then she set a course for San Francisco, arriving there on 14 November, interrupting her passage only long enough to search unsuccessfully for the British ship *Inverna,* which had gone missing.[33]

The *Thetis* did not escape unscathed from the rigors of these strenuous polar cruises. For this reason, the Bering Sea Patrol headquarters diverted her as often as possible in later years from extended periods of sea duty. To this Arctic veteran fell instead the less hazardous duty of providing a seagoing platform for transporting the federal judges and their staffs of the U.S. court to such isolated settlements along the western Alaskan coast "as it was necessary for the court to visit," thus enabling law and order to reach even the most remote areas.[34]

The 1911 judicial cruise made by the *Thetis* was representative. Leaving the search for Bering Sea seal poachers to the revenue cutters *Rush, Manning, Bear,* and *Tahoma,* the *Thetis* began her leisurely passage up the Alaskan coast. After picking up the "floating court," consisting of a judge, an assistant U.S. marshal, a clerk, and a stenographer, at Juneau, Alaska, the *Thetis* cruised toward Unalaska, stopping at various settlements along the way.

After touching at the Bering Sea Patrol headquarters, the revenue cutter continued on to Naknek, taking aboard a prisoner and a witness for transportation to Nushagak on Bristol Bay in the Bering Sea. Here, at the largest canning factory town in the area, a grand jury made up of Capt. C. S. Cochran, commanding officer of the *Thetis,* who acted as jury foreman, and two other cutter officers conducted "considerable investigations . . . in the week that the court was in the town."[35] The cases tried dealt not only with poaching but also with murder, arson, assault with a deadly weapon, and selling liquor to the natives.

Its business finished at Nushagak, the "floating court" rode the revenue cutter back to Unalaska. It stayed long enough to convict and sentence four Japanese to prison terms for poaching before continuing on its coastal journey. This judicial cruise slowly but steadily turned the *Thetis* into a floating jail. After disembarking both her prisoners and the "floating court," she returned to other, more service-connected duties. It was through the *Thetis* and other Bering Sea Patrol revenue cutters that a semblance of order—a thin veneer of civilization, so to speak—was brought to the more isolated regions of the frontier settlements along the Alaskan coast.

Meanwhile, the passage of the years, coupled with rugged Arctic duty, had taken its toll of the *Thetis.* An official service description of the vessel in 1913 not surprisingly contained the ominous phrases "being over 31 years," having "outlived her usefulness," and "would cost considerable to put her hull and machinery in first-class condition."[36] The old Arctic veteran, however, hung on for another three years. She was again decommissioned on 3 June 1916, and the following entry was made soon after in the official records: "Placed out of commission at San Francisco."[37]

The same year, the W. and S. Job Company of New York purchased the *Thetis* for twenty-four thousand dollars. This marks the beginning of the last major turning point for the ship. Her new owners converted the former revenue steamer into a sealer, and the *Thetis* worked out of Newfoundland for the next thirty-four years.

By 1950 the *Thetis* had finally outlived her usefulness, after a seagoing career spanning sixty-nine years. Her inevitable end—unique though it was—came at St. John's, Newfoundland. An official of the sealing company that owned her recalled that, after her figurehead had been detached and "any fittings useful were used by other ships of the sealing fleet, . . . the hull was turned over to the public for firewood with the result the police had to be called to quell the riot."[38] What still remained of the *Thetis* "was towed outside of St. John's to Freshwater Bay (about two miles) and grounded and so remained until she broke up."[39]

Thus, ignobly, yet with her customary flair for the unusual, did this gallant old Arctic veteran pass from the maritime scene. Perhaps it was fitting that the vengeful seas—so skillfully cheated innumerable times amid polar ice packs, Arctic gales, and storm-tossed waves—finally claimed her. Only the *Thetis*'s figurehead, faithfully preserved by a museum in Newfoundland, remains to remind anyone of her passing.[40]

# FIVE

# Exploring Uncharted Regions

The Senate's ratification of the purchase of Alaska on 9 April 1867 cleared the path for a systematic exploration of the newly acquired land. Because ships had long visited Alaska navigators knew most of its coastline, but they found the available Russian and English charts of the region often inaccurate and the hinterland a geographical blank. One of the initial official actions of the United States, therefore, called for an American ship to carry the flag and U.S. officials north to Sitka to speed the orderly transfer of sovereignty from the Russian authorities there, and then to make a reconnaissance cruise westward.

On 4 June 1867, Secretary McCulloch instructed Capt. William A. Howard, who was at the time stationed at the Treasury Department's headquarters, to "proceed without delay" to San Francisco to take charge of the revenue steamer *Lincoln* for the purpose of performing the reconnaissance. His expedition had orders "to acquire a knowledge of the country," not only for the "protection of the revenue" but also for "the information of Congress and the people,"[1] paying particular attention to areas valuable for commerce, the probable haunts of smugglers, and possible sites for customhouses. Besides performing a reconnaissance of the coast, the captain would also take soundings, locate sites for lighthouses, and look for areas for coaling. Unalaska Island in particular, his instructions read, should be examined thoroughly as a potential coaling station. All the while, the expedition should chart the locations of fishing banks and collect a general description of the land, its climate, and its resources. Lastly, the expedition was to collect specimens of the flora and fauna.

Built in 1864 by the John F. Fardy Brothers at Baltimore, Maryland, the *Lincoln* had a length of 165 feet, a beam of 26 feet, and a draft of 10 feet. She had been sent to the West Coast via Cape Horn two years previously. Capt. John W. White already commanded the revenue steamer and remained in command for this 1867 expedition, which was under the overall charge of Howard as senior captain; Howard also described himself as a special agent of the U.S. Treasury Department. Room also had to be made aboard the revenue cutter for five officers of the U.S. Coast Survey party headed by George Davidson and their scientific equipment; a civilian doctor from San Francisco, A. Kellogg, who would serve as surgeon; and Lt. George W. Moore of the U.S. Revenue Cutter Service. Since both Captain White and Doctor Kellogg were experienced naturalists, the treasury secretary expected them to "prosecute diligently" the investigations desired by the Smithsonian Institution. Captain Howard's orders called for him to voyage north to Sitka, establish diplomatic communications with the Russian authorities, and then continue westward to the Aleutians. Lieutenant Moore would remain at Sitka as an agent of the U.S. collector at San Francisco—in reality, the sole U.S. representative at the Russian colonial capital—and "superintend the discharge of cargoes permitted to land by the Russian authorities."

Once the revenue steamer *Lincoln* had been reported ready for sea, Captain Howard directed her to depart San Francisco on the morning of 21 July. A week later she stopped at Victoria, on Vancouver Island, to load coal. Davidson landed a transit with which he hoped to test his chronometer and other equipment, but poor weather prevented a good observation. Captain Howard delayed sailing for another day in hopes of better weather but had to depart when conditions did not improve. The U.S. Coast Survey party made another attempt at Fort Rupert, a Hudson Bay Company station at the northern end of the island, while the engineering crew made adjustments to the new propeller, but neither the sun nor stars could be sighted. As the *Lincoln* continued its voyage to Sitka, the heavy rain and fog also doomed the survey party's efforts to verify landmarks between Canada and Alaska.[2]

Once the weather cleared, the revenue steamer moored off the town of Sitka at 10 A.M. on 12 August. Captain Howard, along with all U.S. Revenue Cutter Service and U.S. Coast Survey officers, paid a formal call to Prince Maksonoff, the Alaskan governor who also controlled the Russian

American Fur Company. The visit was returned the following day by the Prince and his wife. Ten days later, with diplomatic obligations out of the way, fresh supplies of coal and water aboard, and Lieutenant Moore established ashore, the *Lincoln* resumed her journey westward.

On the 26th, battered by heavy winds and a driving rain, the cutter anchored off the island of Kodiak. Captain Howard paid a visit to the local commander of the Russian American Transportation Company there. After touring the company storehouses and the island, Howard concluded that Kodiak was "more important in a commercial or agricultural point than Sitka," and he recommended that a customs officer be stationed there, "with a good sail-boat capable of encountering bad and heavy weather."[3] En route to Unalaska the *Lincoln* continued to take soundings at intervals for fishing banks, as her instructions required. On 5 September her soundings revealed "an excellent bank with sixty fathoms water. . . . We soon commenced catching some of the finest and fattest codfish I ever saw," reported Captain Howard, "two at a haul weighing from eighteen to thirty-five pounds and from thirty-two to thirty-seven inches in length."

After an approach to Unalaska through thick rain and fog, the *Lincoln* anchored at 3 P.M. on 6 September in "Hooloot harbor, eleven fathoms, good holding ground and perfectly land-locked, in fact." Captain Howard reported it as being "one of the best harbors I ever saw. There are, however, several equally as good in this island." Calling upon the local authorities and using a letter from Prince Maksonoff, Captain Howard arranged to take two hundred tons of coal placed there years before by the Union Telegraph Company. Since the progress of the revenue steamer had depended solely upon steam this late in the season, her coal bunkers needed to be replenished for the return trip. The cutter's crew and passengers, meanwhile, set up the observatory on shore, along with a tent for the transit and flags for surveying the harbor. In addition, parties were sent out to assess the surrounding country.[4]

While there, the *Lincoln*'s executive officer, 1st Lt. Daniel B. Hodgsdon, led a party consisting of the surgeon, assistant engineer, a U.S. Coast Survey geologist, two seamen, and four local natives in an ascent of a volcano some fifteen to twenty miles distant, to determine whether it was active. Neither the Russians nor the local Aleuts had ever visited the volcano or knew of anybody who had. The four-day expedition proved to be "a perilous one, being along the sides of very steep mountains and still steeper ravines, often having all we could do to keep from being hurled into the abyss below."[5] The expedition members succeeded in hoisting the revenue ensign—and leaving it flying in the strong winds—on Mount Makushinsky's highest pinnacle (5,691 feet) on 9 September 1867.

After another month of exploratory cruising the *Lincoln* entered Dixon's passage, the southernmost boundary of the new American possession, and crossed it at 4 P.M. on 4 November, thereafter entering the harbor of Fort Simpson and anchoring. "Thus ended the observatory cruise of the Lincoln," Captain Howard reported, "regretting so little has been effected, by the lateness of the season, the extremely boisterous and rainy weather, as also the tardiness of the commissioners, which kept us many days that might have been employed in examining the eastern archipelago and the main shores bordering on British Columbia."[6] In the years to come, many other cutter skippers would echo these comments on the first cruise.

After returning to San Francisco on the evening of 18 November, Captain Howard completed his final report of this 1867 Alaskan Expedition. In it he made the point of having been absent four months (less two days) and having sailed or steamed 6,297 miles, "without the loss of a man or an accident of any kind." His report clearly reflected his ability to write a coherent narrative, with all the necessary attention to details and emphasis on those areas considered of importance to his superiors. Besides giving a detailed report on the five areas he had been asked to pay particular attention to, as well as offering his general impressions and conclusions, the Alaska Expedition commander also included separate reports, written by knowledgeable people who had accompanied him, on such diverse scientific fields as botany, coast surveying, conchology, geology, meteorology, and native languages. He collected and forwarded every bit of information available to him, such as a list of the names of 1,968 inhabitants of Unalaska that had been derived from the archives of the local Russian Orthodox Church.

Despite the ratification by the Senate of the purchase treaty and the formal transfer of Alaska at Sitka on 18 October 1867, the bitter controversy surrounding this unique acquisition did not end. The House of Representatives, where pockets of opposition persisted, still needed to appropriate the necessary funds. The foes of expansion often quoted the records of the *Lincoln* during its Alaska expedition, especially as to fogs, storms, and other navigational dangers. Captain Howard had admitted that, if his revenue steamer had been left anchored in Sitka harbor on the night of 20 October 1867, instead of getting underway in "a heavy rain, blowing a gale from southeast," she "could not have escaped destruction," even after reaching a safe anchor-

The cutter *Nunivak*, commanded by Lt. John C. Cantwell, patrolled the Yukon River.

age; he had described the gale as "increasing and roaring overhead like a train of railroad cars running with great speed."[7] Despite this serious opposition, the appropriation bill finally passed on 24 July 1868, being signed into law by the president on 27 July.

Earlier that same year the Treasury Department had ordered its revenue steamer *Wayanda* to begin the next surveying and discovery voyage to the new possession. The steamer had no sooner entered Cook Inlet than her skipper, Captain White, late of the *Lincoln*, landed parties ashore at various places to explore the natural resources. He even sent an expedition by boat up the Kukuy River. Captain White later reported that the east shore of the inlet could become a fine agricultural country supporting a dense population. Interestingly enough, close to a century later the New Deal planners selected this site for their Matanuska Valley farming experiment.

At Kenai, on the Cook Inlet, Captain White made a chart of the harbor. There he also observed coal veins "over an area 40 by 50 miles, so thick that it seems one vast bed," with the coal coming "in cube blocks, bright and clean," having "excellent steam quality" and leaving a "a clean white ash."[8] Like the *Lincoln,* the *Wayanda* found and recorded the locations of extensive fishing banks. "The smaller codfish are in the shallower waters, nearer the shore, of 20 or 30 fathoms," Captain White reported, "but the best fisheries are farther out in 70 or 80 fathoms."

The *Wayanda* also visited the Pribilof Islands in the Bering Sea, home of the famous rookeries of fur seals. The fur companies there, Captain White discovered, had taken advantage of the departure of the Russian authorities to slaughter the fur seals wantonly. Only the inability to hire more Aleuts to do the killing and harvesting of hides had prevented them from wiping out the fur seal herd entirely, while their use of liquor as payment threatened to bring starvation to the local Aleuts. "I put a stop to the slaughter," Captain White wrote, "broke every whiskey-barrel and poured the contents on the ground," prohibited the traders from killing "any seals except a limited number of the two-year old males," and "required them to pay the Aleuts in provisions, clothing, and other needful articles."[9] He subsequently recommended that the United States make the Pribilof Islands a federal reservation to protect both the fur seals and the Aleuts on them.

Other revenue cutters followed the initial—and somewhat random—northern deployments of the *Lincoln* and *Wayanda.* These voyages greatly eased the way for the frontiersmen eager to develop the new land. The cuttermen and their official passengers recorded soundings, prepared charts, made hydrographic observations, and furnished sailing directions for the Alaskan waters. Through their observations, much hard-earned scientific and geographical knowledge became known. In the years to come, the wakes of the revenue cutters sent north each spring would crisscross the emerging history of this new U.S. possession.

The landmark 1880 voyage of the cutter *Corwin,* with Capt. Calvin L. Hooper in command, ushered in systematic Arctic cruising to the northern waters. Earlier cutters occasionally had put their bows over the Arctic Circle, but after 1880 cutters routinely plowed the Arctic Ocean. Captain Hooper's primary mission, in addition to his normal U.S. Revenue Cutter Service tasks, called for locating the missing exploring steamer *Jeannette,* under the command of Lt. George W. DeLong, USN, and discovering the fates of two overdue whalers, the *Mount Wollaston* and *Vigilant.* Hunting whales in the polar fall could be risky, and some six hundred men on thirty-three whalers had become trapped and lost in the ice pack within the previous decade. The *Jeannette* Expedition's goal had been the North Pole, and its patron, James Gordon Bennett of the *New York Herald*, had purchased, outfitted, and sent the steamer north amid much publicity and fanfare. Lieutenant DeLong planned to touch first at Herald Island to build a cairn as a record of their progress, and then to proceed polarward along the eastern coast of Wrangel, leaving similar records at twenty-five mile intervals. The mystery of the *Jeannette*'s disappearance had focused worldwide attention upon the Arctic Ocean and the resultant relief attempts.

The revenue steamer *Corwin* had a length of 143 feet, a width of 24 feet, a draft of 11 feet, and a hull reinforced for working in polar ice. She steamed out of her home port of San Francisco on 22 May 1880, arriving at Unalaska on 3 June. Continuing northward, the *Corwin* touched at the islands of Nunivak and St. Lawrence before encountering a whaling bark whose captain reported having sighted the three missing ships the previous fall, some forty miles southeast of Herald Island. Captain Hooper came within sight of Herald and Wrangel islands, some four hundred miles into the Arctic Ocean, by early September, but his attempts to work his cutter closer to the islands through the leads in the ice pack proved unsuccessful. With the Arctic winter and its ice barrier now closing in, the *Corwin* abandoned her search for the season and headed south, stopping at Unalaska before returning to her home port. Although convinced that the lost whalers had perished, Captain Hooper had "no fears for the safety of the *Jeannette*," believing that she was safe and capable of spending "another year at least" in the Arctic.[10]

He and the *Corwin* headed north again with the same goal on 4 May 1881. Three distinguished naturalists—Dr. Irving C. Rosse, ship's surgeon; E. W. Nelson of the U.S. Signal Service; and John Muir, already well known for his studies on glaciers—joined this cruise, providing an expertise not normally found among cuttermen. In time this practice of transporting scientists became traditional in Alaskan waters, the cutters serving in the role of courier to the scientific world.

After a thirteen-day journey, the *Corwin* stopped at Unalaska to load coal and the relief supplies needed for her Arctic cruise in search of the *Jeannette* and the missing whalers. The cutter then pushed on into the Arctic Ocean and headed for Asia to check on the numerous reports from Siberian natives who claimed to have sighted a wreck that was almost certain to have been one of the missing whalers. After steaming "along the Coast to the westward, tracing the edge of the shore-ice," from "three to six miles wide," John Muir wrote in his journal, "we reached the end of the open lead" in the vicinity of Kolyuchin Island by June 1, "having thus early in the season gained a point farther west than the *Corwin* was able to reach at any time last year. At this point the firm Coast ice united with the great polar pack."[11]

Captain Hooper knew that any survivors of ships trapped in the ice would seek the safety of the icebound Asian shore, and, in this event, the delay of even a single day in their rescue could mean life or death. With his ship's passage blocked, he landed a sled party the next day on the frozen ocean and dispatched it northwest along the coast to render aid to any shipwrecked men who might be found (this expedition is further detailed in chapter 7).

Once the dogsled expedition had returned, the revenue steamer turned back to Saint Lawrence Island and to Saint Michaels, Alaska, before turning north again to the Bering Strait, touching at all the islands in the strait and, according to Nelson, spending "the remainder of the summer visit[ing] in succession the entire Alaskan Coast line from Bering Strait to Point Barrow, including Kotzebue Sound and on the Siberian shore from the Straits to North Cape."[12] The *Corwin* also resumed her search for traces of the *Jeannette*, shuttling back and forth to follow leads northward in the ice barrier between America and Asia. Doctor Rosse described how "a series of gales and snow storms continued throughout the summer. Even as late as July 18, the decks were covered with snow and hail, and a bitter cold wind penetrated our winter clothing."[13]

Hoping to find some sign of the *Jeannette*, the *Corwin* "came to anchor in the midst of huge cakes and blocks about sixty-five feet thick within two or three hundred yards" of Herald Island on the evening of 30 July, after being "pretty roughly bumped" and forced "to steam her best."[14] John Muir, using the mountaineering skills he had honed in the Sierras, made the first ascent of the "sheer granite cliffs" and described the "midnight hour I spent alone on the highest summit—one of the most impressive hours of my life."[15] He and others searched the six-by-two-mile island for three days but discovered no signs of the DeLong Expedition. "A nearly grown young" white fox transferred to the *Corwin*, Nelson later recalled, proved to be "extraordinarily intelligent, inquisitive, and mischievous, and afforded all of us much amusement and occasional exasperation."[16]

Having failed to find any signs of the DeLong Expedition, Captain Hooper departed for Wrangel Island, where no human had ever claimed to have set foot. His initial attempts, like those of 1880, failed to find leads through the ice. Persistence finally paid off on 12 August. Dawn revealed "less, firmly packed" ice, and the cutter steamed "without difficulty" for eight miles before encountering "craggy blocks extremely hard and wedged closely," just two miles from the open water near the beach. Captain Hooper threw "the throttle wide open" and forced this last barrier, to "anchor less than a cable's length from a dry gravel bar."[17]

After going ashore, the captain and his landing party first built a cairn of rocks on a hill. They placed a record of their visit and a copy of the *New York Herald* within and raised an American flag, to claim the territory for the United States. They next searched the island but found no evidence that the *Jeannette* or any other vessel had ever landed there. Although Muir complained of a "far too short" stay to permit "anything like as full a collection of the plants of so interesting [a] region," he did admit collecting twenty-seven plants from "an area of about half a square mile."[18]

The *Corwin* continued searching and performing her regular duties until 2 September. Then, while attempting yet once more to force an ice passage to the northwest in search of clues to the fate of the missing explorers, Captain Hooper suffered several setbacks. The rudder was lost off Herald Island, and that, coupled with miles of heavy pack ice, his "ice-breaker, made of heavy boiler iron," being "broken by the pounding of the waves" and battered by one "storm-day" after another amid heavy seas, convinced him that the open season was over.[19] After a new rudder had been jerry-rigged, the *Corwin* headed south, pausing at Unalaska only long enough to make necessary repairs before returning to San Francisco.

The *Jeannette*, meanwhile, had become frozen in the ice in September 1879 and had drifted with the polar pack until 12 June 1881. Then, crushed some 150 miles north of the New Siberian Islands, she sank to the bottom, forcing the men to load boats and supplies onto sleds and attempt the long haul to the Siberian Coast. During this dramatic escape across the frozen Arctic Ocean, a fierce gale divided the expedition into two parties. Chief Engineer George Melville led twelve survivors to safety at a Russian village on the delta of the Lena River, but DeLong and twenty crew members perished.[20]

The missing *Jeannette* expedition inspired two other 1881 relief cruises besides that of the *Corwin*. The U.S. Navy purchased a whaler already on the Pacific Coast, renamed her the USS *Rodgers,* and dispatched her polarward. Her orders called for a journey along the northern coast of Siberia until the ice pack blocked further passage, and then the landing of dogsleds to continue the search. Upon reaching Herald Island and discovering that the *Corwin* had already anticipated her and dispatched a dogsled expedition, she went into winter quarters on the Siberian coast of the Bering Sea.

At the suggestion of James Gordon Bennett, the navy also dispatched the USS *Alliance* to cruise that year in the waters north of Scandinavia and Russia, where the drifting polar ice conceivably could have dragged the trapped *Jeannette*. This small warship, although not designed for forcing a passage through ice packs, had been reinforced against the less dangerous scum ice and floes. Besides seeking reliable information about the *Jeannette,* her orders called for the collection of scientific information. Departing Hampton Roads, Virginia, on 16 June, the warship first touched at Newfoundland, Iceland, Norway, and Spitsbergen and then headed polarward. She successfully worked her way along the ice pack as far as latitude 80 degrees north before retracing her trackline and arriving at New York on 11 November.

The *Corwin* made five annual Arctic cruises in all, establishing the patrol routes and activities that later cutters would follow. During her 1884 and 1885 cruises, she launched the longest and most extensive explorations ever conducted by cuttermen on Bering Sea Patrol. The expedition belatedly brings into the spotlight of history the work of Lt. John C. Cantwell.

# SIX

# Lt. John C. Cantwell, Explorer

The concept of an expedition up the Kowak (now known as Kobuk River) to discover its headwaters in the then-unknown Alaskan hinterland had its genesis in the mind of Capt. Michael A. Healy after he assumed command of the *Corwin* and her Arctic duties. A passenger on his 1883 cruise, Lt. George M. Stoney, USN, had the task of delivering gifts to the Siberian natives around St. Lawrence Bay, who had given aid and comfort to the crew members of the USS *Rodgers,* destroyed by fire in winter quarters. After their delivery he grew restless, being confined to the *Corwin* until her return to the United States.

At Kotzebue Sound, Captain Healy authorized the naval lieutenant to use a small boat, one cutterman, and supplies to make an exploration of Hotham Inlet. The two explorers came across the Kobuk delta and proceeded up the winding river some forty to fifty miles. Both Captain Healy and Lieutenant Stoney officially reported the discovery of the Kobuk River and urged their respective superiors to carry out further explorations. In truth, despite evidence of earlier European association with the lower portion of the Kobuk, the naval and revenue officers deserve the credit for effectively opening this waterway. By stressing interservice rivalry, Lieutenant Stoney subsequently obtained naval backing for his 1885 and 1886 Kobuk expeditions.[1]

The fact that the naval officer and cutterman traveled east captured Captain Healy's interest, because of certain known geographic facts of Arctic Alaska. The Colville River flowed north into the Arctic Ocean just to the east of Point Barrow; the Koyukuk River in approximately the same longitude ran south into the Yukon River; and the Kobuk River lay midway in latitude between their mouths and emptied westward into the Hotham Inlet and then the Chukchi Sea, just north of the Bering Strait. Captain Healy reasoned that the headwaters of all three lay close together, perhaps in a mystical big lake that the natives along the coast frequently mentioned. If that were true, perhaps these river routes could be utilized as escape routes for whalemen trapped in the ice near Point Barrow. Even the most superficial survey of this portion of the Alaskan mainland, the revenue officer felt, would both benefit the scientific community and attract the interest of commercial interests, thereby enriching the nation further. The expedition seemed to whet the appetite of the revenue cutter officer selected to lead the exploring party.

With official permission to test his theory having been obtained, Healy had already made the necessary preparations for the planned exploration when the *Corwin* neared the mouth of the Kobuk River during its regular patrol duties in 1884. The expedition he had organized consisted of 3d Lt. John C. Cantwell, in charge; 2d Asst. Engineer Samuel B. McLenegan; Q.M. Horace Wilbur; Frank Lewis, fireman; James Miller, miner; and Andre Fernda, guide and interpreter (an overview of Cantwell's career is given in chapter 2). They would use the cutter's steam launch plus two small boats for additional supplies and camping equipment.

While anchored off Cape Krusenstern in Kotzebue Sound on 8 July, Captain Healy gave written orders to Lieutenant Cantwell. They concisely spelled out the Treasury Department's desire "to ascertain the extent of the Kowak River, together with the character of the country through which it runs, the number and extent of its tributaries, the number, condition, habits, and customs of the inhabitants, and, in general, everything of interest to science and commerce relating thereto." They also called for Cantwell and his party "to proceed to the mouth of the said river and begin the compilation of the data required, extending your explorations as far toward the source of the river as is possible with boats, and until the 20th day of August, 1884, when you will rejoin the *Corwin* at Hotham Inlet."[2]

Captain Healy mentioned several possibilities likely to occur and offered his preferred courses of action. Should the Kobuk River prove not long enough for such an expenditure of effort, he wrote, "you will turn your attention to the survey and exploration of Selawick Lake, or any navigable stream which you may discover in the neighborhood." He noted the persistence of rumors about jade being located in the unknown hinterland and remarked that "if this supposition should prove true the discovery would be one of great value." Trading with the local inhabitants "to secure their help in case of need" was permitted, but the *Corwin* commander cautioned the expedition members not "to excite their cupidity or awaken their distrust." If a "collision" could not be avoided, Captain Healy instructed Lieutenant Cantwell to "try and make good your retreat without bloodshed. If, however, this be impossible, act with firmness, decision, and moderation." Then, so typical of those penny-pinching days of the U.S. Revenue Cutter Service, he "particularly" cautioned the expedition leader "to be economical in the expenditure of your ammunition and provisions."

The "young and buoyant" Cantwell possessed the "true explorer's instinct," while his "somewhat dour" second in command, McLenegan, appeared to live up to the stereotypical image of the engineer, being "inclined to take a work-a-day attitude towards the whole project"; both, however, "had a scientific turn of mind, a sailor's eye, and unquenchable desire to see around the next bend in the river."[3] Captain Healy's cruise report benefited greatly from their keen observations, insights, and explanations. "The explorations of the bank of the Kowak River are the first ever recorded," wrote Treasury Secretary Hugh McCulloch as he forwarded the 1884 report to the speaker of the House of Representatives, "although the river has been known through information furnished by the natives for thirty years."[4]

The Kobuk River Expedition departed the *Corwin* on 8 July but made little progress until after the Indian guide, Natorak, whom Captain Healy had sent to accompany them as a guide-interpreter, caught up two days later and pointed out the real mouth of the river. "The course of the river was exceedingly tortuous," reads Cantwell's journal entry for the eleventh, "and we sometimes found ourselves, after running two hours, back within a quarter of a mile of our starting point."[5] Twice the cuttermen discovered coal in the riverbanks and filled their bunkers, only to find it "useless" and to be forced to throw it out and load wood instead. Encountering their first rapids on the sixteenth, they pushed on and, despite the overturning of their steam launch, managed to reach the calmer waters upstream without any loss.

Finding the Native Americans friendly, the explorers often spent the night as welcome guests in their villages. At one village Cantwell treated a native for colic. On another occasion the natives became convinced that the revenue officer was a shaman after watching him work with a sextant. They begged the white witch doctor to use his magic to make their hunting more

Drawing of the steam launch being pulled during the Kobuk River Expedition.

successful, and Cantwell had "no alternative but to promise plenty of deer"—until he "nearly lost" his patience. Whenever possible, and primarily to prevent delaying the expedition, the Americans persuaded the villagers—usually by gifts of tobacco—either to hunt fresh meat, catch fish, cut wood, or help paddle the small boats.

The closer he came to the legendary "Ashiganok or green-stone mountain," the more Cantwell became enchanted by the stories and legends surrounding it. The Native Americans warned "that whoever goes to that mountain and brings away any stone will be afflicted with some dreadful malady ever afterwards, and that the stone belongs to the natives and not to the white men." Early on the eighteenth, he first spotted "a high serrated mountain" up ahead, and Natorak confirmed its identity. "All day," Cantwell reported, "we have been steaming toward the mountain of the mysterious green stone; sometimes standing up plain to our sight and sometimes obscured by heavy masses of clouds, its presence was ever felt, and it seemed to me to hold within its shadows some mysterious charm, some fascinating secret which must be wrested from its grasp."

Then, within mere days, he experienced his first real setback, a shoal blocking the river almost from shore to shore, where the current ran so swiftly and so strongly that it was almost impossible to move the boat. Aware of both the necessity of abandoning the steam launch in favor of smaller vessels and their closeness to "the mountain of the green stone," the revenue officer decided not to delay his expedition. Instead, he instructed McLenegan and the miner to remain and explore the mysterious mountain; he took the steam launch "back to a place where she could be left in safety."

Upon his return in a birch bark canoe a mere three days later, he greeted McLenegan and Miller, who were returning from the mountain "in a terribly exhausted condition." The two displayed "haggard and bloodstained" faces and were wearing torn clothes and, in place of their worn-out boots, pieces of blanket. They had brought back specimens of green stone, believed to be either jade or nephrite. Because of the men's condition, Cantwell sent them back to the steam launch to rest, while he, Andre, Natorak, and two locals serving as paddlers pushed up the river in the skin boat.

Later that day, 24 July, Cantwell recorded passing "a remarkable clay bluff, some 150 feet high and three-quarters of a mile long," where "Mammoth tusks abound," some being "eight inches in diameter." As the sun was setting they came upon "a deserted village" and, having sent the tent back to the steam launch, slept in a vacant hut "safe from the rain."

Three more days of paddling through spongy tundra brought Cantwell to a plain stretching toward the mountains. From the local inhabitants, he learned that most of the Indians he had observed fishing on the Kowak River lived near its headwaters and made winter sled journeys to the headwaters of the Koyukuk. They also informed him that "the sea could be seen from the mountains on a clear day" and, on "the other side of the mountains where they hunt there is a river by which the sea can be reached in five days." The revenue officer confidently entered into his journal, "This is doubtless the Colville River."

The expedition's goal now appeared almost within grasp, but by this time the skin boat had become "thoroughly saturated" and required constant patching, seriously delaying progress. Determined to push on, however, Cantwell paddled up a small twisting branch of the Kowak River to the nearest village, where most of the inhabitants had never seen a white man. "They crowded around me," he reported, "examining my clothing, etc., with the greatest curiosity. My watch was source of never-failing interest to all."

More seriously, "a consultation in which the entire village joined" revealed the disappointing news "that no boats suitable for our purpose could be obtained, as the frail birch-bark canoes they use in fishing are never taken as far as the head of the river." Moreover, about twelve days would be needed to reach the head of boat navigation, and then another day's march on foot would bring them to two waterfalls.

Undeterred, Cantwell returned to the Kowak River at a point about thirty-five miles farther upstream. Twenty of his hosts helped in carrying the skin boat over tundra "covered by snow," through "a dense thicket" of willows, "mud and water sometimes knee deep," and over stumps and past two lakes, before plunging into a "morass" to regain the Kowak. Launching his skin boat, Cantwell "paddled away up stream," boldly continuing his quest.

Forced to stop to make repairs to the badly leaking boat, Cantwell reconsidered his options. The conditions facing him forced the leader to make a radical change in plans on the evening of the twenty-eighth. Some 275 miles still remained to the waterfalls, a journey of twelve days, but his local guides had promised to stay for only eight and already agitated to return. The expedition had food for only five days and, being some 125 miles from the steam launch, would need "seven days to get a fresh supply of provisions." The skin boat was in a highly unsafe condition, and its loss would place his "party in a very bad position." Hence the expedition leader decided to return to the steam launch and "there to make a fresh start, . . . working day and night to get both boats as high as the rapids, and then renew the attempt to reach the water-fall with the skin boat."

On the way back down the river, the skin boat became so weakened by the opening of a seam as to require immediate repairs and a day of drying out. Cantwell, on 30 July, could not resist visiting Jade Mountain, some twelve miles distant. He and Andre found that the "whole mountain seemed to be composed" of the green stone, and the two collected seventy-five to one hundred pounds of specimens.

During the trip back the next day, Cantwell confessed in his journal an inability to describe the true extent of the pain and exhaustion he had suffered on this expedition. He had worn his boots through, and the pieces of blanket tied around them did not prevent his feet from becoming cut, bruised, and so swollen that the boots had to be cut off. Exhaustion impelled him to send a message, via a shaman of the local village, to McLenegan, requesting that he bring the launch upstream to his position.

The reply, brought back by the shaman, was that the fireman had let the water in the boiler run low, burning the tubes badly. Since the engineer could not quickly repair them, McLenegan wanted to know if Cantwell could make it downstream. Cantwell promptly set off, reaching the engineer's camp at about 3 P.M. on 2 August. He and his second in command at first discussed the possibility of reaching the head of the river but then examined their situation more realistically. The two discovered that the steam launch was "scarcely in condition to go *down* stream," while any attempt "to make her stem the current" would be a "useless waste of time." Cantwell also noticed with alarm "the rapidly falling river"; knowing of "the many shoal places and rapids below" their present position, they "considered it best to make [their] way back to the mouth of the river while [they] yet had time enough to do so in safety." By midnight, with none having "had a moment's sleep" for over forty-eight hours, they turned in, "wet and hungry, but too tired to care for anything but rest and sleep."

They spent the next day in overhauling and repairing their equipment. Cantwell intended to make this return as quickly as possible in order to reach Selawik Lake in time to explore it, and they departed early on 4 August. The party bent to their oars and began pulling the inoperable steam launch, knowing they had 225 miles of river to travel. The "great number of shoals" made the journey downstream "very dangerous," as did running the rapids. Whenever possible the cuttermen "ceased pulling" and let the steam launch "drift with the current." One day the river carried them fifty miles without the necessity of rowing. The downstream trip was uneventful and ended on 7 August.

The expedition members made camp at the river's mouth. They spent the next two days in numerous small jobs, as well as in assisting Cantwell in sounding the many other mouths of the Kowak and preparing for the trip to Selawik Lake. Its entrance lay nearby, for the lake was merely an extension of Hotham Inlet.

At 6 A.M. on 10 August, Cantwell, Andre, and Natorak began their exploration of Selawik Lake; their "light skin boat glided over the waves, covering fifty-three-and-a-half miles" the first day. The next day the explorers made forty-three miles. A strong wind on 12 August kept them shorebound, with Cantwell logging their track line and progress and then teaching Andre to write. The next day the explorers advanced over thirty-five miles and, over the next two days, saw a gain of fifty-nine miles, so that they arrived back at their camp near the entrance of the lake on 16 August.

By 20 August, as per his orders, Cantwell returned to the site of his first encampment on Hotham Inlet. The next day he found a cache of coal from the *Corwin,* along with a letter from Captain Healy. His new instructions called for him to find out "the number of the Indians who annually make this spot a rendezvous for trade, and to examine the shoal lying off the inlet with a view of discovering a channel to the sea." The revenue officer readily accomplished the first task, although it did cost him some labor, but he failed completely with the second one. Even after five hours of soundings, he could not find a depth of greater than one fathom across the bar.

The hospitality of his hosts at the temporary trading village completely overwhelmed Cantwell. "The chief of the Kotzebue Sound Eskimos, who took a violent fancy to me, acted as my guide through the village," Cantwell later wrote; the inhabitants threw huge "bear, wolf, and deer skins" before him to walk on, and he was followed around by "great crowds of men, women, children, and dogs, who kept up a continued howling and hustled each other about in great good humor; and upon arriving at [the chief's tent he] invited me inside." Inside his tent, the chief insisted that his guest eat from "a disk of white whale blubber," which tasted like "solidified codfish oil." Pleading "a late and hearty dinner," Cantwell declined a second helping. The trading rendezvous, he learned, occurred from the middle of July to the latter part of August. The methodical Cantwell personally counted nearly two thousand attendees and estimated that another six hundred had already gone back to their homes. During his return to the expedition's camp, the revenue officer experienced a final honor: "little boys ran ahead and picked berries for me to eat."

On 30 August, Cantwell drew "alongside the *Corwin* and reported [the party's] return on board to Capt. M.A. Healy." The expedition had traveled a total of 1,104.9 miles, spending fifty-four days on the trip—forty-three underway—journeyed 370 miles up the Kowak River, and covered 204.9 miles in exploring Selawik Lake and vicinity. "We are the pioneers of the river," Captain Healy flatly stated in his letter of transmittal to the secretary of the treasury, while including evidence to downplay the role of the U.S. Navy expedition of the same river and time: "I would respectfully call attention to the fact that the head of the river was not reached either by our party or the naval expedition, and the most interesting portion of the river remains unexplored. As far as I can learn, the naval expedition ascended about four hundred miles, and that from the *Corwin* three hundred and seventy-nine— little or no difference. Lieutenant Cantwell had reached his highest point and was returning when he met the expedition under Lieutenant Stoney."[6]

Although it was overshadowed by the significance and magnitude of his 1884 Kowak River expedition, Cantwell that same year made the first foot reconnaissance of the recently formed portion of Bogoslov Island in the

Lt. John C. Cantwell, probably at the time of his expedition up the Kobuk River.

Bering Sea. "The sides of the new Bogoslov rise with a gentle slope to the crater," the intrepid explorer reported, and, at first, his ascent proved easy. But soon, "at every step, my feet crushed through the outer covering and I sunk at first ankle-deep and later on knee-deep into a soft, almost impalpable dust which arose in clouds and nearly suffocated me." Nearing the summit he managed to walk on rocks and boulders, which were somewhat cooler and furnished a better foothold. His examination of the crater remained "unsatisfactory," because of "the clouds of smoke and steam arising and obscuring the view." The revenue officer did discover one "curious fact," however, the "entire absence" of either "lava or cinder," although these had been observed on all other volcanoes examined in the Aleutian Islands.[7]

Their 1884 failure to reach the headwaters of the Kobuk deterred neither Captain Healy nor Lieutenant Cantwell, for both planned a second attempt. Upon the senior officer's advice, the junior wrote his superiors in Washington, admitting his ignorance of the many obstacles encountered, describing his resultant mistakes that had prevented success, and expressing his belief that he deserved another chance. That winter, approval was forthcoming. The summer of 1885 found Captain Healy disembarking Lieutenant Cantwell on his second Kobuk Expedition.[8]

A valuable member of this group proved to be Charles H. Townsend, a naturalist of the Smithsonian Institution. On 20 June 1885, Captain Healy found him already on St. Paul's Island in the Bering Sea, having been sent to Alaska by the U.S. commissioner of fisheries to gather data on seals, fish, and other wildlife. Quickly convinced that the labors of this trained observer "would be of great value to science and of much interest to the public," the captain offered to let him become part of Lieutenant Cantwell's expedition.[9] "The opportunity of accompanying the *Corwin,* afforded through the courtesy of Captain Healy," Townsend recalled, "was one which I gladly availed myself of, as it enabled me to visit a remote and usually inaccessible region."[10] His observations during this expedition, recorded in his official report, ensured the scientific success of the *Corwin*'s second exploration up the Kobuk River.

The other members consisted of William G. Marsh, seaman; Frederic Lewis, fireman; and Myninck, an interpreter taken on board at St. Michael's. The cutter's steam launch, which had been overhauled and remodeled before departing San Francisco, once again served as their primary means of transportation.[11] They also had a locally built skin boat, about twenty-eight feet long, with which to haul supplies, equipment, and fuel. Once ashore, Lieutenant Cantwell intended to hire Native Americans and buy additional skin boats whenever needed and available.

Departing the *Corwin* off Hotham Inlet on 2 July, Lieutenant Cantwell made good use of his experience gained the previous year, and nine days later he had reached a position "one day's journey from the highest point reached by the Stoney expedition in 1884." They had traveled so fast that Townsend had had little opportunity for gathering scientific data. The revenue lieutenant now decided to leave the steam launch, and the two cuttermen to operate it, with the scientist for his use in making a collection, while he himself pushed on.

The next day, Lieutenant Cantwell set out with the natives he had hired in a skin boat he named the *Pioneer.* He had provisions for twenty days. On 16 July, having endured extremes of cold and heat, hordes of mosquitoes, and the dangers of wilderness traveling, he "rounded a high, rocky bluff and came suddenly in sight of a seething mass of white water bursting its way through a gorge composed of perpendicular masses of slaty rock two hundred to three hundred feet high, surmounted by a forest of spruce and birch. The channel was completely choked with sharp-pointed rocks, past which the water flew with frightful velocity, breaking itself into mimic cascades of foam and spray."[12]

Here, at the head of boat navigation, the expedition leader quickly determined that the only hope of reaching the Kobuk's headwaters "was to get the boat past these rapids." The first of many portages turned out to be over a mile long, while shorter ones later on often proved the more dangerous.

At last, on the afternoon of 21 July, Lieutenant Cantwell reached the outlet of a lake known by the natives as Car-loog-ah-look-tah. His guides had already told him that this lake was the headwaters of the Kobuk River; its name meant Big Fish Lake. Entering this tributary, they soon encountered yet another rapids obstructing their passage and landed to reconnoiter. After climbing the bank, the lieutenant "struck out across the tundra" toward the higher elevation, where his Indian guides said that the lake forming the river's headwaters could be seen. The revenue officer "climbed up the sides of the hill and looked away toward the north. Four or five miles away, and almost completely surrounded by mountains from twenty-five hundred to three thousand feet high, the blue sparkling waters of the long-sought lake burst upon my view. The sensations of pleasure and triumph which took possession of me as I gazed upon its waters, now for the first time seen by a white man, amply repaid me for the long tedious journey."[13]

Being so close to his ultimate goal, and his skin boat being in such "dilapidated condition," Lieutenant Cantwell continued on foot, reaching Big Fish Lake some two and a half hours later. After making a temporary camp on the beach, he "began at once the work of taking observations, photographing, sketching, etc." Finding his way around the lake blocked by "dense growth of willows," the revenue officer climbed the mountains bordering the southern side of the lake and "obtained a magnificent view of the entire lake and country in every direction." The lake proved to be about eight miles long and three miles wide.

After completing his exploration of the lake, Lieutenant Cantwell returned to his skin boat on 24 July; he launched her and, once reaching the Kobuk River again, headed upstream. The lieutenant pushed the boat until the river became too shallow to proceed farther. He could see an unbroken line of mountains ahead of him and knew no river could flow through them.

Although believing his mission had been accomplished, Lieutenant Cantwell continued scouting the area and retreated only when the heavy rains threatened to make the gorge impassable. He then started the descent of the Kobuk River at once and in earnest. The following days became all jammed together into jumbled memories of "shooting the rapids," having the skin boat spin out of control and smash into rocks or overturn, finding "some means of protecting her rotting sides and bottom from the rocks and gravel beds which we found it impossible to avoid running over," dangerously narrow gorges swollen by muddy torrents, "a terrific rain-storm," and similar navigational horrors. Yet they survived them all and, finally, one day "the sun rose clear and bright in a sky that was free from clouds."

About 8 P.M. on 27 July, Lieutenant Cantwell's small party reached the last native village they had visited during the upstream trip. There a message awaited that the launch had sustained damage in a rapids and appeared lost. Despite their weariness they resumed their downstream journey. No longer did they have to spend hours paddling, for the swift current now bore the craft along at a rapid pace. Shooting the last rapids before reaching the steam launch proved an ordeal. As the revenue officer later described this event, "With a rush and a roar we plunged past huge bowlders [sic] fringed with foam, so close sometimes as to enable us to touch them with our hands, and then over jagged rocks lying beneath the surface."

Within minutes after clearing these rapids they arrived at their destination, only to find a note from Townsend dated 19 July. It informed them that the party had safely refloated the launch and made a new camp ten miles downstream. The two parties were at last united and celebrated the event with a meal of fresh bear meat.

The homeward journey for the entire party began the next day, 28 July. The expedition made a leisurely voyage, stopping along the way to make observations and gather specimens of the flora or to send men up hills to assess the surrounding countryside.

Lieutenant Stoney's second expedition, of 1885–86, had meanwhile been wending its way up the Kobuk River. This time the naval explorer headed inland with three other officers, an assistant surgeon, an assistant engineer, ten enlisted men, and two Indians with their families. His expedition had liberal supplies of provisions (enough for twenty months), boat gear, equipment, hand tools, scientific instruments, and trade goods. Even a portable steam saw mill had been brought along, for Lieutenant Stoney planned to built a semipermanent camp and to winter over. For transportation he had a specially designed sixty-foot flat-bottomed steamboat, a steam launch, and two small boats.

Ironically, on 11 August this lavishly manned and equipped naval expedition met the revenue cutter's much smaller party, returning downstream after having already located the source of the Kobuk. For the second year in a row, Lieutenant Cantwell had upstreamed his rival.[14]

Resuming his data-gathering journey to the river's mouth, the revenue officer found "little of interest to relate," although he did mention photographing the legendary Jade Mountain. Having sighted their cutter at 8:30 A.M. on 27 August, his expedition broke camp for the last time, and its members were soon safely on board the *Corwin* once again. Lieutenant Cantwell "immediately made a short report of [his] explorations to Captain Healy," thus ending the second Kobuk River expedition.[15]

Second Assistant Engineer McLenegan also reported back from his exploration of the Noatak River on this same date, having been gone the same number of days as Lieutenant Cantwell. That river, discharging into Kotzebue Sound about thirty miles north of the Kobuk River, had previously been "known only from native accounts, for there is no record of its ever having been visited by white men."[16] Captain Healy had believed that the same reasons called for the explorations of both rivers. Why he selected McLenegan for this difficult and dangerous task remains unrecorded, but the engineer, being both young and healthy, had already demonstrated his exploring abilities as a member of the *Corwin*'s 1884 expedition.

McLenegan had been able to obtain neither Native American interpreters nor paddlers and so had decided to get by with his "own slight knowledge of the language" and the assistance of Seaman Nelson from the cutter's crew. They had been forced to travel by canoe, for the river's shallowness and rapids made that the best available vessel. Their craft, a three-hatch bidarka (a skin boat more commonly known as a kayak), had been obtained in Unalaska. It was twenty-seven feet long and two feet wide, and its top portion was entirely closed except for the circular hatches.

The engineer and seaman made their farewells on 2 July and headed north toward the mouth of the Noatak River. For most of the next two months, they became as one with their canoe and paddles. Through mountains with "rocky cliffs," turbulent waters, thick forests, wide marshes, and empty tundra, the two explorers made their way, often forced to shoot rapids, carry the canoe on portages, and work in cold waist-deep waters for hours on end. After twenty-seven days of paddling they reached the head of boat navigation, some five hundred miles inland, and then abandoned their canoe to continue on foot. At last, when the Noatak River "had degenerated into a mere rambling creek," Engineer McLenegan realized that its headwaters had been reached for all practical purposes. A large number of lakes dotted the countryside, all drained by the river. He concluded that the topography made it impossible to trace the river to a single source, and that none of the many rivers were navigable. Convinced that they "had achieved all that lay in [their] power," the engineer "determined to retreat without delay."

Not only had Seaman Nelson fallen ill with a fever but in addition provisions were rapidly dwindling and the weather had changed for the worse. An accurate description of their exciting adventures on the return trip, McLenegan later lamented, "would require an abler pen than mine," for "the dangers encountered on the ascending journey were now doubled." As in the earlier part of the expedition, they again surmounted all obstacles and, finally, glimpsed the sea.

In his official report, Captain Healy emphasized the ordeals endured by both Lieutenant Cantwell and Engineer McLenegan and their men. "Both expeditions experienced many difficulties and hardships," he wrote to the secretary of the treasury, "which at times seemed insurmountable. Their perseverance and labor overcame their trials, and they succeeded in reaching the head of canoe navigation of both rivers; a feat which was never before achieved, and one which has hitherto been considered impossible of accomplishment in the time given."[17]

Over the years, the scientific, commercial, and practical benefits subsequently derived from the *Corwin's* explorations of the Kobuk and Noatak rivers proved incalculable. William H. Dall, an authority on Alaska, characterized McLenegan's reconnaissance of the Noatak as "extremely creditable."[18] The sketch map made by the revenue engineer, for instance, remained the most reliable one available until into the twentieth century. In fact, according to one history of U.S. Arctic explorations, the U.S. Revenue Cutter Service published "the best reports" of any governmental agency.[19]

The U.S. Revenue Cutter Service's active—and prolonged—participation in the exploration of Alaska, both on its own and in collaboration with other organizations, did not occur without casualties. The service possesses the dubious distinction of experiencing the largest number of fatalities of any U.S. governmental agency engaged in these efforts. The greatest single loss came on 6 June 1891 off Icy Cape, Alaska, while carrying out departmental instructions to land a U.S. Geological Survey expedition. One of the boats from the *Bear* capsized during this ship-to-shore maneuver, resulting in the drowning of the revenue officer in command, four cuttermen, and an expedition member. [20]

The penultimate and final exploring efforts by a revenue cutter came in 1900. In that year, First Lieutenant Cantwell, commanding the revenue steamer *Nunivak,* stationed year-round on the Yukon River, launched two reconnaissance expeditions. Cantwell had maneuvered to become the commanding officer of this cutter, probably because of the isolated location of the ship and the chance he would therefore have for further exploring.

As 1900 dawned, the *Nunivak* was laid up in winter quarters about a mile up the Dall River from its mouth on the Yukon River, some one thousand miles inland from the Bering Sea. On 11 January her commander dispatched 3d Lt. Eugene Blake, Jr., and Asst. Eng. H. N. Wood with a dog team and sled for the purpose of making a trip over the Koyukuk trail "to the mountains which form the divide between the headwaters of the Dall and the Koyukuk rivers to ascertain the nature of the country and to gain practical knowledge of winter traveling."[21] The first night they had to make camp and sleep in a tent in a temperature of minus fifty-six degrees Fahrenheit. When the next morning the two officers found it "impossible" to break camp, load the sled, and continue, they "left all standing and beat a retreat to the ship."

After the extreme cold broke, Lieutenant Blake and Engineer Wood made a fresh start on the twenty-first with four dogs and the empty sled, returning to their former camp and then continuing onward. They mushed for three days before the trail crossed the Dall River.[22] Continuing on, they took the wrong fork in the trail and ended up on the north fork of the Dall River. Since the commander's orders had called for a detailed "look into this creek," the two revenue officers spent the next three days exploring it. Besides finding some traces of quartz- and ruby-bearing rock in abandoned mining holes, they also ran into two prospectors and gained more current information on the Koyukuk Trail. The expedition rejoined the main trail on the twenty-ninth, and the two explorers mushed on for three more days before stumbling upon an empty cabin, a mere thirteen miles from their goal—the divide. They left their outfit secured in the cabin the next morning and started out on snowshoes.

The revenue officers had climbed to within a mile or so of the top by 11 A.M., when the wind suddenly knocked both down. After deciding "that it would be unwise to proceed farther," they used a pocket aneroid barometer to measure their elevation—fifteen hundred feet above the Yukon River—

and then returned to the cabin. The morning of 2 February remained stormy. Having but few provisions remaining, the lieutenant and engineer decided to begin retracing their path. Nothing "worthy of note" occurred on the return trip, and the expedition ended upon their arrival at the cutter on the evening of the fifth.

Five months later to the day, cuttermen from the revenue steamer boarded the Alaska Commercial Company's steamer *Leah,* bound for the headwaters of the Koyukuk River with passengers and freight from Dawson, Northwest Territory. Since Lieutenant Cantwell desired "some information in regard to the traffic on that stream," he arranged for 2d Lt. Bernard H. Camden to journey aboard the *Leah* for the trip.[23] The revenue lieutenant made his reconnaissance, returning on the twentieth. He reported having "mapped the Koyukuk from its junction with the Yukon to a point 450 miles upstream" in addition to boarding and examining "all vessels found engaged in commerce on the river."

In his official report, Lieutenant Camden described at some length his discoveries. The Koyukuk River, despite draining some thirty-thousand square miles, was muddy, narrow, and sluggish. "Its course is constantly changing," he recorded, "frequently turning through 180 [degrees] and heading in parallel but opposite direction, so that the river is not only difficult to navigate, but very tedious to follow on account of the many sharp turns in the channel."[24] He found wildfowl and large game, such as bear, moose, and caribou, plentiful, and estimated the number of natives living along the river to be not more than three hundred. After presenting a detailed rundown of the Koyukuk mining district, he predicted the possibility that, once the problem of food and supplies had been solved, it would "rank with any of the gold fields known in Alaska at the present time."

Thus ended the period of significant exploration by revenue cutters. By 1900 the overall picture of Alaska's geography had been acquired and, for all practical purposes, the U.S. Coast and Geodetic Survey became the major federal agency devoted to scientific exploration in Alaska. Once the *Nunivak* was decommissioned, revenue cutters seldom sailed Alaska's inland waters, and even less frequently dispatched exploring parties ashore. Interestingly, the officer who had commanded the Revenue Cutter Service cutter, Lt. John C. Cantwell, led both the expeditions that had initiated the American exploration of the interior of western Alaska.[25]

# SEVEN

# The Smithsonian's Navy

One time-consuming, routine-disrupting, inconvenient, annoying, and sometimes even irritating U.S. Revenue Cutter Service activity in the far north has continued down to the present day, to the almost uniform disgust of both past and current U.S. Coast Guardsmen. Since few, if any, other vessels traveled in these northern regions, the revenue cutters and their crews found themselves being drafted as the government's passenger and freight handymen. They performed as a federal general-purpose service handling passengers, mail, and freight, and doing taxi, towing, rescue, ambulance, census-taking, and a myriad of other duties.

This practice started with the initial July 1867 voyage to Russian America of the U.S. Revenue Cutter Service cutter *Lincoln*. That ship carried the sole official U.S. representative, five U.S. Coast Survey officers and their equipment, and two experienced naturalists, with orders to "prosecute diligently the line of investigation prescribed by the Secretary of the Smithsonian Institution."[1] In the years to follow, the cutters carried almost everything capable of being transported, including shipwrecked mariners, Alaskan residents, Native Americans, foreigners, government convicts, explorers, judges, scientists, and teachers, as well as construction materials, food, mail, medicine, scientific specimens, trading goods, and even large quantities of live reindeer.

### *"Yes, Doctor, You Have But to Ask"*

The cuttermen often reported fulfilling many of the desires of the Smithsonian Institution in only the most casual manner. One example was in June

1884, when the revenue steamer *Corwin* cruised among the hunks of ice floating in the Bering Sea. Her commander, Capt. Michael A. Healy, simply reported the shooting of several banded seals with the intention "of procuring specimens for the Smithsonian Institution, but they sank as soon as they were killed."[2] The following year he mentioned stopping the *Corwin* at Halls Island to permit Charles H. Townsend, a naturalist of the Smithsonian Institution, to land and kill a polar bear for the museum.[3]

On 9 April 1899, shortly after learning of his assignment to command the revenue cutter *Nunivak* on the Yukon River and its tributaries, 1st Lt. John C. Cantwell contacted the Smithsonian Institution. He offered to cooperate with it in scientific work "in that region, so far as compatible with [my] official duties." The secretary of the Smithsonian wrote to the Treasury Department on 24 April stating that Cantwell could provide a valuable service to the National Museum.[4] The Treasury Department granted permission on 2 May.

A representative 1903 request involved transportation. James Judge, a treasury agent on St. George Island, one of the Pribilofs, had obtained the skeletons of two whales for display in the National Museum. The Smithsonian wanted a revenue cutter to stop at the island, take the skeletons aboard, and deliver them to Seattle. The Treasury Department, in turn, authorized Capt. John F. Wild, commanding the *Bear,* to convey these skeletons. His orders, however, left the decision "entirely" up to him. Captain Wild decided not to perform this service. [5]

The captain's actions brought about an exchange of correspondence the next year between Richard Rathbun, the head of the National Museum, and the secretary of the treasury. Rathbun stressed the importance of the whale skeletons and how much the Smithsonian would appreciate having them brought to Washington. Later, on 29 July, he wrote directly to Capt.-Cmdt. Charles F. Shoemaker for assistance. A handwritten notation on the filed correspondence reads "Put in Bear's orders."[6] Since no additional correspondence ensued on this matter, the mission was apparently fulfilled in 1904.

Two years later, Rathbun made an even more unusual request. Of the many and varied Smithsonian requests, this 7 February 1906 entreaty was perhaps the strangest: "The natives of Alaska often abandon their dead in the neighborhood of their settlements," the senior Smithsonian scientist explained, "where the skeletons are sometimes to be found in greater or less numbers." The U.S. National Museum desired a series of these skeletons "for use in the study of the physical characteristics of these aborigines, a line of investigation which has already been extended to many races." Rathbun suggested that the medical officers aboard the cutters serve as scientists. Probably in hopes of gaining an affirmative reply, Rathbun praised the efforts of earlier U.S. Revenue Cutter Service officers.[7] The Treasury Department granted approval on 9 February 1906.

When permission was obtained, the Smithsonian forwarded copies of a pamphlet prepared by Dr. Alex Hrdlicka, a noted anthropologist of the U.S. National Museum. It contained instructions for the cutter's doctors.[8]

Other scientific organizations also routinely made requests for assistance of the U.S. Revenue Cutter Service. In 1900, for instance, Capt Francis Tuttle cooperated with the Geographical Society of Philadelphia in an "interesting scientific experiment." He had his cuttermen aboard the *Bear* distribute fifteen of their "Melville-Bryant Drift Casks in the Arctic Sea north of Alaska."[9] Another assist to scientists occurred in mid-October 1907, after major volcanic eruptions had transformed Bogoslof Island. Capt. Henry B. Rogers, commanding the *McCulloch,* detailed 1st Lt. Bernard H. Camden to inspect the island and note any changes that might have occurred since the cutter's visits earlier that year. His report, accompanied by a sketch and five photographs, quickly became a highly desirable item. Many prominent organizations requested copies, among them the American Museum of Natural History in New York City and the Geographical Society of the Pacific in San Francisco.[10]

The exception that proves the rule concerning the Treasury Department's overly generous treatment of scientists and scholars is probably its refusal to give favorable consideration to one such request, even when supported by a senator. On 17 May 1905, Prof. Joseph Schafer, head of the History Department at the University of Oregon, proposed using his summer vacation, accompanied by his spouse as a research assistant, to visit Alaska and gather historical information. His itinerary called for stops at Sitka and other historic fur trade centers as far west as the Pribilof Islands. This trip, the professor explained, would permit him to gather data and prepare himself for writing a history of the territory. In exchange for passage on a revenue cutter, he would make a bibliographical report available to the Library of Congress. Senator B. R. Tillman of Oregon provided a letter in support of the professor's request.

Despite the senator's recommendation, the secretary of the treasury refused the request. The secretary wrote Tillman that no cutter would be making the transit from Seattle to Sitka, and he pointed out that the vessels were already overbooked by those on official business.[11]

## The Cutter Mailmen

The difficulties encountered in delivering the mail in remote areas proved many and varied. One cutter ran into most of them in mid-1905 while attempting to perform an ordinary mail run. On 20 June at Dutch Harbor, Alaska, the steamer *Perry* loaded the mail for Atka, Attu, and Pribilof islands, as well as clothing donated for the destitute Aleuts on Atka and Attu. A strong gale delayed her departure until the following morning, when the weather moderated. The *Perry* had no sooner cleared harbor than the wind made up again and the sea rose so that her commander, Capt. William H. Roberts, felt it more prudent to run for shelter at Dutch Harbor until the storm passed.

Captain Roberts began his journey again, and again he ran into another tempest that lasted until 23 June and forced the *Perry* to the west. He decided to continue on to Attu rather than turn back for the Pribilof Islands. The revenue captain believed this course of action safer, since his coal supply might not hold out. Captain Roberts sighted his destination early on the morning of 27 June, entered Chicagof Harbor, and anchored off the Aleut village. The revenue captain immediately learned from the island's inhabitants of four Japanese schooners anchored in nearby Saranna Bay. He quickly sailed to the ships, inspecting them and their sixty-five hundred seine-caught salmon. The shipmasters had conducted their fishing in accordance with the existing salmon regulations. Captain Roberts, however, did find preparations "for setting a floating trap running out from the beach." He accordingly ordered the Japanese schooners to leave Attu within twenty-four hours and had their camps ashore torched once they had departed.

The *Perry* delivered both the mail and a portion of the donated clothing before putting to sea during the morning of 29 June. After a much appreciated smooth cruise the *Perry* came to anchor in Nazan Bay, Atka Island, the following morning. Shortly thereafter the wind again rose to gale force, and Captain Roberts found it necessary to drop both anchors during violent williwaws off the nearby mountains. Eventually, Captain Roberts and the *Perry* delivered the mail and the clothing sent by the Women's National Relief Association.[12]

Bad weather conditions did not permit a departure until the morning of 2 July. After the cutter put out to sea, the wind soon increased to a gale with heavy following seas. The *Perry* anchored off the village on St. George Island in the Pribilofs the following afternoon. Her signal for a mail delivery prompted a negative reply because of dangerous breaking surf on the beach. Captain Roberts remained at anchor until the early morning of 4 July before getting underway and proceeding to the East Landing, St. Paul Island, where he signaled a mail delivery. The reply here requested the *Perry* land the mail by one of her small boats at the West Landing, since the low tide did not permit any launching from shore. Once her small boat had returned, the cutter retraced her trackline to the village on St. George. Finding the sea peaceful, she landed the mail and took aboard outbound mail before departing that afternoon. After a full-speed run, the *Perry* docked at Dutch Harbor on the afternoon of 5 July.

Some activities involving the mails did not fall within the category of routine picking up, carrying, and delivering. One such occurred during the mid-1900 smallpox quarantine of vessels entering the harbor of St. Michael. "All mail originating at Nome or that had lain in the Nome post-office was fumigated on board this vessel," reported Surg. James T. White, R.C.S., of the cutter *Nunivak*. They accomplished this task "by first perforating the letters and then subjecting them to the fumes of burning sulphur, burned in a box with a crated bottom for want of a better apparatus." The cuttermen then delivered the fumigated mail to the St. Michael post office.[13]

On 7 July 1908, Capt. Andrew J. Henderson sailed the *Thetis* out of the anchorage near Nome to seek the passenger steamer *Ohio,* last seen on 29 June, to check on the safety of her passengers. William McManus, district superintendent of the Railway Mail Service, also sailed aboard the cutter in hopes of retrieving sixty sacks of mail from the vessel. Sighting the *Ohio* on 10 July, the *Thetis* immediately shaped a course for her. Summoning her master to his cabin, Captain Henderson first mentioned the public resentment over his failure to land his passengers as scheduled. He then warned the master that "unless he consented to follow the THETIS to Nome [he] would take the mail and such passengers as [he] could carry from him." The master agreed to accompany the cutter in convoy but still did not want to enter the ice.[14] With the *Ohio* following, the *Thetis* started working through the ice and made the passage safely. The two vessels anchored off Nome the next morning. The *Ohio* unloaded her passengers, baggage, mail, and a small quantity of freight before proceeding to St. Michael to finish discharging.

In the case of the U.S. mails, as in other matters, persistence often succeeded in wringing cutter assistance out of the sometimes parsimonious Treasury Department. When acting secretary of the treasury C. D. Hilles denied a transportation request, the postmaster general immediately challenged this decision. He argued that a misunderstanding had taken place, since the Post Office Department merely wished to request "that the inspectors be granted the privilege of traveling on Revenue Cutters between post offices in Alaska in event it so happened that the Revenue Cutters would, in their regular course, ply between offices or points which the inspectors desired to visit and which would enable them to economize and save time and expenses. The disadvantages of travel in Alaska are extraordinarily great at best, and it is believed that if the inspectors were granted this privilege, not only days but sometimes weeks of time would be saved the inspectors in their work."[15]

In a swift reversal of policy, Acting Secretary Hilles informed the postmaster general on 27 July 1909 that the revenue cutters in Alaska would transport these two postal inspectors. The same day, he issued new guidelines to Capt. William V. E. Jacobs, commanding the Bering Sea Patrol Fleet, and Captain Henderson, commanding the *Thetis.* The acting secretary authorized them to transport these two postal inspectors should the cutters under their "command touch at any points they may desire to visit." He cautioned them, however, against diverting from any regular duties "to perform this service."

## Census Taking

Whenever a national census became necessary, the cutters plying northern waters had to transport the special agents of the Census Office about the Alaska Territory. Even more surprising, the Treasury Department approved a 22 April 1890 request by the superintendent of the census that Captain Healy, commanding the *Bear,* be commissioned as "a Special Agent of the Eleventh Census." As an official census taker, Captain Healy had the task "of making the population and social statistics of the Diomede Islands in Bering Strait and King's, Nunivak, St. Lawrence, Sledge, and Nunivak Islands in the Bering Sea." This action saved the government the cost of transporting additional officials. Hence a revenue officer on an Alaskan cutter became an official census taker.[16]

## On a Mission for God

The cutters on northern cruises routinely transported missionaries and others on church business. One commanding officer explained his reason for carrying two young students of the Russian Mission School at Unalaska: There existed "no other means of transportation." An instruction from the commander of the Bering Sea Fleet to a cutter commander in 1896 best illustrates the practice of the U.S. Revenue Cutter Service: "The Rev. S. H. Rock, a Moravian Missionary, having made application for passage to Nushagak on the 'Wolcott' and there being no other way by which he can reach his destination before August, you are directed to furnish him the desired transportation. It being understood that he will pay for his subsistence as provided for in the Regulations."

The Treasury Department regularly issued instructions such as the following one to cutter skippers: "You are directed, in the course of your cruising the present season, not to interfere with the regular duties of the vessel, to convey Dr. J. B. Driggs from Nome to Point Hope, and Mr. A. J. Knapp, from Point Hope to Nome, on Church business."[17] Cuttermen also provided other kinds of assistance, as Captain Healy informed the secretary of the treasury: "The Catholic Mission, having purchased the condemned Steam Schooner 'Challenge,' found her machinery in a sad state of repairs. They requested aid from the 'Bear' to put it in working order, which request was granted."[18] On another occasion he reported his inability, because of the large number of shipwrecked mariners aboard the *Bear*, to transport the body of the recently deceased Archbishop Seghers from St. Michael to Victoria, British Columbia.

### At the Beck and Call of Congress

It was rare indeed that a request from Congress—which holds the federal purse strings—failed to win a ready acceptance from either the Treasury Department or the U.S. Revenue Cutter Service. The presence of congressional interest lies heavily upon much of the surviving correspondence in the National Archives.

From 9 to 19 July 1903, Capt. Washington C. Coulson and his officers and enlisted men of the cutter *McCulloch* played host to the nine members of the Senate Committee on Territories. The four senators and the five others of their party remained with the revenue steamer during a 3,406-mile cruise from St. Michael to Nome, the Pribilof Islands, and various points along the southern coast of Alaska and British Columbia, disembarking finally at Seattle. When they expressed a desire to visit the canneries on Kodiak Island by way of Karluk Strait, Captain Coulson agreed. Not being sufficiently acquainted with this inland passage, he secured the services of a pilot off a merchant vessel and successfully made a very satisfactory trip, remaining as long as the senatorial party desired. The customary thank-you

The cutter *Tahoma* was lost in the Bering Sea. Some of the survivors celebrate their rescue.

note penned by the committee, whose chairman was Sen. N. P. Dillingham of Vermont, exuded flowery praise. It exulted that such "a voyage [had taken place] without a single disagreeable occurrence to mar its delights" and concluded with a most kind wish: "May the McCulloch sail only to add additional glory to her flag, and Captain Coulson, his officers and men live to ripe old ages and enjoy peace, plenty and happiness throughout every one of their days."[19]

Sometimes the Treasury Department succeeded in reducing the scope of a congressional request. For example, on 3 April 1905, Rep. James A. Tawney, chairman of the Committee on Industrial Arts and Expositions, wrote the secretary of the treasury about their forthcoming visit to the opening of an exposition in Portland, Oregon. The overwhelming majority of congressmen, he complained, had never visited Alaska and possessed no knowledge of the territory. This ignorance did not help them in passing good laws for Alaska. As a partial solution to this problem, he suggested that one or two revenue cutters transport his committee members on a three-week trip to Alaska to familiarize themselves with conditions in the district and become acquainted with the country and the people.[20]

The treasury's brief, negative, and prompt response came three days later: "The most spacious revenue cutter in the service will accommodate five first cabin passengers. By so doing the captain has to bunk with the minor officers." Moreover, explained the departmental secretary, the "guests on revenue cutters have to pay their own board," and even his own assistant secretary would have to use a passenger boat on his upcoming trip to Alaska. In the judgment of the treasury secretary, "the steamship companies will be very glad to extend to the Congressional committee complementary passage." The official did offer the use of a revenue cutter at Portland to escort them around the harbor. But when the committee chairman replied that this seemed reasonable, the Treasury Department official replied that they would do their best but refused to promise the use of the cutter, as operational commitments might make the trip impossible.

### Providing a Helping Hand to Destitute Natives

While searching for survivors of the SS *Pelican,* long overdue and believed lost, the revenue steamer *Grant* visited Attu Island. Her commanding officer, Capt. Jefferson A. Slamm, found the island's seventy-three inhabitants "very Destitute" in "some of the necessities of life" as understood by the cuttermen. As a result, those on the *Grant* gave the natives all the spare clothing they had. Upon discovering many inhabitants "suffering from hereditary tertiary syphilis," the ship's surgeon did "much to relieve temporarily, the afflicted."[21] The cuttermen aboard the *McCulloch* on its mid-July 1908 visit to the native village at Akutan Harbor also supplied their own clothing to "some of the more scantily attired" Aleutians and distributed food.

More often, the revenue cutters made special trips, and cuttermen showed a unique knack for revising or improvising arrangements and cutter schedules to make possible the distribution of the boxes of clothing supplied by charities. Those boxes donated by the Women's National Relief Association in 1905 received special handling. In the early part of the year, the revenue steamer *Manning* made two trips to the islands of Attu and Atka to distribute the clothing to the destitute inhabitants.[22] Having a surplus of clothing left over on their second voyage, the cuttermen made a detour to another island with needy residents and distributed the extra clothing there. Later in the year, the *Manning* picked up additional boxes of donated clothing in Seattle from a local hardware company and conveyed them to Dutch Harbor. Since the *Manning*'s cruising area did not include the Aleutians, the cuttermen placed the clothing in a storehouse to await the arrival of other cutters that could complete the delivery. When the master of a merchant vessel offered to deliver free of charge those charity items destined for the inhabitants of St. George and St. Paul in the Pribilof Islands, the cuttermen at Dutch Harbor readily loaded them aboard the steamer. The cutter *Bear* later delivered the boxes earmarked for the unfortunate North American natives on St. Lawrence Island.

### Even Private Citizens and Businessmen Sometimes Need a Lift

From time to time the U.S. Revenue Cutter Service provided passage and transportation for private citizens and businessmen, their families, and belongings. Captain Coulson, for instance, furnished a Mr. Williams of Tacoma and a Mr. Ames of Nome with passage from Dutch Harbor to Seattle aboard the revenue steamer *McCulloch* "on account of urgent business interests."[23] Five years later, on 27 May 1905, a revenue cutter transported Morris Marcus, of L. Foster & Company, an import/export wholesale grocery, from Nome to St. Lawrence Island and then to the Seward Peninsula.

The following December, Henry Koenig requested passage for himself, his wife, four sons, some whalebone, and a few boxes on the revenue steamer making the Arctic cruise in 1906 from Point Hope to Nome. When queried for his views, Capt. Oscar C. Hamlet recommended approval by the U.S. Revenue Cutter Service chief: No commercial transportation existed, he said, and Koenig was "a worthy man who never gave the Revenue Cutters any trouble, has furnished us much valuable information and assisted us materially in building the School House at the Point two years ago." Captain Hamlet also mentioned his recent granting of passage on the steamer *Bear* for "Mr. C. Brower and his Son from Point Barrow" for the same reason: unreliable commercial passenger service, which consisted solely of Arctic whaling ships.[24]

### Support Your Local Sheriff and Courts

As is to be expected from a law enforcement agency, the U.S. Revenue Cutter Service did more than its share in supporting the enforcement of U.S. law throughout the Alaska Territory. A good example of how a revenue cutter rode to the rescue began with a telegram in early 1899 from the governor of Alaska to the secretary of the interior, who, in turn, notified the attorney general on 12 May "that the Judge of the District Court for Alaska contemplates a trip through Alaska for the purpose of administering the new code which goes into operation on the first of July, and particularly of that portion of it in regard to the issue of licenses." Furthermore, the "greatest difficulty in the way is the want of means of transportation." The official went on to point out "that a term of court begins at Juneau May 10th" and the court, after issuing licenses in southeast Alaska and elsewhere, would reach St. Michael about 10 August. "If a Government vessel could meet the party and bring them back by way of Unalaska and other places, the whole work could be accomplished in an orderly manner."

The governor wanted "the matter be brought to the attention of the President, the Secretary of the Treasury, and yourself" and "orders be given to have a government vessel at the point indicated for the use of the Judge of the Court."[25] The attorney general, in turn, referred the entire matter to the treasury secretary, asking only to be advised as to any action taken. Approval for the use of a revenue cutter for the Alaskan judge was forthcoming four days later, on 16 May.

Within two years, the use of a revenue cutter for Alaskan judges seemed to have been established. Judge Melville C. Brown of the first division of the district of Alaska did not bother invoking the name of the president, governor, or secretary of the interior. He simply asked the attorney general on 7 March 1901 for a revenue cutter to "report to [him] at Juneau on 1st of June for [his] trip" to Cook Inlet, Kodiak, and other places in the northern and western part of his division, "in order to determine by my own personal observation the judicial necessities of that country." He also made the unusual request that, if the "accommodations" on the cutter were "ample" enough, he wished to take with him his "clerk and stenographer, who is a young woman, and whose services I shall very much need on the trip. Please have the usual order 'no women allowed' excluded from the orders requiring the Cutter to report to me."[26] Within mere days after the attorney general agreed to these requests, the Treasury Department had agreed to assign the *Rush* to Judge Brown for his trip.

The rationale of "no other means of transportation" apparently worked virtually every time. The U.S. commissioner for the Colville District, Alaska, used this justification to request that the revenue cutter making the annual 1904 Arctic cruise "transport for my deputy not more than two tons of provisions as far as Pt. Barrow"; he gained approval. Four years earlier, for the same reason, the revenue cutter *McCulloch* delivered both office furniture and supplies to the U.S. court in Nome.[27]

Sometimes the federal authorities in Alaska Territory needed armed support from the cuttermen to enforce the peace. While at Unalaska in September 1907, Captain Henderson, commanding the *Thetis,* first sent six cuttermen to prevent the crew members of the Japanese sealing schooner *Kaiwo* from stowing away on a departing American steamer; they left two armed sentries on the dock to prevent any further desertions. Later, as the *Thetis* started to warp the *Kaiwo* down the harbor, eleven of the Japanese crewmen lowered a boat and attempted to land. Captain Henderson promptly dispatched an armed boat with an officer and crew to return the deserting Japanese to their vessels; they succeeded only after "a display of force."[28]

In a similar case, Capt. Dtelf F. A. de Otte no sooner made his cutter fast to the wharf at Sitka on 13 May 1909 than a U.S. marshal came aboard and alerted him of the need to transport thirty Japanese prisoners to Juneau for trial on charges of violating game laws. After receiving a departmental cablegram approving this action, Captain de Otte loaded the prisoners aboard the *Rush* on 16 May and landed them at Juneau the same day. Two months later, after a conference between Capt.-Cmdt. Worth G. Ross and the Bureau of Immigration in the Department of Commerce and Labor, the Treasury Department ordered the commanding officer of the *Thetis* on 22 July 1909 to "Convey aliens detained by district attorney at Teller to Nome, Alaska, and turn them over" to the deputy collector of customs. The following month, again in compliance with departmental instructions, the revenue cutter *Perry* transported a deputy U.S. marshal and seventeen prisoners off a Japanese sealer from Unalaska to Valdez.

### *"Teacher's Pet"*

Educators bound for—or already in—the territory of Alaska found willing allies in the cuttermen serving on this northern frontier. Seldom did one of their requests for assistance fail to evoke a successful response. Without the revenue cutters plying the waterways to the more remote schools, the task of educating the native inhabitants of this vast land, let alone the children of the explorers, prospectors, and pioneers seeking to develop its natural riches, would have proved impossible.

At the request of the secretary of the interior in 1897, the Treasury Department directed the commanding officer of the revenue cutter *Bear* "to render such protection as he can to the teachers of the schools under the supervision of the Bureau of Education, Department of Interior" and to prevent "the unlawful killing of domestic reindeer by the Eskimo," as well as to impress "upon the native parents that they will be punished to the full extent of the law for killing their infant children."[29] The Bureau of Education often called upon the services of both the cutters and their crews. In March of

1900, for example, the Bureau requested the Treasury Department to issue instructions to "the Commanding Officers of the Revenue Cutters cruising in Bering Sea and the Arctic Ocean" to extend to those activities involving the transportation of reindeer "such friendly offices as are not incompatible with the rules of the Revenue Cutter service and existing laws."

After receiving reports in 1903 of discontent among the natives of St. Lawrence Island, the Bureau of Education assigned another person, thinking "it best to have this extra man there in case of any disturbance." The revenue steamer *Thetis* provided passage from Nome for Thomas Richards, "formerly a boatswain in the Revenue Cutter Service, and a thoroughly reliable man."[30] Two years later the bureau again requested—and again received, as it had the previous fifteen navigational seasons—passage for its general agent of education for the district of Alaska, which enabled him to inspect and establish schools and reindeer stations in the remote area of the Bering Sea and Arctic Ocean.

Such simple transportation requests became routine over the years. The *Thetis,* for example, furnished passage in 1904 to a man and wife team of teachers and the general superintendent of schools and reindeer stations in northwestern Alaska. Two years later the same cutter transported another male teacher from Nome to Icy Cape and, in 1909, allowed the assistant superintendent of government schools to travel on her annual arctic cruise. By that time, the practice had evolved so that commanding officers were issued specific instructions while making the customary Arctic cruise. The captains were told that they should "furnish necessary transportation to permit education officials to inspect the schools and reindeer stations on the shores of Bering Sea and the Arctic Ocean," and they were to "give transportation from Nome, or from points north of Nome, as occasion arises, to teachers going to or returning from United States public schools along the coast of Arctic Alaska north of Nome, which places are difficult of access and cannot readily be reached by commercial vessels." Lastly, the skippers of the revenue cutters were to "carry the mail and packages of school supplies from Nome to Diomede, Shishmaref, Deering, and Kotzebue."[31]

There were always unusual requests. In 1893, Captain Healy, of the *Bear,* authorized L. M. Stevenson, the school teacher at Point Barrow, to use a room in the U.S. Life-Saving Service Refuge Station there as a schoolroom. The same year Healy placed 3d Lt. Chester M. White in temporary charge of the Reindeer Station at Port Clarence from 5 July until his relief by W. L. Lopp of the Bureau of Education on 19 July. On behalf of the same bureau, the *Rush* carried J. L. Brown, a government school teacher at Unalaska, on one of the Bering Sea Patrol missions in 1909 to check on Canadian and Japanese sealing vessels putting in at Akutan Harbor. Brown visited the native village located there.[32]

### General Handyman

The number of requests fielded by both the Treasury Department and U.S. Revenue Cutter Service for transportation, as well as for other services, were legion, and it would require another volume to adequately cover them all. Probably the best example of a local request concerned the city of Tacoma on Puget Sound in Washington State. In 1906 the city's citizens planned an elaborate Fourth of July celebration, including a parade of vessels in the city's harbor. Although preferring the *McCulloch,* they said that they would appreciate any revenue cutter that could participate in these festivities. In the end, the service instructed the commanding officer of the *McCulloch* to arrange his movements "to take in stores at Puget Sound, participate in the exercises referred to and be in readiness to sail from Seattle not later than the 5th of July next."[33]

From the Department of Agriculture in 1901, interestingly enough, came a request to furnish F. A. Walpole, an artist, with passage "to Alaska for the purpose of making drawings of the useful and prominent native plants of that region." Although Walpole planned to visit only Unalaska and Port Clarence, "the necessities of his work" might require "additional transportation to points at which revenue cutters may touch on their official trips."[34] The service granted this request for passage, as it had those of 1899 and 1900. C. C. Georgeson, special agent in charge of the Alaska Experiment Stations, Department of Agriculture, was taken from Seattle to Unalaska.

The Department of Commerce and Labor often requested cutter assistance, primarily on behalf of its Bureau of Fisheries. Such a request for the services of a revenue cutter came on 28 April 1906. The Bureau of Fisheries wanted to send W. C. Marsh, a pathologist in the Division of Scientific Inquiry, "to the Pribilof Islands to enable him to make certain studies of the fur-seal herd on those islands." Naturally, there being "no local facilities for getting from one island to the other," the bureau requested the services of a revenue cutter, which the Treasury Department granted.[35] Three years later a similar request resulted in the revenue cutter *Manning*'s transporting an assistant agent of seal fisheries, also of the Bureau of Fisheries, E. W. Clark, and his wife from Unalaska to the Pribilof Islands.

The U.S. Revenue Cutter Service usually assisted the Bureau of Fisheries in making its inspections of Alaskan salmon canneries to enforce U.S. laws and regulations. Where else could sea transportation to these remote sites be obtained by a federal agency? The catching, curing, and canning of salmon and other fish products of Alaskan waters, coupled with that of the states of Washington, Oregon, and California, had developed into a business of great promise by 1905. The property employed in this industry totaled thirty million dollars, the number of men and women employed exceeded forty thousand, and the annual value of the output of the factories reached about twenty-eight million dollars. An estimated five hundred thousand Japanese were also engaged in the fishing business, mostly importing salt salmon. As the Japanese lost their foothold on their primary sources of salmon along the Siberian coast, the secretary of the Commerce and Labor Department warned his counterpart in the Treasury Department on 1 May 1905 of the American fishermen's fears that the Japanese "will swarm into Alaskan waters if some preventive action is not immediately taken." The existing law imposed a tax on salmon canneries and salteries, but it had been levied only on those operating on shore by citizens, not those on ships manned by aliens. Hence, the Department of Commerce and Labor instructed its Bureau of Fisheries "to make a thorough investigation during the coming fishing season relative to the encroachment of aliens upon the Alaskan salmon fisheries in order that a full report of the conditions prevailing may be made to Congress at the next session, for such action as it may deem necessary. This Department believes that the Revenue Cutter Service of your Department can render valuable aid in this investigation without interfering with its regular duties, by reporting the number of alien fishermen its officers discover in Alaskan waters, and by collecting and reporting any other information bearing upon the subject."[36]

As a result, on 16 May, the treasury secretary recommended, and President Theodore Roosevelt the same day approved, the selection of the revenue cutter *Perry* to "make the regular cannery cruise in Alaskan waters" and to patrol the North Pacific Ocean and Bering Sea to preserve the fur seals.[37] Between 8 July and 25 August 1905 the cutter cruised 3,826.6 nautical miles in support of the bureau's inspection of twenty-two salmon canneries. She carried H. M. Kutchin, special agent for the Bureau of Fisheries, to conduct the inspections, and C. M. Clegg, assistant district attorney, third district of Alaska, to collect the taxes.

Interestingly enough, two years earlier the emphasis had been on uncovering illegal Chinese, either in the canneries or on merchant vessels. Aboard the *Perry* on her 1903 cannery cruise, the cutter had carried an inspector of immigration to examine the documents of all Chinese encountered and to certify that they were legal. Since no facilities existed for "transporting the large number of Chinese whose certificates" had been found to be defective, the inspector of immigration notified his counterparts at Seattle and San Francisco "to apprehend them upon their arrival at those ports as they all must—there being no other means of transportation—return on the cannery vessels."[38]

As a result of an 1899 request from the War Department, a revenue cutter convoyed the steamer *Ducheskay* from Juneau to Cooks Inlet, prepared to tow her if necessary. At the request of the Lighthouse Board in 1906, the *Thetis* furnished passage to a carpenter from the U.S. Corps of Engineers, Portland, Oregon, to Scotch Cap, Alaska. When the supervising inspector-general of the Steamboat Inspection Service, located in the Treasury Department, asked in 1899 for passage on the revenue cutters in Alaskan waters for his steamboat inspectors, the necessary authorizing instructions were issued quickly. The same year, the *Perry* transported, among others, the governor of Alaska, the commissioner of education for Alaska, the commissioner of agriculture for Alaska, the deputy collector of customs, and a U.S. marshal. Seven years later the Treasury Department designated the *McCulloch* to be "at the disposal of the Governor to enable him to visit towns and settlements in southeastern Alaska and on the southern coast as far west as it may be practicable to go, and that the vessel be at Juneau August 15, next."[39]

### Aiding Explorers, Both Domestic and Foreign

On many occasions, far too many to relate here, the U.S. Revenue Cutter Service provided assistance to explorers sailing around or traversing the interior of Alaska. In one instance, just providing a few days lodging for a reconnaissance party led to an exciting adventure for two revenue officers. The expedition's leader, Lt. H. J. Ericksen, U.S. Army, had been ordered to seek out the best route for the army telegraph line being constructed along the Yukon River. The party arrived at Fort Shoemaker, the winter quarters of the river steamer *Nunivak*, two days after Christmas in 1900. Lieutenant Ericksen, perhaps mellowed by holiday cheer one night, invited any of the revenue officers who would to accompany his party.

First Lt. John C. Cantwell, the commanding officer, still eager to explore, and 3d Lt. William J. Wheeler both volunteered, in order to learn about "life on the trail by actual experience." During their twenty-three-day trip along the Yukon from the Dall River to the mouth of Beaver Creek, they slept in "thin cotton tents" and subsisted on the "simplest kind" of fare, "consisting of beans, bacon, and baking-powder biscuits with large quantities of tea to help fill up the yawning cavity which always seemed to be present in our stomachs." The weather varied from being "very disagree[ably]" hot to temperatures of minus sixty-five to minus seventy-two degrees Fahrenheit, as a result of which cold the men were forced "to remain in camp for nearly two weeks." Yet upon their return to Fort Shoemaker, both cutter officers "felt that in spite of the hard trip we had been amply repaid for all our labor by the experience that had been gained."[40]

Most of the time, the Treasury Department looked favorably upon forwarding the goals of explorers, whenever feasible. Even when no federal agency, foreign government, or scientific organization sponsored the expedition, both the Treasury Department and the service readily offered the assistance of their cutters.

In late 1902, for instance, one LeRoy Pelletier wrote to Capt.-Cmdt. Charles F. Shoemaker about his polar expedition, funded by a newspaper syndicate. Pelletier's party consisted of three "hardened Arctic travellers," a five-dog sled team, and equipment that weighed approximately two tons. They planned to start their journey at Point Barrow, head straight for the North Pole, and then press on to Franz Josef Land or Greenland, depending on conditions. Pelletier sought permission for passage on a cutter for his party. Captain-Commandant Shoemaker promptly gave his permission.[41]

A somewhat similar case occurred six years later, when the noted Arctic explorer Vilhjalmur Stefansson and R. M. Anderson conducted an ethnological and zoological expedition for the American Museum of Natural History along the shores of the Arctic Ocean in the vicinity of the Mackenzie River. They went into this region in the summer of 1908, planning to remain there until 1910. When Director W. C. Bumpus of their sponsoring museum in New York City requested the transport of over a ton of supplies by the *Thetis* north to Point Barrow in the summer of 1909, approval was quickly forthcoming. The Treasury Department also granted permission to the commander of the *Thetis,* Captain Henderson, to issue Stefansson "a permit to take Eskimos with him on whaling vessels as a part of his expedition."[42] The cutter also carried mail for the Arctic explorer.

Two years earlier, Captain Henderson had recommended the granting of a permit to Ejnar Mikkelsen of the Anglo-American Expedition in the Arctic to carry one or two native hunters, each "accompanied by not more than one wife," to the eastward from Herschel Island in a whaling ship and back again. Captain Henderson suggested that both Mikkelsen and the master of the whaling steamer be required to "execute in writing" that "they will not permit anyone employed either on board the vessel or in the expedition to have illicit or carnal intercourse and relations with any female who may be authorized to accompany the expedition, either on board the vessel or on shore or on the ice."[43]

Ernest deK. Leffingwell, another member of the Anglo-American Polar Expedition, meanwhile, had sought help from the superintendent of the U.S. Coast and Geodetic Survey. The expedition had ended up at Flaxman Island, Alaska, with its members scheduled to start leaving for home in 1907. Leffingwell, however, wished to remain another year at his own expense. The explorer requested transportation of supplies to his location.[44]

The superintendent of the U.S. Coast and Geodetic Survey, O. H. Tittman, informed Captain-Commandant Ross of Leffingwell's situation and plans, and requested that a cutter transport the needed supplies. In order to impress Leffingwell's worth upon Captain-Commandant Ross, Tittman added: "Mr. Leffingwell is the son of a clergyman and a fine specimen of manhood. He is a graduate of Chicago University where he specialized in physics and geology. He spent a short time at this in the Arctic Ocean. . . . Two or three years ago when the Anglo-American Polar Expedition was organized he went down the Mackenzie River, joining Mikkelsen in the Arctic Ocean."[45]

In reply, Captain-Commandant Ross warned that his cutters "seldom go far beyond Point Barrow," but he did promise to "carefully look into the matter and see what can be done when our ships start north next season." Before the end of March 1908, Leffingwell learned from Captain Henderson, commanding the *Thetis,* of his having official "permission to transfer a reasonable amount of supplies as far north and east as he may be able to go next summer."[46]

The following year Ross again agreed to assist Leffingwell, since the explorer intended to turn over the results of his "surveys and investigations to certain branches of the Government." Although the U.S. Revenue Cutter chief offered to make arrangements "to receive on board the THETIS, for transportation, five or six tons of your outfit," he declined to "guarantee" their landing at Pt. Barrow, stating that delivery would occur only "if conditions will permit."[47]

Sometimes the assistance given fell in the realm of search and rescue, as did the 10 March 1905 request from the consulate of Norway and Sweden in San Francisco. Consul Henry Lund wanted the U.S. authorities to be aware of the Arctic expedition of eight men in the little forty-seven-ton sloop *Gjoa*, under the command of the noted Arctic explorer Capt. Roland Amundsen, which had left Norway in 1903. The explorers had planned to establish the exact location of the north magnetic pole and then "penetrate the much sought after Northwest passage north of this Continent and come out next Autumn, or that of next year, via Behring Strait to this port." If the captains of the revenue cutters should come across the sloop *Gjoa* or any of its crew and they needed assistance, Consul Lund stated that any help proffered would be highly appreciated.[48] In reply, the Treasury Department promised to provide the commanders of all revenue cutters assigned to cruise Alaskan waters during the 1905 navigation season with the pertinent correspondence and to direct them to seek information about the *Gjoa* expedition. Interestingly enough, on 4 September 1905, Capt. William H. Roberts, reporting on his cruise of the *Perry* in Alaskan waters, stated that he had not met anyone having any knowledge of any member of the *Gjoa* expedition reaching either the Arctic Ocean or the Bering Sea, despite his having cruised 8,272.4 nautical miles, boarded seventy American and seven foreign vessels, and visited twenty-two cannery ports.

The reaction of the Treasury Department and U.S. Revenue Cutter Service to the 1909 request of the leader of the Kamchatka Expedition, organized under the auspices of the Imperial Russian Geographical Society, demonstrated their usual response. Scientist Vladimir Jochelson requested transportation around the Aleutian Islands in vessels of the Revenue Cutter Service to enable him to conduct studies of comparative ethnology and ethnography and to make scientific diggings and excavations. He wished to be picked up at Unalaska in April 1909, be provided passage to Attu, the Pribilof Islands, Atka, and the village of Nikolsky on Umnak Island, and then be taken back to Unalaska, from where a Russian naval vessel would return the scientist and his party in the spring of 1910 to the Kamchatka Peninsula. The Treasury Department responded typically, stating that the cutters dispatched in 1909 to the Bering Sea would be issued orders instructing their "commanding officers to do all that can be done to assist Mr. Jochelson in making his investigations, so far as the same will not interfere with the regular duties required of the vessels."[49]

For the officers and crews of the revenue cutters on their long deployments to the far north, the amount of "tacked on" duty must have made them wonder if they were sailors or merely general laborers. How the crews felt about being assistants to the Smithsonian Institution, explorers, mailmen, census takers, transporters, and anyone else with enough influence to wrangle a berth aboard a cutter is not recorded. If their attitudes were similar to those of the U.S. Coast Guard crews of the 1960s, many grumbled at the additional work involved. In the case of explorers needing supplies hauled, the sailors aboard the cutters, after all, were the ones doing the hard, cold work of loading and unloading, and their names would never be mentioned in the reports that would make many famous. Some of the sailors, then as now, looked forward to something that would break up the monotonous sea routine. Most of the sailors never groused over helping those in actual need. Someone in the secure warmth of an armchair may wonder just what was the worth of the additional duties performed by these men. The noted Alaskan historian William R. Hunt points out that "without the transportation made available by the Revenue Service, the islands and mainland of the Bering Sea would have been virtually inaccessible to scientists . . . and the progress of knowledge would have been considerably slower."[50]

# EIGHT

# Through Ice and Howling Gale

Search and rescue (SAR) by default fell upon the U.S. Revenue Cutter Service in Alaska, especially in the Bering Sea and Arctic regions. The small cutters could be depended upon to go to the aid of anyone in distress, and, while many whalers would pick up stranded people on the beach, the castaways could then be forced to remain in the northern regions until the ship returned to the United States. As the hunt for whales led further and further into ice-choked seas, cutters like the *Bear* and *Thetis,* designed for polar travel, became necessary. The modern-day U.S. Coast Guard makes much of their search and rescue heritage from the U.S. Revenue Cutter Service, yet the service has very little material on the rescue efforts of the cutters that sailed in Alaskan waters. Recruits and cadets usually hear about the Overland Expedition of 1897–98, on which 1st Lt. David H. Jarvis, 2d Lt. Ellsworth P. Bertholf, and Surg. Samuel J. Call, all from the cutter *Bear,* set out in the dead of an Arctic winter from Nelson Island, Alaska (approximately three hundred miles south of Nome), driving a herd of reindeer to be used to provide food for beset whalers. Their destination was Point Barrow, and the entire trek covered an incredible fifteen hundred miles. That expedition, of course, was a major rescue and its story is well worthy of being told. It has, however, been told and retold by many writers. There were other instances of SAR by the U.S. Revenue Cutter Service in Alaska, and it is those forgotten cases that we will examine.[1]

One of the earliest known SAR operations for the service in the Bering Sea began on 30 July 1879, when two seamen off the American brig *Timandra* came into Unalaska on another boat. They said that the *Timandra,* bound from San Francisco via Honolulu to the Arctic on a trading voyage, had wrecked on Nunivak Island on 23 May. The two sailors said that eight of the crew were still on the island. The cutter *Rush,* commanded by Capt. George W. Bailey, sailed on 4 August, after hurriedly finishing coaling; the *Rush* completed the four-hundred-mile voyage to Nunivak Island on 7 August. Upon arrival, the cuttermen found the brig a total wreck near the beach. The *Timandra*'s crew had managed to save the principal portion of the cargo, which consisted of trade goods and "a quantity of breech-loading arms and ammunition, and one hundred barrels of rum, the latter articles taken on board at Honolulu." All the rum had been destroyed when the vessel went aground, leaving Captain Bailey only the repeating firearms and ammunition to be seized as contraband. He then sailed back to Unalaska with everyone aboard except for two crewmen who volunteered to stay and care for the cargo until their employer could send another ship for them the following year. According to Captain Bailey, the 119-ton *Timandra,* and other ships fitted out by the same owners, had "traded in these waters for several years, and invariably traded liquors, breech-loading arms, and ammunition, contrary to and in violation of law, but could not be caught in the act."[2]

On the 1881 *Corwin* cruise in search of the lost exploring ship *Jeannette* and two missing whalers, the *Vigilant* and the *Mount Wollaston,* Capt. Calvin L. Hooper, on 2 June, launched an unusual SAR effort on the Siberian coast. Captain Hooper knew that any survivors of ships trapped in the ice would seek safety on the icebound Asian shore and, in this event, the delay in their rescue of even a single day could mean life or death. With his ship's passage blocked, he ordered 1st Lt. William J. Herring to take charge of a dogsled expedition along the Siberian coast. According to the noted naturalist John Muir, writing in his journal, about five miles northwest of Koliutchin Island, Captain Hooper had the Chuckchi interpreter, Chuckchi Joe, ask his companion what he thought of beginning the expedition at this location. Chuckchi Joe replied: "He says it's good; it's pretty good, he says." To which Captain Hooper replied, "Then get ready, Mr. Herring for your journey." The expedition had orders to scout to the northwest at least as far as Cape Jarkin, to "seek intelligence" about the missing ships. Lieutenant Herring's party included 3d Lt. William E. Reynolds, Cox. Gissler [or Gressler], Chuckchi Joe and another Chuckchi to act as guides and drivers, plus twenty-five dogs, four sleds, a light skin boat for crossing any open water, and provisions for two months.[3]

The search party mushed over rough terrain amid dismal weather as far as Cape Wankerem and questioned the inhabitants of nine native settlements before discovering that three hunters who might have information resided in a village near the cape. The natives told Herring through Chuckchi Joe that while hunting they had spotted a large ship without masts locked in the ice. Upon reaching the vessel the three hunters saw that the masts had been chopped down, and they found a pair of horns on the end of the jib boom with an illustration of the ship drawn upon them. Because of flooding, they could not go into the hold. The natives next went into the cabin, where they found four men who had been dead a long time, three lying in their bunks and one on the deck. They then took some articles from the ship and went ashore. Lieutenant Herring offered tobacco for the items that the men had brought, and they accepted this exchange. Another party of natives came by and reported that no ships had been seen any farther to the northwest. The *Vigilant* had been said to have had deer horns nailed to her jib boom, so the fate of at least one of the whaling ships had come to light. Since this evidence strongly indicated that both whalers had been crushed by the ice, the sled expedition then mushed to the rendezvous location for pickup by the cutter. Lieutenant Reynolds later reported on the "great kindness" of the natives and their generosity at all of the villages they visited. At one of the villages, as the cuttermen were served dinner they received good tea in "handsome China cups" that the village chief had bought from the Russians.

On 29 June, near Cape Serdzekamen, the sled expedition spotted the *Corwin*. Stormy weather prevented the cutter from putting a small boat ashore, and the cuttermen thus ended their journey with some excitement. Lieutenant Herring had the party venture out onto the ice, and when the *Corwin*'s boat came close enough, the crew threw a line "to the most advanced of the party, who was balancing himself among the heaving bergs," and pulled them "from the tossing, wave-dashed ice which momentarily threatened to engulf them."[4]

The revenue steamer continued pursuing her regular duties, including the performance of less dramatic SARs. On 8 June, for example, while his cutter was anchored near the northwest end of Saint Lawrence Island, Captain Hooper took advantage of good weather and searched for the wrecked ship *Lolita,* which had gone ashore a few miles to the north of their anchorage the previous fall.[5] The search failed to locate the ship, however. Bad weather and the approach of the Arctic ice pack delayed the *Corwin*'s departure again until 10 June. Then, using his expert seamanship, Captain Hooper maneu-

The *Bear* working with a ship in the ice.

vered the cutter along the edge of the pack and made good his escape into open water. The revenue captain, still refusing to give up hope of finding the remains of the *Lolita,* resumed his search. His persistence paid off, and the *Corwin* came upon the ship's remains five or six miles down the coast. From the wreck, the sailors of the revenue cutter obtained iron, blocks, tackle, spars, and "two barrels of oil," all of which the cuttermen had to drag over ice "covered with sludge and full of dangerous holes."

The following month, on 25 July, Captain Hooper steamed northward in an attempt to reach Point Barrow. By using the steam launch towing a lifeboat, the cuttermen in the small craft managed to locate and offer aid to the whaler *Daniel Webster,* then trapped in the ice near Point Barrow. When the revenue steamer finally worked her way through the ice to the ship in mid-August, the cuttermen learned that the *Daniel Webster,* "nipped" (that is, crushed) in the ice, had sunk, and the whalers in the area had rescued all of her crew. The *Corwin* took nine of these rescued men aboard for transportation back to the United States.

On her Arctic cruise three years later, the *Corwin,* now commanded by Capt. Michael A. Healy, again participated in a number of SAR operations.

A request for assistance reached Captain Healy on 8 June 1884 during an early stopover at St. Michael. The previous year, the Golowin Bay Mining Company of San Francisco had sent the schooner *Alaska* with twenty men aboard to work a silver mine up the Fish River, a tributary to Golowin Bay, but had so far received no news about them. The company asked Captain Healy "to ascertain, if possible, their fate or condition." Healy sailed on 8 June for Golowin Bay.[6]

Arriving the following afternoon, Captain Healy immediately dispatched 1st Lt. David A. Hall to the mining camp, where he found the four men who had wintered there and learned that the *Alaska* had left Golowin Bay on 21 October 1883 with sixteen men and a cargo of seventy-five tons of galena ore. Despite a thorough search, Healy reported no sighting of the ship. He later learned that the crew of the *Bowhead*, as well as some other whalers, had spotted a schooner, bottom up, in the spring of 1884 to the west of the Aleutian Islands. His failure to find any sign of the missing schooner, in conjunction with the reports from the whalers, led Healy to conclude that the *Alaska* had foundered in heavy weather and that all hands were lost. The *Bowhead* would also become a subject for a search and rescue effort.

On 20 August at Point Hope, Healy received a letter from Capt. E. E. Smith, master of the *Bowhead*, informing him that his ship had been crushed by the ice thirty miles to the northward of Icy Cape. He further stated that he was in a destitute condition and requested the aid of the *Corwin*. Healy again proceeded northward in the ever-present thick fog, arriving at Cape Sabine, where Captain Smith awaited the revenue cutter at a coal mine. The *Bowhead*'s skipper came aboard in the morning, and Healy shaped a course toward Icy Cape.[7]

The loss of the *Bowhead* came as a surprise to Healy and others in the north. The two-year-old whaler had a reputation for being one of the strongest and best built in the fleet, constructed especially for whaling in the Arctic. Captain Smith, furthermore, had a reputation for being one of the best in the business—and yet the ship had sunk within ten minutes, barely giving the crew enough time to escape with the clothes on their backs.

Captain Healy continued working the *Corwin* through dense fog, growing more and more concerned as the cutter encountered thicker and thicker ice. Near midnight of 22 August, the revenue cutter came to anchor under Point Belcher near some whalers, their position in the murk being evident only from the sound of the ships' bells. Captain Healy sent over boarding parties to inquire if anyone knew the whereabouts of the crew of the *Bowhead*.

The boarding parties returned with both good and bad news. Healy learned that the sailors from the wrecked whaler were safely aboard the ships now anchored nearby the *Corwin*. A rumor persisted, however, that part of the fleet had been carried away into the pack ice by the strong currents present in that location. If this rumor proved correct, Healy knew that "their loss was certain." Healy weighed anchor and began to search. He found the bark *Helen Marr* being pushed ashore by ice. The cuttermen put a line aboard the bark, and the *Corwin* towed the ship to safety. Healy then carefully navigated the cutter through the thick fog and picked his way between ice floes until he had accounted for all the whalers.[8]

By the afternoon of 24 August, Captain Healy had guided the *Corwin* through rising winds, snow squalls, and threatening weather to come within ten miles of Point Barrow, before finally being halted. He decided to end this SAR operation early the next morning, after having taken on a total of twenty-two *Bowhead* survivors and the homebound mail of the whaling fleet. Healy turned the *Corwin*'s bow southward, collecting more of the *Bowhead*'s survivors, an army scout, four miners who had wintered over at the silver mine, and fifteen prisoners (six white and nine Japanese). There were a total of ninety-eight passengers on board by the time the *Corwin* arrived at Unalaska on 11 September. Because of the overcrowding, the *Corwin* could give shelter from the rain, storms, and cold to only one-half of the people on board at a time. Nor could the town of Unalaska provide either food or accommodations for so many. Fearing that an epidemic might be the result, an opinion shared by his ship's medical officer, Healy departed on 25 September for San Francisco, arriving there on 5 October.

Four years later, Captain Healy, now in command of the *Bear*, found himself in a similar situation. Once the revenue steamer *Rush* had relieved the *Bear* from her duties around the Pribilofs, Healy sailed north for Point Barrow, arriving there on 2 August 1888. He found the wind steadily increasing, and by night the cutter pushed through an easterly gale.

The captain of the *Bear*, along with the skippers of eight whalers, sought shelter under the lee of the Sea Horse Islands. During the night, however, the wind veered to the west, making the anchorage a poor one for the whalers, although the *Bear*'s length permitted the cutter to ride better. Dawn found only one of the whalers still near the revenue cutter, the rest having dragged their anchors—burning up their windlasses, tearing up their decks, demolishing their hawse pipes, and generally damaging their ground tackle. After the gale slackened, Healy rendered assistance to any ship requesting help.[9]

The whaling barks *Mary and Susan, Young Phoenix,* and *Fleetwing,* all of New Bedford, Massachusetts, and the schooner *Jane Grey,* of San Francisco, wrecked on 3 August. About 150 sailors now became destitute, so Healy took them aboard the *Bear.* Later he arranged that these shipwrecked men take the place of sailors aboard the whalers who were sick, while the sick who were relieved were taken aboard the revenue cutter for transportation to San Francisco. In all, the *Bear* carried 102 shipwrecked whalers upon departure from Point Barrow on 8 September. As she steamed southward that day, a lookout spotted the schooner *Ino* of San Francisco aground at Cape Smyth, with seas breaking over her. Healy hove to for the night near the schooner and next morning took off the captain and fourteen sailors, now bringing the total number of passengers aboard the *Bear* to 117.

The following day, the *Thetis,* at that time a naval steamer under the command of Lt. Cdr. William H. Emory, USN, hove into view. Commander Emory "kindly sent on board for the whalers twenty five suits of clothes and provided the ship with an anchor and fifteen fathoms of chain" to replace those given to the bark *Ohio,* which had lost her anchor during the recent storm. Because of the number of men now aboard the *Bear,* Healy again feared an epidemic and shaped a course directly to San Francisco.

Upon their arrival in San Francisco, the masters of the shipwrecked whalers wrote the secretary of the treasury, expressing their thanks for the assistance of Captain Healy and the crew of the *Bear.* Speaking on behalf of every shipmaster and individual in the whaling fleet, they stated that "the presence among us of the Rev. Cutter Bear with her experienced and energetic commander . . . gives us increased confidence to pursue our dangerous sailing."[10]

The perils of the Alaskan waters continued to occasion a never-ending stream of SAR operations, with only the lonely revenue cutters present to offer immediate aid. An account of the vessels lost in the Bering Sea during the 1900 sailing season alone included one steamship, one stern-wheel steamer, eleven schooners, one barkentine, three tugs, and three barges.[11] The 1900 cruise report of the cutter *Manning* mentioned that besides conducting hydrographic surveys, the cutter's crew rescued passengers from the stranded barkentine *Leslie D,* wrecked on Nunivak Island.

The cutter *McCulloch* also gave SAR assistance to several ships. When the schooner *Prosper* made "signals of distress" on 6 September 1900, the revenue cutter, even though riding out a storm at Sledge Island, left the safety of a sheltered harbor and immediately departed into the teeth of the storm,

Lt. Cdr. Godfrey L. Carden, Gunner Hendricks, and the boat crew that took the secretary of commerce through high surf to visit the seal rookeries on St. Paul Island in 1910.

making for the schooner's location.[12] Once on the scene, the cuttermen passed a towing hawser to the *Prosper* and took off five shipwrecked sailors from the schooner. The *McCulloch* then took the ship in tow and brought her to the roadstead at Nome. Then, after the steamship *Orisaba* wrecked at St. Michael on 17 September, the *McCulloch* remained standing by the ship for several days. On 19 October, off Sledge Island, the anchored steam barge *President*, with machinery broken down and its crew cold and hungry, requested a tow to Nome. As the sea is relatively shallow at Nome, the revenue cutter held the barge on her tow line all night, until relieved by a tug in the morning. When a schooner brought word on 24 September that the SS *Cleveland* had run aground, the *McCulloch* immediately got underway for the east side of Sledge Island and stood toward Cape Rodney. The cuttermen were able to locate the *Cleveland,* even in the heavy snow squalls. Darkness prevented any approach to the ship, grounded near the beach. A revenue officer in a small boat rowed to the *Cleveland,* only to discover that nothing could be done to help her, the bottom being stove in and open to the sea. In the end, the captain and five crew members remained on board to protect the cargo, and the cutter transported the other eleven sailors to Nome.

The existing records of the U.S. Revenue Cutter Service mention many other SAR activities in Alaskan waters during the first part of the twentieth century. More often than not, a search by revenue cutters to find a missing merchant vessel failed completely. Such an unsuccessful SAR mission occurred in connection with the overdue steamers *Portland* and *Jeanie* in the summer of 1902.

In preparation for this mission, Captain Healy, now in command of the *Thetis,* took aboard eighty-six tons of coal and departed Nome on the night of 23 June. Thick fog the following day forced Healy to anchor off Cape Prince of Wales. Since his latest information confirmed that the two missing steamers had been seen drifting northward, the *Thetis* got underway on the twenty-fifth and stood to the northward and eastward, working her way through heavy drift ice to about twenty-five miles south of Cape Thompson. Heavy ice stopped the cutter from proceeding any farther in that direction, and Captain Healy then shaped a course to the westward, coming to anchor on 28 June off Cape Serdze, Siberia. Questioning of the local Siberian natives failed to uncover any pertinent information. Healy then moved the *Thetis* along the edge of the pack ice to Point Hope. From 30 June to 12 July the cuttermen attempted to establish communications with the people ashore, but the ice proved too heavy to enter. "We anchored at times," Healy later wrote, "but the swiftly moving drift ice and the continuous fogs almost impenetrable in character greatly hindered our movements." Then, on 12 July, he learned from the whaling steamer *Narwhal* that both the overdue ships had reached port safely.[13]

Three noteworthy SAR operations occurred in 1903. A sharp lookout aboard the cutter *McCulloch* spotted a small boat making signals of distress some one hundred miles from St. George Island on 19 July. The endangered craft turned out to be an otter boat belonging to the Japanese sealing schooner *Sifu Maru* of Hakadate. It contained one white man and two Japanese who had gotten separated from their vessel in a fog three days before and were making for Dutch Harbor, about ninety-eight miles distant. The men were all suffering from lack of food and loss of sleep. The three were taken aboard the cutter and given food, and their boat was hoisted aboard the *McCulloch*.[14] Two months later, on 6 September, the cutter *Manning* arrived at Unalaska with the passengers and crew of the schooner *Abbie M. Deering,* wrecked on Baby Island, Akutan Pass. Captain Healy, at the request of the collector of customs, took thirty-three of these destitute people on board the *Thetis* for transportation to either Valdez or Sitka, both scheduled stops on his cruise. Later that same day, Healy called away a fire-fighting party, along with others from the cutters *Rush* and *Manning,* to fight a blaze aboard the American ship *St. Francis,* lying on the opposite side of the wharf from the *Thetis.*[15]

The most significant SAR operation of 1907 also involved the cutter *McCulloch.* On 8 September the SS *Dora* relayed a rescue request to Capt. Frederick M. Munger, Bering Sea Patrol commander. The message stated that "the ship JOHN CURRIER had been wrecked on Unimak Island, near Nelson Lagoon, and crew without food, except fish and flour, and in urgent need of assistance."[16] The patrol commander placed the *Thetis* on standby and sent the cutter *Perry* at once to the Pribilof Islands with orders for the *McCulloch* to proceed at her best possible speed to the scene of the disaster. She was to investigate the matter and, if the report was true, to transport the people to Dutch Harbor. On 12 September the *McCulloch* rescued 243 shipwrecked and destitute persons from the *John Currier,* bound from Nushagak to Astoria, Oregon, and wrecked near Nelson Lagoon, Unimak Island. The cutter took them to Unalaska, feeding them for five days. They were then transferred to the *Thetis* for further transportation to Seattle.[17] Prior to the arrival of the *McCulloch,* the castaways had been forced to take shelter for almost a month on the beach. The *Thetis* kept her galley open all night on 13 and 14 September to cook food for the survivors, lending her small boats to catch fish for that purpose, before making the passage southward to Seattle.

During her Arctic cruise from 11 July to 18 November 1908, the *Thetis* "steamed 10,854 miles, assisted three vessels in distress," and searched unsuccessfully for the British steamer *Greenwich,* overdue on her trip from Nome to St. Michael.[18] When the cutter finally came across the missing ship on her original course and apparently undamaged, her master explained that his ship had gone "ashore on the mud flats to the southward of Stuart Island," but he said that his vessel had suffered no damage and that he had resumed sailing toward St. Michael. Sometimes assistance to distressed ships took the form of ice-breaking, a routine operation for the *Thetis.* While carefully making her way through the ice pack on 14 June, she encountered the steamer *Umatilla* of New York, bound from Seattle to Nome, with freight and passengers. At the request of her master, the revenue steamer went ahead of the merchant ship for the remainder of that day and all of the next, "pushing ice cakes out of the way and making leads" through the ice for her to follow.[19] Although separated at times by darkness and fog, they came together for the last time on 20 June and proceeded together until in sight of Nome. The *Thetis* then steamed back to help another merchant vessel with passengers that was also bound for Nome but hesitant about entering the ice. The 1909 Arctic cruise report of the *Thetis* reads very much the same. The cutter "steamed 9,764 miles, rendered five cases of assistance to vessels in distress, made a search for one that was overdue at St. Michael," and "made unsuccessful efforts to reach two vessels which were subsequently released by their own efforts."[20]

The role of the revenue cutters in search and rescue in Alaskan waters, especially in the Bering Sea and Arctic, is a commendable one. While every cutter and captain provided some search and rescue almost every patrol, two captains should be singled out for special mention. Capt. Calvin L. Hooper was the personification of the determined revenue cutter skipper who would go to great lengths to search for a missing ship. He was arguably one of the best Arctic navigators the U.S. Revenue Cutter Service produced. The other officer was Capt. Michael A. Healy, the controversial ship handler par excellence and indefatigable sailor when a ship went missing. Most of those who sailed in the western and northern Alaskan waters knew, whether they were an officer or sailed before the mast, that if they were in distress Captain Healy would make every effort to find them.

Lastly, there were the officers and crews who sailed in the cutters. Both had to suffer long hours in an extremely hostile environment. Anyone who has stood lookout watches in the ice pack knows how ineffective heavy clothing can seem when the polar winds howl across the frozen sea and seem to cut into your very soul. Both officers and enlisted men worked at many unusual assignments during this period. One wonders if 1st Lt. William J. Herring, 3d Lt. William E. Reynolds, or Cox. Gissler [Gressler] ever in their wildest imagination pictured themselves mushing over the frozen Siberian landscape with a dog sled in search of whalers. An officer might receive some recognition for his work, but those who sailed before the mast earned very little, if any, acknowledgment. On the great Overland Reindeer Expedition, for example, a crewman who began the trek but later was detailed back to the *Bear* never has received any credit for his participation—only the three officers are mentioned. It is hoped that someday the U.S. Coast Guard might see its way to recognizing the efforts of both the officers and men of the U.S. Revenue Cutter Service in saving lives in Alaskan waters.

# NINE

# Doctors, Natives, and Cutters

Not until mid-1914, a year prior to the demise of the U.S. Revenue Cutter Service, did Congress finally authorize the secretary of the treasury to establish a regularized medical corps for the service.[1] The act directed the doctors assigned to the cutters to provide medical and surgical aid to American deep-sea fishermen.

Previously, only the rare cutter in the lower continental United States sailed with a surgeon aboard, while most of the ships bound for Alaskan waters carried medical help, a practice that had begun with the surgeon sailing aboard the *Lincoln* on the initial 1867 Alaskan voyage. These revenue cutter doctors treated all in need of medical attention, be they fishermen, whalers, sealers, traders, missionaries, trappers, prospectors, Native Americans, or foreigners. Even cuttermen without medical degrees volunteered their first aid or curative expertise to those injured or incapacitated by illnesses. Hence, from their initial entry into Alaskan waters, these predecessors of the U.S. Coast Guard dispensed medical or surgical aid as a matter of course.

Information on this unique role of the U.S. Revenue Cutter Service in the early frontier days of Alaska is practically nonexistent. Only a sentence or two in the two standard histories of the U.S. Coast Guard even mention this activity. This chapter is an effort to shed light on this little-known humanitarian role of the U.S. Revenue Cutter Service.[2] To avoid repetition, only representative examples of medical assistance have been selected. The examples demonstrate unique types of assistance.

Some examples of medical assistance already have been discussed. Third Lt. John C. Cantwell, for example, treated a Native American for colic during the 1884 Kobuk River Expedition. When the *Thetis* discovered five whaling ships trapped in the ice off Point Barrow during her 1906 Arctic cruise, the ship's doctor not only checked on the physical health of the crews but also inspected the sanitary conditions aboard the stranded whalers. Other examples were interspersed throughout the activities of the revenue cutters plying the Alaskan waters.

Assist. Surg. Robert White, U.S. Marine Hospital Service (USMHS), accompanied the revenue steamer *Rush* on her 1879 cruise as medical officer. With the approval of the commanding officer, Capt. George W. Bailey, he freely gave both "professional assistance and medicines" to the inhabitants of the various settlements at which the steamer touched during the cruise. "These services were extensively required, as at most of the points in question the natives and whites, alike, are without medical attendance of any kind other than such as is furnished by the native 'shamans.'"[3] The resources of these Native American doctors, according to Surgeon White, "are almost wholly limited to the employment of sorcery and incantations for exorcizing the evil spirits that are supposed to be the cause of all serious disease."

Ironically, the first natives that Surgeon White treated turned out to be Canadians rather than Americans. Prior to entering Alaskan waters, the *Rush* touched at Fort Simpson in British Columbia, a village of nearly a thousand inhabitants, some of whom required medical aid. The ship's surgeon first encountered an Alaskan settlement of some three hundred Native Americans at Kazan Bay. As at Fort Simpson, White found many of the locals suffering from "various chronic syphilitic affections" and a few others from advanced stages of pneumonia. With the cutter's pilot serving as an interpreter, the surgeon prescribed and furnished the appropriate medicines. The first significant settlement in Alaskan territory came at Fort Wrangel, where there were about seventy-five permanent white settlers, although the population swelled in the spring and autumn from the influx of miners on their way to and from the gold mines inland. About three hundred members of the Stikleen tribe also resided there permanently, their numbers increasing greatly when the adjoining tribes came to trade. Surgeon White observed that these Indians suffered from ailments similar to those suffered by other natives living along the coast, where they were at the mercy of the damp climate, exposure to the elements, and their limited diet, especially in the winter. To his surprise he learned that death during childbirth, however, was almost unknown.

At Sitka, the territorial capital, the medical officer acquired extensive information on the prevalent Alaskan diseases and the native remedies for treating them. "The use of 'bear's gall' for arthritic and rheumatic affections," he reported, "is universal among the Indians, as well as by the Russians, Creoles, and Aleuts of the islands." Since so many white traders, merchant seamen, and even cuttermen had used this remedy and praised its effectiveness, Surgeon White recommended "further inquiry into its properties and observation of its effects." He also noted that its fame had spread outside the territory, for the gall bladders of bears with their dried contents readily sold for $5.00 each in San Francisco.

On the thousand-plus miles of coast between Sitka and Kodiak, Surgeon White found "hardly a vestige of civilization," the country being "very sparsely peopled." His official report ends with observations on the medical conditions among the Aleuts of the Seal Islands and the Aleutian Chain as far west as Attu Island. Although they differed markedly in their habits, mode of life, and means of support from the Native Americans of the mainland, their ailments were similar. Besides those diseases already mentioned, the most prevalent ones, the doctor observed, had been made worse "by frequently recurring colds, and living in close, unventilated huts."

The islanders, Surgeon White reported, had had only limited knowledge of how to treat illnesses prior to the coming of the Russians. "Bleeding with a rough lancet, which every Aleut formerly carried, was, and is still so to some extent, resorted to in every real or fancied disturbance of the health." He told of seeing the scars made by these deep punctures on the older Aleuts by "the score or the hundred." In Surgeon White's opinion, the Aleuts submitted almost apathetically to their illnesses and his treatments, made no complaints, and seemed resigned to either getting well or dying. They had "little fear of death, meeting it with the same apathy and resignation that they would any necessary event of their daily life." Rarely did the Aleuts shed tears over their own possible death or that of a close relative or friend. Apparently they regarded death as a temporary state and spoke of their dead as being merely "asleep." Despite the hardships and dangers of their lives, the Aleuts of the island chain did not have an excessive death rate among the adults, the annual figure being merely thirty per one thousand of the population. Yet those Native Americans living on the Pribilofs did have an excessively high death rate, a rate three or four times that found in the larger cities of the continental United States. As with so many other strange things about the Alaska of that day, the ship's medical officer, despite his scientific training, proved "unable to assign any reason for the excessive mortality." He did suspect that its cause lay in the "almost wholly inactive life" that the residents of the Pribilof Islands lived for nine months each year, most of which time they spent "in their excessively hot, badly-ventilated houses."

The *Corwin* began its 1885 Arctic cruise in late April, but a broken crankpin in the engine off Cape Cheerful in the Aleutians forced a return to San Francisco. There, Capt. Michael A. Healy awarded a contract for repairs to the Risdon Iron Works, whose employees "labored night and day, and finished the work in one week."[4] Returning to Unalaska on 19 June, the *Corwin* recorded its first instance of medical assistance on a visit to Golwin Bay. Captain Healy dispatched the ship's surgeon "to visit the mining camp to ascertain the condition of the white men and Indians there, and to render medical aid if such was required." The second one came as the cutter anchored off her coaling station at Point Spencer on 27 June. Encountering three Arctic whaling sailing ships, soon to be joined by three steam whalers, the surgeon aboard the *Bear* "rendered medical assistance to those of the whaling fleet that required it." In early July he unsuccessfully tried to help "an officer of the *Stamboul* who was somewhat demented, and who, a few days later, committed suicide." Captain Healy noted in his report that he had "frequently observed slight symptoms of insanity, and this has also been noticed by the surgeon of this vessel when visiting vessels of the whaling fleet professionally."

As 10 August dawned, the *Bear* and some thirty vessels of the whaling fleet remained at anchor off Point Marsh to the north of Icy Cape, Alaska. Captain Healy described this day as "the most eventful of the season, and [one that] will long be remembered by the whaling fleet and the crew of the *Corwin* as a day of calamities." A heavy squall suddenly capsized the mail boat and dumped its occupants into the water. The cuttermen promptly launched their surfboat, rescued the six struggling men in the water, and landed them on the nearest whaler, "on board of which the doctor was then officially visiting." When the storm snapped one of the anchor cables of the whaler *George and Susan* and ran her hard aground, some of her crew panicked and launched lifeboats in an attempt to reach shore. The "very heavy" surf "swamped both boats and drowned three of the crew," with the remainder "landing on shore in an exhausted and semiconscious state."

An hour later, the *Corwin* "anchored in the breakers ahead of the bar"

*Mabel,* whose position was considered a dangerous one."[5] The cutter's surf-boat managed against great odds to run a line to her, but, when the whalers failed to haul the *Corwin*'s towing hawser on board, the ship parted her cable and went ashore, breaking up almost instantly. Once the gale abated enough to permit a boat from the *Corwin* to reach shore, the doctor assisted all those who were hurt.

The captains of the two wrecked ships requested transportation for themselves, their officers, and their crews on board the *Corwin* to San Francisco, and Captain Healy readily granted it. Some of the cutter's wardroom officers objected to having these officers at their table, since the Treasury Department had refused to reimburse them for feeding the officers of the wrecked *Bowhead* who had messed with them the previous year. With "the forecastle being entirely unsuitable for an officer" in his opinion, the revenue captain arranged for them to be "received into the cabin mess and fed at my personal expense, the crowded condition of the cabin necessitating the setting of a first and second table."[6] In all, fifty-four additional men came aboard. Captain Healy also brought the two whaleboats from the wrecked *George and Susan* aboard the *Corwin,* since her own boats would prove inadequate in case of disaster.

As the shipwrecked crew members came aboard the *Corwin,* they received assignments to help the cutter's crew. Every time that the cutter stopped to take on water, Captain Healy had soap provided to these men and compelled them to go ashore to wash themselves and their clothing. Some of these whaling crewmen "were the filthiest I have ever seen, and seemed to have no idea of personal cleanliness. The duty of making them keep themselves and clothing clean, in order to avoid a contagion which filth might cause in such crowded quarters, was anything but pleasant."

One seaman, formerly of the bark *Napoleon,* had been rescued upon her sinking and taken on board the whaler *Reindeer.* Her captain had amputated the toes on both his feet, which had become badly frozen during this shipwreck, because there was not a surgeon in the Arctic. The *Corwin*'s doctor subsequently examined the man and performed necessary further amputation. Aboard the cutter the sailor received good care, and one of the crewmen from the *Corwin* was detailed to attend to him personally. The sailor improved, and, upon arrival in San Francisco shortly before noon on 11 October, he was sent to the marine hospital.

The revenue captain made only one further mention of actual medical aid being given. The cutter stopped again at Golwin Bay on 3 September, and

One of the dangers of the Bering Sea Patrol was poor charts. The cutter *Perry* on the rocks near St. Paul Island in 1910.

the ship's surgeon visited a schooner loading ore from the mine about thirty miles inland. Once again he found the health of those at the mining company excellent and the relations between the miners and Indians friendly.

Captain Healy, however, did feel strongly enough about having doctors aboard cutters in the far north to state, "The value of the services of a medical officer in the Arctic cannot be too highly estimated, the attendance on the officers and crew of the *Corwin* forming but a small portion of the duty which he is called on to perform. The Alaska Commercial company employs one doctor at Ounalaska and two at the Seal Islands, but they are so far removed from the Arctic that their services are seldom, if ever, called into requisition by any of the whaling fleet. The crews of the fleet comprise upwards of one thousand men, and a large percentage of these are annually treated by the medical officer of the *Corwin*." Healy went on to say, "When the *Corwin* first went north the Indians had a great repugnance to receiving medical attendance from a doctor, but would resort to their shaman to cure all their ailments. Now, however, the doctor is sought by them in all their ills, and their faith in his power is truly surprising."[7]

In 1896, the service established a hospital in a house at Dutch Harbor for use by its Bering Sea fleet during the navigational season. The North American Commercial Company owned this building but let the government use it free of charge. The medical officer assigned there normally treated not only the cuttermen but also the local residents, mostly consisting of natives, and the crews of the many merchant ships stopping there.

The U.S. Revenue Cutter Service appointed Dr. Gardiner P. Pond as its Bering Sea fleet surgeon at this hospital for the 1897 season. His report from a U.S. Revenue Cutter Service hospital, albeit a temporary one, possesses a certain unique quality. He opened his hospital for patients on 26 June. The medical officer treated forty-nine cuttermen, about an equal number of merchant seamen, and twenty-seven natives without admission to the hospital. He admitted only five cuttermen and four merchant seamen. An ordinary seaman off a schooner by the name of Healey Hughes remained the longest in the hospital, being admitted on 29 July with acute inflammatory rheumatism and discharged on 17 September.

Surgeon Pond closed the seasonal hospital on 17 September with the discharge of his last two patients. Before leaving he packed supplies of drugs and instruments and left them in the North American Commercial Company warehouse to be disposed of as the fleet commander ordered. In his final report, he stated that the building furnished to him had been large enough for all who had needed admission.[8]

On 18 September 1897, Capt. Calvin L. Hooper, commander of the Bering Sea Patrol Fleet, forwarded the fleet surgeon's hospital report to the secretary of the treasury. He complained in his transmittal letter that "the present system, after two years' trial," remained "not entirely satisfactory," being "a make-shift unworthy of the Government."[9] The fleet commander recommended that, before another navigational season began, steps be taken to establish a marine hospital and a full-time doctor at Unalaska.

A total of 375 people, mostly natives, lived in the settlement at Unalaska, Alaska. Merchant vessels, primarily sealers and whalers, also stopped there in large numbers during the summer, while some remained all year. The "most frequent demands for the Doctor," Captain Hooper explained, came from the U.S. government school, the Russian Orthodox church school, and the "Mission Home in Unalaska, for children who cannot go to Dutch Harbor, and in consequence the doctor is kept traveling between the two places during the patrol season, and then both settlements are left for nine months without a doctor." A hospital located in the settlement at Unalaska, the fleet commander continued, would serve the cuttermen of the Bering Sea Patrol Fleet just as well as the existing one, since the cutters touched both there and at their headquarters in Dutch Harbor. He concluded by arguing that "the largely increased commerce of Unalaska and Dutch Harbor fully justifies the maintenance of a Marine Hospital, and I recommend that one be established."

His recommendation, unfortunately, died stillborn, as had others concerning the establishment of a hospital. Within just ten years of the initial *Lincoln* cruise into northern waters, an earlier cutter captain made a similar request. Capt. George W. Bailey, in his official report as commander of the *Rush* on her 1879 cruise, told the story of how the Aleuts of the Bering Sea, whom he had first visited in 1868, had had the services of a doctor once a year under Russian rule. Since the Americans had assumed control in 1867, Captain Bailey explained, the only ones to benefit from the skills of a physician had been "the Seal Islanders, those who have lived near the military posts, and others who have been prescribed for by the different surgeons who have accompanied this vessel during the last three years. The trading companies keep their different stations supplied with considerable quantities of medicines, but the want of a knowledge how to dispense it is strongly felt." The natives at the Unalaska settlement had become so desperate for medical aid under American rule that they had "started a fund (now amounting to fifteen hundred dollars) for the purpose of erecting a building suitable for a hospital, where the different diseases peculiar to these people may be treated. It would, no doubt," continued the revenue captain, "be a worthy charity on the part of the Government to have a surgeon stationed here, say one from the Marine-Hospital Service, who, besides giving his attention to the people, could also attend the sick seamen of the different vessels calling here during the summer, and who are by law entitled to hospital relief."[10]

As late as 12 November 1909, Capt. A. J. Henderson, then commanding the *Thetis* on its Arctic cruise, recommended that a hospital be established for sailors of the U.S. Revenue Cutter Service. Captain Henderson pointed out that there was hospital furniture stored at Nome that could be used in supplying any new hospital.[11]

During his four months aboard the steamer *Bear* on its 1899 cruise, Surg. R. N. Hawley, RCS, reported the health of the ship's company as "remarkably good." He treated only three men suffering from serious illness and two having minor accidental injuries, with all but one recovering and returning to duty. This exception, Fireman Anton Anderson, spent most of the time unfit for duty and was still in bad health when the steamer returned to its home port of San Francisco in November. "His trouble," Surgeon Hawley believed, was "Malarial in its origin," dating from his service with the 4th Wisconsin Volunteers for eight months in Alabama during the Civil War. He recommended that this cutterman be sent to the U.S. Marine Hospital for further treatment.[12]

During the Arctic portion of the cruise, Surgeon Hawley observed many of the crew suffering from "severe colds and influenza, and a few mild cases of rheumatism." All made fast recoveries, and the amount of time lost on account of illness proved negligible.

On 28 and 29 July at Port Clarance, Hawley visited four whaling steamers, examined twenty sailors and prescribed medicines for them, fitted and supplied four men suffering from hernia with trusses, and dressed the knife wounds another had received during a fight. Later, at Cape Prince of Wales, he visited whaling ships to examine and prescribe medicines for several crew members.

Among the destitute miners taken on board at Kotzebue Sound on 23 and 24 July, the surgeon found "some 30 cases of scurvy, ranging in severity from helplessness to convalescence." All these cases, he pointed out in his report, displayed visible improvement upon their departure from the *Bear* on 27 July and their being turned over to the army surgeon at St. Michael.

Every place that the revenue steamer remained long enough for the local natives to come aboard, Surgeon Hawley provided medical assistance to all who requested it. The most prevalent diseases among them, he found, resulted from "their mode of life, unsanitary surroundings, and climatic influences." At both Point Barrow and Kotzebue Sound he found that influenza had become epidemic, with some of the cases resulting in pneumonia and death.

Surgeon Hawley concluded his medical report by calling attention to the alarming number of smallpox cases reported in the vicinity of Puget Sound. Since many ships probably would leave ports on the Puget Sound for the north next season, he suggested precautions be taken to prevent any spread of the disease in the isolated areas, where its consequences could be disastrous. Lastly, he mentioned the prevalence of typhoid fever at Cape Nome and St. Michael and suggested "that all possible precautions be taken in the future, as on this cruise, in regard to the drinking water supply of the ship."

The following year, Surg. James T. White, RCS, served as the medical officer of the revenue steamer *McCulloch* during her trip (26 May–26 June 1900) from San Francisco to St. Michael. His services provide a fairly representative picture of the normal medical practices aboard a revenue cutter in Arctic waters at the beginning of this century.

Overall, Surgeon White found the health on board good and the sanitary condition excellent, with no sickness having been "caused by lack of cleanliness or poor sanitation."[13] White reported an average of two sailors a day answering sick call, with most of them suffering from constipation, cuts, and bruises. He did recommend the discharge at Port Townsend, Washington, of one cutterman, because of a physical disability. The medical officer also examined and passed eight men for enlistment on the *McCulloch*. While at Dutch Harbor, Surgeon White visited five merchant vessels and a barge, rendering professional services to eight of their crew members and two passengers, plus dispensing medical supplies and medicine to two of the ships.

The U.S. Revenue Service Cutter *Nunivak* had the primary mission of enforcing customs and navigation regulations on the Yukon River and a secondary one of enforcing the laws of the United States. Departmental orders for the first commanding officer of the *Nunivak* called upon 1st Lt. John C. Cantwell to extend assistance to others.[14] To fulfill a significant portion of these instructions, especially medical, Surgeon White, late of the revenue steamer *McCulloch,* served as the ship's medical officer from 1 July 1900 until 30 June 1901.

His first crisis came on 2 July, when smallpox appeared in Nome and the threat of its sweeping "the Yukon Valley like wildfire" caused the general commanding the Department of Alaska to establish a quarantine against all vessels from Nome and all other points on the coast to the westward.[15] The revenue cutter took a position at the entrance to the harbor of St. Michael and maintained a constant surveillance and patrol of the port until the lifting of the quarantine. Surgeon White set the period of quarantine for vessels at fourteen days, with the general lowering it to an unrealistic eight days on the twenty-first, but the quarantine ended five days later. In all, the ship's surgeon boarded thirty-nine vessels and detained twenty-one of them at Egg Island. He also had all the mail originating in Nome or handled by its post office brought to the *Nunivak* and fumigated before being delivered to the St. Michaels post office.

The influenza that first showed up among the natives at St. Michael in early summer grew to epidemic portions and soon spread to the white population. In some cases a fatal attack of pneumonia followed the influenza, causing a very high death rate. The next illness to appear, measles, first struck the natives, but by 11 August it had "appeared among the white people." Besides treating four cuttermen with influenza and one with measles, the surgeon also visited the inhabitants of the nearby native camps across the harbor to provide medical aid.

The revenue steamer departed St. Michaels on the evening of 13 August for her trip up the Yukon River before the end of the navigation season. On

27 September, 1,082 miles from the mouth of the Yukon, she entered the Dall River and tied up to the bank. All hands were at once made busy getting the boat ready for the eight months' winter siege to come. Here, one mile up the Dall River and about thirty miles south of the Arctic Circle, stood Fort Shoemaker, their winter quarters. It had been erected the previous fall and named in honor of Capt. Charles F. Shoemaker, who had been responsible for the cutter's being in the Yukon.

The following extract from the official report of Surgeon White effectively summarizes his activities:

> The trip up the river had been a most interesting and instructive one. We had visited 20 villages and stations with a total population of 925, and had personally attended 245 sick people, both native and white. Treating natives medicinally is most unsatisfactory in many respects. In the first place, not speaking their language, it is hard to make them understand what you wish to convey. In reply to your questions the answer would be almost always, 'Me sick inside. . . .' But the greatest difficulty is to overcome their superstitious belief in the power of their shamans, or medicine men, a superstition which still exists, notwithstanding the teachings of the missionaries. It was decided that, instead of leaving any considerable amount of supplies with the natives, to leave such food and medicines as they might need with the missionaries, the agents at the several trading posts, and with others equally responsible. In this way we rendered assistance to some 2,500 natives residing on or near the Yukon River, and we were assured by many this spring that if we had not done so the suffering and destitution would have been many times greater than it was.[16]

A few descriptions in this report stand out starkly. The ship's surgeon characterized the village of sixty-five inhabitants at Petka Point as "one of the worst we saw on the river. The people appear to be in abject poverty, their houses and tents are filthy, and no effort seems to be made to have either order, cleanliness, or comfort." He found in a very small tent "a man very sick with pneumonia and covered up beside him was the body of another native who had been dead several days." Just twenty miles further upstream, the *Nunivak* stopped at a village of five houses and found most of the people sick either from influenza or measles. One small house, occupied by some sick villagers, Surgeon White described as "dark, damp, and dismal, the fireplace was cold, and an odor of rotting fish permeated everything. The inmates were lying about on their beds, some covered, some uncovered. In one corner was a girl of about fourteen years, entirely nude, whose body was covered with the red rash of measles. Food and medicines were left for the use of these poor people, and we hurried on." A mere quarter of a mile farther on, they found another village where all were "sick with measles and influenza, and many had died. The surviving members of this community were half starved and helpless, and after burying the dead and leaving food and medicines for the living we were compelled to proceed on our way up the river."

Probably "the most miserable little village imaginable" proved to be Dog Fish, fifteen miles above the mission run by the Russian Orthodox Church at Ikogmute. The cuttermen found only eight survivors out of the original forty inhabitants. "They seemed utterly indifferent to our presence, and did not appear to care whether they were helped or not." Once again, the cuttermen had no recourse but to leave food and medicine.

Another seventy-five miles, and the revenue steamer visited the Holy Cross Mission at Koserefsky, run by Jesuit fathers and the sisters of St. Anne. Some 150 Native Americans lived at the mission, with about three hundred more in the immediate vicinity. Surgeon White saw the following cases: "One case pulmonary tuberculosis, 2 cases dysentery, 2 cases pneumonia, 1 gunshot wound of foot (amputated), 1 injured hand, caught in sawmill (amputated two fingers), 1 boy totally blind from some purulent inflammation in infancy."

At Grayling, a winter rendezvous for trading, only thirty-two out of the original sixty-five villagers were still alive. Of these, the medical officer found "10 sick—2 with dysentery, 3 acute conjunctivitis, and the remaining suffering from pulmonary complications following influenza." He discovered only women and children at the Pioneer Coal Mine, the men being away hunting. Six turned out to be ill: "2 with influenza, 2 pulmonary tuberculosis, 1 pneumonia, and 1 infant suffering from starvation, the mother not having sufficient milk to feed it."

Throughout the winter, the revenue cutter crew enjoyed good health, with no serious cases of illness occurring and but few accidents. Only a few cases from the dispensary report proved worthy of note. In late November, following the first real cold weather, a number of throats became "simply inflamed and irritable," probably from the cold air. "Catarrhal conditions of the nose and throat became worse during the winter," with a couple of cases being "quite aggravated." Only one incident of snow blindness occurred, although no one wore smoked glasses or eye shades. Frostbite of the nose, cheeks, and ears proved common, but none of the cases were serious.

With the approach of spring came "a condition resembling a mild form of scurvy" brought on by the crew's "continuous living on preserved foods, whether salted or canned." The cuttermen first complained of constipation and headaches, followed by "a skin eruption, red blotches over the trunk and limbs, accompanied in most cases with diarrhea." The numbers affected became so alarmingly large that fresh moose meat had to be purchased and issued as an extra ration.

The ice in the Dall River did not break until 15 May 1901, with the Yukon clearing two weeks later. In sharp contrast to his reporting of the trip upstream, Surgeon White concluded his official medical report by noting, "The trip down the river was uneventful. We stopped at the more important villages, but most of the natives were away preparing to catch the salmon that would soon come up the river. At Nulato there were three cases of whooping cough and as we proceeded down the river the number of cases became greater. At Anvik nearly all of the mission children were suffering from it. At Koserefsky was seen a young boy whose feet had been frozen the winter previous, necessitating a secondary amputation of four toes on one foot and three on the other. It was impossible to get any data regarding the death rate of the previous winter, but from what we could learn it must have been very great. The condition of the natives this spring, however, was very encouraging and there was every prospect of a good and profitable season ahead of them."[17]

During her 1903 cruise, the U.S. Revenue Cutter Service cutter *Rush* carried Surg. Howson W. Cole, Jr., RCS, who came aboard at Seattle. His first significant case occurred on 30 July at Sitka, when one of the crew members experienced "an attack of Hysteria."[18] The surgeon had him taken to the Naval Hospital ashore and, since his condition had not improved by departure time, he left him there.

While at Dutch Harbor, he and his colleague from another cutter examined three sailors on the merchant vessel *St. Francis* to determine whether they were "shirkers or not." Finding nothing the matter, the surgeons told the sailors to turn to. Surgeon Cole also rendered assistance to a British marine from HMS *Shear Water,* since her surgeon was on shore leave in Dutch Harbor. His next significant case came at sea on 9 September. The wardroom steward reported that he had not passed any urine for three days. Upon examination, the *Rush*'s surgeon discovered a filiform stricture so tight that his smallest instrument failed of passage. Unable to pass a catheter into the bladder, he had to resort to drugs. These finally caused the passage of "a small amount of urine, which was very ammoniacal in odor & very turbid from the large amount of pus present," indicating an acute inflammation of the bladder in addition to the stricture. When the patient developed "a peri-naeal abscess" a day later, the medical officer opened, cleaned, and drained it. Lacking the proper facilities, he had to delay operating, despite the patient's alarming bladder symptoms, until arrival at Sitka. Rushing him to the Naval Hospital, Surgeon Cole and a naval doctor operated on him, while the medical officer from the revenue steamer *Perry* gave the anesthetic. The operation proved successful, with the steward reporting for duty eighteen days later. While in Sitka, the *Rush's* surgeon assisted the naval doctor in all his operations. When a cutterman slipped off the sidewalk and fractured his left kneecap, the two successfully operated on it, opening up the joint and removing the blood clot.

Every time the revenue steamer anchored off a Native American village, Surgeon Cole treated all who needed or requested medical assistance. He ministered mostly to individuals suffering from tuberculosis or rheumatism, although there were a few with heart problems. The ship's surgeon did record noticing marked evidence of syphilis in many of the very young children.

The *Rush* had no sooner anchored at Klawock on 4 November than a request arrived summoning her surgeon to come, for "three old Indians" had "drank 9 bottles of 'Wizard Oil' between them." He found two of them dead, having died some three or four hours previously. Since each bottle contained half an ounce of opium and thirteen ounces of wood alcohol, each drinker had ingested "enough to kill a number of people." The medical officer reported doing all that he could for the one still alive, who displayed the typical symptoms of opium poisoning, "but the oil had a day's start on me & he died the next morning."

The cutter next put in to Klingquan. Surgeon Cole traveled by canoe to a village three miles inland to treat a reportedly bad case of tonsillitis and, while there, also rendered medical assistance to all others who requested it. At Yaku-tat he treated quite a number of natives, whose prevailing diseases were tuberculosis and rheumatism. At Hooniah, aided by 3d Lt. Leon C. Covell, the ship's surgeon successfully "operated on a native boy, who had an extensive abscess just below the left groin & just under the Femoral artery."

Surgeon Cole concluded his annual cruise report with a discussion of the more prevalent diseases he had found among the natives encountered. Tuberculosis easily ranked as most common, with rheumatism being also "quite prevalent." The next most common disease proved to be syphilis, with the doctor noticing "marked evidences of it in the very young children." He saw very little of gonorrhea, and of smallpox not a case.

Surg. Henry Horn, RCS, who served aboard the *McCulloch* from 30 June to 2 November 1904, echoed Surgeon Cole's conclusions of the previous year. "The prevalence of venereal diseases and tuberculosis, in Unalaska," Surgeon Horn wrote in his final report, "is something frightful. Every single native family and most of the whites are tainted."[19] He also reported that treatment of the cuttermen aboard the vessel for venereal disease "exceeded all the other cases combined." Of the treatments he performed, 383 were for "syphilis, 247 for gonorrhea, and 7 for chancroids."

Out of the *McCulloch*'s complement of sixty men, thirty-seven (60 percent of the crew) applied for medical treatment. The only accident of note occurred to a coal passer. The surgeon had to lance a badly infected index finger on the victim's left hand. Although the patient had to be off duty for twenty-nine days, the operation saved his finger. The only case of "peculiar medical interest" proved to be "one of jaundice, in a syphilitic suspect, which ushered in the secondary eruptions." If the Treasury Department permitted him, he planned to publish the full reports of his treatment in a medical journal. He noted one other case, "more on account of the rarity than for any scientific value." After "washing down paint work, with a strong solution of salt water soap suds," a seaman "developed a case of severe dermatitis of the hands." It proved so severe that even twenty-four hours later his right hand was swollen to "twice its normal size" and "was exquisitely painful." Not until four days later did he recover enough for the medical officer to allow him to return to duty. As in previous cruises aboard the cutters plying these northern waters, Surgeon Horn observed many cases among the crew involving problems with the nose, throat, and lungs.

He also treated thirty cases off the revenue cutter. Two patients had to be referred elsewhere for adequate medical care. One, a member of a whaling ship crew, had an "advanced case of diabetes, probably due to malignant disease of the pancreas," and Surgeon Horn ordered him sent to San Francisco. The other, also on a whaler, was suffering from appendicitis. The ship's medical officer did not operate on him, as the cutter lacked "proper facilities," but instead sent him to the doctor at Unalaska. Surgeon Horn gave a detailed explanation in his final report of "the impossibility of doing any important surgical work in the sick bay" of the *McCulloch* "as it stands at present." He requested that his recommendations for improvement be "authorized at once."

Surgeon Horn's report on the 1904 patrol is typical of all the patrols that went before and after. Like their counterparts in the U.S. Army, posted in isolated forts scattered throughout the West, the surgeons who accompanied the cutters to an even wilder region in addition to dispensing medical care also provided an educated view of daily life and of the natives. It is difficult to assess the impact that Surgeon Horn and his colleagues made upon Alaska, but it is obvious that many people owe their lives to these doctors who served without fanfare on the Alaskan frontier.

# T E N

# Law Enforcers or Humanitarians?

T he purchase of Alaska brought the United States face to face with a problem that plagued decision-makers from the time Europeans first set foot in the New World: What about the indigenous people? In the vast new territory there were at least some thirty to forty thousand natives—mostly Aleuts, Athapaskans, Eskimos, Haidas, Tlingits, and Tsimshians. What policies would the United States follow in regard to these people? As seen in previous chapters, the cuttermen all too often found themselves the sole representative of the U.S. government on the Alaskan frontier. Since their primary mission long had been law enforcement, their first contacts with natives were marked with a rigorous enforcement of the law: They demanded respect be paid to the national flag, and they ruthlessly crushed any attempt by the Alaskan natives to challenge the authority of their new rulers. As the years passed, however, the cuttermen witnessed more and more of the suffering that the local inhabitants endured as a result of disease, famine, the severity of their environment, and drink. In time, those serving under the revenue ensign grew to appreciate the intrinsic goodness of these people and, instead of considering them potential enemies, began regarding them with compassion. They ended by helping the Alaskan natives in any way possible, even circumventing rules and regulations to do so.

Before any policy concerning the natives could be enacted, however, logically there had to be a territorial government. But in this case of a noncontiguous acquisition, logic did not prevail. Instead Congress merely extended the existing U.S. laws governing commerce and navigation. In the absence of any legal civil government, the task of ruling the land fell to the military commander of the occupying U.S. Army troops. The soldiers, however, lacking any water transportation, exercised real control only over the areas immediately surrounding their garrisons at Sitka and Forts Wrangell, Kodiak, Tongass, and Kenai. "For ten years after the purchase," wrote an early U.S. Coast Guard historian, "the federal government was represented in the new lands by a few troops in scattered garrisons, by a collector of customs at Sitka, and by cutters cruising along the full sweep of the coasts."[1]

When the U.S. Army withdrew its soldiers in 1877, the task of governing the new possession next fell to the U.S. Treasury Department, whose local representative was the custom collectors. The withdrawal of the soldiers triggered an outbreak of lawlessness. Emboldened by illegal liquor, the natives brawled in the streets, looted unguarded government buildings, behaved insolently, and uttered threats against both life and property. The Sitka settlers intensified their petitions to the federal government, clamoring for armed protection and blaming the unrest upon the widespread consumption of illegal liquor. Only the presence of a revenue cutter or naval warship could limit the trading of liquor for furs. In response to the petitions, the Treasury Department, as was their wont, pleaded a lack of funds as an excuse for not stationing a revenue cutter at Sitka. The rest of the national government simply ignored the pleas.

The long-festering problem spilled over into a night of horror on 6 February 1879, with inebriated natives rioting in the streets and the residents locking themselves inside their houses, prepared to defend their lives to the last bullet. Fortunately, some friendly natives persuaded the others to return to their village. The next morning, since the federal government had not responded to any of their demands for protection, the whites dispatched a desperate plea for help to the nearest British military post, on Vancouver Island. Capt. H. Holmes A'Court of the HMS *Osprey* no sooner learned of their plight than he turned a blind eye to diplomatic niceties, upped anchor, and set sail toward his besieged American cousins. His warship came scudding into the Sitka Harbor on 1 March 1879, her decks cleared for action. Overwhelmed by a display of force, any native harboring hostile intentions quickly faded into the brush.

The U.S. government, meanwhile, unaware of A'Court's action, had learned of the threatened massacre and decided to intervene at once. The nearest armed government vessel turned out to be the revenue cutter *Wolcott,* in Port Townsend, Washington. On 18 February the secretary of the treasury sent a telegram to Capt. James M. Selden "to take on board the necessary supplies and proceed with all practicable dispatch to Sitka." Captain Selden sailed north the next day and, "notwithstanding the frequent snow storms and boisterous weather," put into Sitka Harbor on 2 March. He quickly learned that the arrival of the *Osprey* had "found the citizens in great alarm as they were momentarily expecting" an attack, and that they "had little hopes of holding out long, unless assistance came to them." The following day Selden informed the secretary of the treasury: "The arrival of Captain A'Court has undoubtedly averted this calamity for the present and the deepest gratitude is felt toward him for his prompt answer to their appeal."[2] The Royal Navy captain, believing that the revenue steamer could not provide adequate protection, offered to remain until an American warship arrived, an offer that the frightened settlers at Sitka readily accepted.

An appropriately named American warship, the twelve-gun sloop USS *Alaska,* dropped anchor in the harbor on 3 April. Although she carried three hundred men, well armed and capable of fighting ashore as infantry, her captain had orders only to make a show of force to discourage the hostile natives, not to garrison the town. His presence no longer needed, Captain A'Court sailed back to British waters, carrying a petition requesting the president of the United States to set up a permanent outpost to protect the Sitka residents. Then, on 14 June 1879, the USS *Jamestown,* commanded by Cdr. Lester A. Beardslee, arrived to relieve the *Alaska.* His orders called for him to restore harmonious relations between the white residents and the local natives and, in the absence of any legal civil authority, to use his own discretion in all emergencies that might arise.

With these terse instructions, the five-year rule of the U.S. Navy over Alaska commenced. From 1879 to 1884, the commanders of the naval vessels stationed at Sitka were the actual rulers of Alaska. In many respects, the U.S. Navy proved to be a more ideal caretaker, since most of Alaska's inhabitants, both natives and whites, resided either along the same coastline, on the many islands, or along the navigable rivers, all of which could be easily reached by sailing vessels. This rationale proved even more accurate in terms of the revenue cutters, for they possessed shallower drafts than the naval warships and could process closer in to shore and farther up the navigable rivers.

Finally, Congress passed and the president on 17 May 1884 signed the First Organic Act for Alaska. This act refused to designate this northern land as a territory, instead describing it simply as a civil and judicial district. To govern this vast land of 375 million acres with a population of some 32,000, of which only 430 were white, the act authorized merely a total of thirteen officials. They consisted of a governor, district judge, clerk of the court, marshal, four deputy marshals, and four commissioners, who had the functions of justices of the peace. Generally, the laws then existing in Oregon became the laws of Alaska as long as they proved applicable and did not conflict with those of the United States. The Organic Act of 1884 did place the problem of controlling this northern land strictly in the hands of a civil government. The U.S. Navy terminated its reign over Alaska on 15 September 1884, when it transferred the USS *Pinta* southward, discontinuing Sitka as the warship's home port.

The federal government had provided only the most basic elements of self-government to the new civil and judicial district of Alaska, and then without any local popular control. The act forbade a legislature and contained no provisions for eventual representative government. In many ways, the United States maintained a strict, almost imperial rule in her new possession, one not unlike those established by European countries in their overseas empires during the days of the "white man's burden." One suggestion urged the use of the new possession as a penal colony, making it the American equivalent of Great Britain's Botany Bay. In truth, the federal government, Congress, and the general public really knew very little about Alaska, either before or after her purchase, and probably cared even less. To many, this mysterious northern possession remained a vast, unknown wasteland until the discovery of Klondike gold in 1896 precipitated a rush from all parts of the world. The first amendment to the Organic Act of 1884 came in 1898 and made provisions for the construction of railroads, as well as for extending the homestead laws to Alaska. Following closely came the passage of the Criminal Codes Act in 1899 and the Civil Codes Act in 1900. Finally, Congress passed and on 24 August 1912 President William Howard Taft signed the Second Organic Act, which provided for Alaskan home rule.[3]

Briefly, that then was the political framework within which the cuttermen operated in the Alaskan frontier from 1867 to 1915. During this formative period, the cuttermen found their activities in all fields, but especially in law enforcement, greatly expanded. In addition to their existing obligations, the government gradually tasked them with a multitude of other major and minor law enforcement duties, the most noticeable one being protecting the fur seal herds. The underlying thread throughout this period proved to be the superb demonstration of self-reliance the cuttermen consistently displayed, especially in their role as the sole representative of the federal government. To them fell the difficulties of operating at great distances from their immediate superior, let alone from those at their service headquarters in Washington, and of solving the problem of interpreting their regulations and orders to meet the new challenges of the far northern frontier. Quite frequently these cuttermen had to make quick decisions and take decisive actions, relying solely upon their innate judgment and their experience. More often than not, the results of their judgments turned out to be so helpful that their example continued to be followed long after the cutterman who had made the initial decision had long departed.

The first substantive report on the indigenous natives by a revenue officer plying the waters of Alaska came about a decade after the cutter *Lincoln*'s initial voyage to the far north. By letter, on 21 April 1879, the Treasury Department directed Capt. George W. Bailey of the cutter *Rush* to cruise "in the waters of Alaska and amongst the islands of the Aleutian archipelago" and make "careful observations" of, among other things, "the pursuits, habits of life, character, etc., of the people" encountered.[4] Having sailed these remote waters for several years, the captain already had "an intimate acquaintance with the natives." Moreover, according to his superior in Washington, "his known good judgment and tact in dealing with these uninstructed people" made him "particularly fitted" for this duty, and his report could be "relied upon for its truthfulness, impartiality, and accuracy." Fortunately for the annals of history, Captain Bailey finished his report mere days before his death. On the morning of 16 October 1879, while the *Rush* steamed southward from Alaska to San Francisco "at about eight knots an hour with a heavy sea running," he came on deck at 4:20 A.M. and complained to the officer of the deck of seasickness, before returning to his cabin. Since none of the crew ever saw the captain again, they "presumed that he went to the side of the vessel and was carried overboard by a lurch of the ship."

Captain Bailey's observations of, and recommendation on, how to stop the large illegal trade in liquor, breech-loading arms, and ammunition with the northern natives proved of particular interest. He suggested that a "revenue vessel be sent to Alaska another year" and that "she be fitted to encounter the ice, and go north at the proper season and visit the Indians of the coast as high as Kotzebue Sound at least. This trade might be broken up by vigorously looking after the people engaged in it." He also expressed his belief that "if the Russian government would detail a vessel to cruise on their side in connection with one of our vessels from our side, this contraband trade in rum, breech-loading arms, and ammunition could be broken up."

Captain Bailey, like other revenue officers, such as Capt. Michael A. Healy, strongly warned of the demoralizing effects of rum. "In my opinion," wrote Bailey, "one of the principal causes of the improvidence of the north-coast Indians, and their neglect to provide food for winter, is the demoralizing effects of the rum sold by the Arctic traders. It is reported that it is sold in such large quantities as to keep whole villages drunk and quarreling the best part of the season—large quantities of it being landed at different places, principally at Kotzebue Sound, and from there distributed to the interior Indians. This is undoubtedly killing them off, or causing them to be careless in providing food for the winter, whereby many of them die of starvation."[5]

Interestingly enough, this initial official report highlighted the threefold problem that would plague the cuttermen in their relationships with the natives. A generation earlier, the Indian Trade and Intercourse Act of 1834 had already prohibited the importation and sale of liquor in "Indian Country." As Capt. William A. Howard correctly reasoned during the 1867 *Lincoln* cruise, this 1834 law still remained in effect. After encountering two whiskey-trading schooners bound from Alaska to Victoria and Port Townsend for resupply, he warned the secretary of the treasury on 17 August 1867 that he expected a continuous war with the Indians unless the liquor trade could be suppressed. After noting that no instructions had been given to him on this matter, he further wrote: "I shall, when our flag has been hoisted over the territory, destroy all liquors brought into it for traffic, and send the vessels away, if under American colors. . . . Until laws or regulations are perfected for the government of this territory, I shall consider it as an Indian reservation, so far as liquors are concerned."[6]

As early as the 1790s, Governor Alexander Baranov of Russian America had banned the sale of liquor to the natives. His successors followed his example, one placing the coastal waters off limits to Americans in 1834 and another declaring all liquor sales illegal. These controls still remained in effect at the time of the Alaskan purchase. Even before the official transfer, the secretary of the treasury had ordered a collector of customs to Sitka to supervise the discharge of cargo and to prohibit the landing of any liquor, firearms, or ammunition. The federal officials then assumed that treaty ratification and congressional action would follow shortly. Not until 1870, however, did Congress finally act. Then it totally ignored the territory issue, instead forbidding the importation, manufacture, and sale of liquor into Alaska, as well as the importation of firearms and ammunition into Saint Paul and Saint George Islands, in an effort to ensure the survival of the fur seal herds there.

*Roy Reinburg, 2d Lieut.*
*McInary, Gunner*
*Johnson, Seaman*
*Pinson, Ord. Seaman.*

A boarding party from the *Perry* remains aboard the Japanese sealer *Tenyu Maru,* seized on 9 July 1909. The schooner contained sixty-three seal skins and one female seal skin. The *Perry's* small boat, under the command of 2nd Lt. LeRoy Reinburg, may be seen alongside the *Tenyu Maru. Courtesy Capt. LeRoy Reinburg Jr., USCG (Ret.)*

Five years later the Treasury Department ordered its collector of customs to impose a total ban upon the "importation of breech-loading rifles and fixed ammunition into Alaska." The widening of the ban from just the Seal Islands to all of the recently purchased territory suggested that fear of Alaska's native population might have been the primary motive behind this order.[7] The exact interpretation of these policies naturally changed from time to time, as did the enforcement procedures. The cuttermen, however, remained responsible for limiting the importation and distribution of breech-loading rifles, fixed ammunition, and liquor to the Alaskan natives from 1867 to 1915.

Smuggling, considered by many to be as American as apple pie, remained a major and constant problem. A multitude of difficulties existed in this northern frontier to complicate the apprehension of contraband trade. Several major problems constantly plagued the law enforcers and made the prevention of such illegal trade almost impossible. These were the proximity of

Canada and Russia; poor communications and isolation from the continental United States; the vast distances and extremely miserable weather; and the lack of available, qualified, incorruptible, and rugged personnel. Complicating the entire situation, the Treasury Department normally preferred to conduct business as inexpensively as possible.

The methods used by the smugglers in Alaska to avoid detection proved to be the normal tricks of the trade employed elsewhere for centuries. Traders and natives, who used canoes to carry contraband items to villages along the southwestern coast, for instance, took few precautions, preferring to depend upon daring and blind luck. Since the customs regulations permitted native canoes and small British vessels to ply the coastal trade without paying any tonnage or other dues, government officials rarely stopped and inspected these small craft. Those larger vessels employed in supplying the canneries and settlements in the Northwest enjoyed a similar freedom. The collector of customs in the ports on the Pacific coast could grant them special permits that allowed sailing in Alaskan waters without requiring clearance from a port of entry. The masters of ships possessing these permits needed only to stop off at Victoria, British Columbia, or Honolulu, Hawaii, load up with liquor and other contraband, and then proceed to Alaska. These collectors also permitted vessels engaged in the Alaska trade for years to carry hundreds of gallons of whiskey aboard as ship's stores, being justified usually as medicinal supplies. The smugglers employing vessels more likely to be searched did not report the illicit articles on their manifests, or devised false labeling and packaging, or simply jettisoned their illegal cargoes upon spotting a revenue cutter.

Interestingly enough, the problem of illegal possession of liquor by the North American natives also plagued the law enforcement organization that many people believed the cuttermen in Alaska most resembled—the Royal Canadian Mounted Police, also called the Northwest Mounted Police, or Mounties for short. The Mounties were noted for their willingness to track whiskey smugglers even into the snow-covered Arctic region.

Like the Canadian Mounted Police, the cuttermen earned a reputation for their relationship with, and treatment of, the natives. Granted, each demanded and enforced a strict adherence to their respective laws, such as the ban on illegal trading of liquor, but they both handled the indigenous people in a benevolent, albeit paternalistic, manner. Most authorities agree that the Canadian record of dealing with natives contained less violence than that of the Americans south of the forty-ninth parallel. Between 1866 and

1895, for example, some 943 military conflicts occurred in the American West, while only six or seven comparable clashes took place in Canada. To many, the credit for that smaller number belongs to the Northwest Mounted Police, who, rather than Canadian army regulars, were the ones that most often dealt with the natives on the frontier. The Alaskan experience, where the rule of the cuttermen lasted much longer than that of the soldiers, sailors, and marines, more closely paralleled the Canadian record. The few armed confrontations, although posing serious risks for igniting a war, appear today as merely minor skirmishes in comparison with the bloody battles that were common during the settlement of the American West.[8]

In many ways, the legendary Captain Healy best typified the normal progression for the average cutterman serving on this far north frontier. In October 1882, Healy put into Sitka for coaling and became caught up in one of the most serious military confrontations with the natives in the history of Alaska. At the time, the forty-three-year-old first lieutenant commanded the revenue steamer *Corwin*.

On 22 October, the Northwest Trading Company tug *Favorite* brought disturbing news to the de facto naval governor in Sitka, Cdr. Edgar C. Merriman. After an accidental explosion had killed an influential Tlingit shaman, who was working as a member of a company whaling party, the medicine man's people had seized two white employees, a steam launch, and other company property. Following their tribal custom, the Tlingits demanded two hundred blankets as compensation for the loss of their shaman, a payment that satisfied their concept of justice. They also tried to capture the white manager of the company whaling station at Killisnoo on Admiralty Island, some seventy-five miles southeast of Sitka, but he managed to escape with his family aboard the *Favorite*.

Commander Merriman considered this demand for compensation claims a direct challenge to his authority. A few weeks earlier, when another Tlingit had died in a company logging accident, the man's tribe had demanded a similar compensation. The naval officer had warned the Tlingits then that they could not demand such death indemnities from the whites and that any future claim of this nature would call for the most severe punishment.

Since the shallow waters around the native villages on Admiralty Island prohibited the use of his warship, the USS *Adams*, Commander Merriman devised a prompt improvisation. He loaded some one hundred marines and seamen, armed with a howitzer and Gatling gun, on the *Favorite* as quickly as possible and sent the tug steaming toward her company whaling station.

First Lieutenant Healy now volunteered his shallow-draft and nimble *Corwin* to assist in this punitive naval operation, an offer immediately accepted by the naval governor. Commander Merriman, accompanied by William G. Morris, the Sitka collector of customs, then embarked on the cutter and soon overtook the *Favorite,* arriving at Killisnoo on 25 October. Finding that the Tlingits had retired with their captives and had seized property at the nearby village of Angoon, the cutter and the hastily armed tug followed.

Collector Morris later reported to the secretary of the treasury that, upon their arrival there, they found the two white men still held prisoner and "the Indians increasing in force and very much excited." Commander Merriman immediately confronted the Tlingit chieftains and rejected their demand for two hundred blankets. He then imposed a fine of four hundred blankets upon them, payable the next morning, for their violation of his earlier warning not to take hostages or make claims of the whites. If they refused to surrender the blankets on time, he would burn their canoes and shell their principal village. The Tlingits proved to be "surly and impertinent," apparently believing that the naval officer would never "put his threat into execution" but was instead merely playing "a game of bluff."

When morning came and passed, Commander Merriman ordered the capture of the two most important Tlingit chieftains as hostages, to prevent any harm to the whites. Then he ordered the canoes set afire. Seeing their means of livelihood in flames, the Tlingits decided to surrender their white hostages. The *Corwin* and *Favorite* then ended the standoff by opening fire with their cannons, Gatling gun, and small arms. Within ten minutes the village lay in ruins, with the inhabitants fading into the safety of the forest. The marines then debarked and finished the job by torching any portion of the houses still standing. Collector Morris strongly believed in "the absolute necessity" of "such harsh measures being adopted," for the Tlingits, "a rich and warlike tribe," had acted "very insolent and saucy towards the whites." He reported to the secretary of the treasury that "the presence and co-operation of the 'Corwin' was most opportune" and especially commended First Lieutenant Healy as "an officer and a gentleman, and a credit to the service. His officers and men conducted themselves well throughout the whole affair, and deserve therefore special mention."[9]

As in their unsuccessful attempts to suppress the illegal trading in liquor, breech-loading firearms, and fixed ammunition, the cuttermen also failed to eradicate illegal fornicating between native women and whalers, traders, miners, and pioneers, although they made huge progress in this effort. According to one cutter captain with many years of Arctic experience, "The old native custom of extending the use of one's wife to guests beneath the roof, which is common to the Alaskan and Siberian Eskimo alike, is responsible in great measure for the carnal intercourse of the Eskimo women with the crews of whaling ships."[10] Often the evils of drink led to the prostitution of native women. "The whiskey traffic," reported one missionary teacher, a veteran of fourteen months in Alaska, to the secretary of the treasury, "is the greatest danger that threatens the Eskimos. It debauches them morally and physically and leads to the prostitution of the native women by the whalers."[11] An article in the Nome newspaper entitled "Trail of Blood" superbly described the actions of one such whiskey trafficker who, according to its subtitle, was "Debauching Natives by the Hundreds":

> Jas. McKenna, the notorious illicit whisky trader reached Bering strait with a cargo of alcohol July 1. After debauching the Siberian coast, he went over to North Alaska, where he always lands more or less of it, and thence he will go to the north coast of Canada, and winter somewhere east of Herschell island out of reach of the mounted police.
>
> He is keeping ahead of the revenue cutter, debauching the natives of three countries and leaving a trail of blood and death behind him.[12]

Other Alaskan missionaries, such as Dr. Sheldon Jackson, emphasized the uncivilized or debauched nature of the Alaskan natives to highlight the needs for their religious services in this far-off land. An untiring advocate, whose affection for the Alaskan frontier bordered on being an obsession, Dr. Jackson never shone more brightly than during his many lectures, at which he bemoaned the pitiful fate of the native woman, especially her sexual license. An inveterate pamphleteer, the good doctor wasted no opportunity to publicize the revolting manner in which so many whites exploited the natives, especially in taking sexual liberties with them. Yet this persuasive missionary, when testifying before the Senate Committee on Education, truthfully reported that the native women looked upon sex in the same light that Americans did washing.

To the cuttermen, probably more than any other of the early federal officers, fell the task of preventing such illicit sex among people guided in religious matters for centuries by shamans (witch doctors). On his first cruise to the Seal Islands as commander of a revenue cutter, for instance, First Lieutenant Healy had "found a terrible state of drunkenness among the natives" and reported that "their sprees are almost continuous among both men, women & chil-

Gun drill aboard the cutter *Bear*.

dren—lasting as long as they can possibly procure the means of getting drunk—neglecting their business and fast bringing themselves to a wretched state of want, depravity & disease."[13] Capt. Oscar C. Hamlet, while commanding the *Thetis* in 1904, told of finding eighteen native women on a whaling vessel planning on wintering over in the Arctic. Captain Hamlet wrote that masters of whaling ships in the Arctic had always carried native women aboard their ships, ostensibly for sewing fur clothing, but more often the women were procured for immoral purposes, as they were not the legal wives of any persons on board. Captain Hamlet went on to say that teachers and missionaries had made complaints to him about some cases in which native girls "of tender years" had been kept as mistresses aboard whaling ships.[14]

Surprisingly enough, the captain's exposure of the mistreatment of native women by the Arctic whalers, when coupled with similar reports from missionaries, federal officials, and others, brought swift remedial legal action. Perhaps the repugnance displayed by the general public upon learning of these incidents played a role. In any case, the decision-makers in Washington took concerted action and soon came up with the idea of having the U.S. district judge at Nome appoint the commanding officer of the Arctic cutter as a U.S. commissioner for the duration of the annual voyage. Such an appointment allowed the cutter officer to adjudicate minor offenses as well as authorize the arrest of persons suspected of having committed felonies. The term U.S. commissioner, as used in Alaska, thus became virtually synonymous with justice of the peace, coroner, probate judge, examining and committing magistrate, notary public, and recorder.

Once armed with this new judicial authority, the U.S. commissioners on their annual cruise into the Arctic made serious inroads in combating the maltreatment of native women by whalers. On the 1906 Arctic cruise, for instance, the U.S. commissioner, and skipper of the *Thetis*, proved to be, appropriately enough, Captain Hamlet. His arrest of Capt. E. W. Newth, master of the whaling ship *Jeanette*, on charges of assaulting a young Eskimo girl resulted in the whaler's transportation on the cutter first to Nome and then south for trial. After Captain Newth pleaded guilty in the U.S. district court in Seattle, the federal judge sentenced him to undergo one day's imprisonment and to pay a fine of twenty-five hundred dollars plus court costs. He readily paid this fine to avoid further imprisonment. That summer, also in the vicinity of Point Barrow, Captain Hamlet discovered eight other whalemen, either masters or officers, who had been keeping Eskimo women on their ships for immoral purposes. The U.S. commissioner prosecuted them for their seduction, imposed fines of two hundred dollars on the whalers, each of whom paid it on the spot, and made arrangements for their transportation back home.

Two years later, Capt. Andrew J. Henderson served as U.S. commissioner during his 1908 Arctic cruise in the *Thetis*. He reported difficulties in obtaining "information concerning the alleged illicit relations between the officers of the whaling ships and Eskimo women." Although his cutter had been in more than usual contact with whalers, his cuttermen had heard nothing reflecting upon the officers of the whaling ships. Captain Henderson and his officers made inquiries at various settlements along the American coast of the Arctic but failed to elicit any information to show that the whalemen had been guilty of carnal intercourse with Eskimo women while their ships had been in American waters. Several of the people interviewed, however, had suggested that threats had been made should anyone disclose what went on aboard ship.

Despite such difficulties, Captain Henderson and his officers accused Frank A. Long, master of the whaling steamer *Jeanette* of San Francisco, of having committed the "crime of fornication" with an Eskimo woman. Their information indicated that this event had taken place earlier that year aboard the whaling ship off Big Diomede Island. They arrested him near Icy Cape on 12 August 1908 and detained him aboard the *Thesis* for trial. The following day, Captain Henderson held commissioner's court aboard the cutter. The accused "pleaded guilty," and Captain Hamlet sentenced him to pay a fine of seventy-five dollars plus court costs. The guilty whaler was given the choice of either being "imprisoned in the District jail at Nome, Alaska, for a period not exceeding ninety days" or paying the fine and court costs, totaling $117.65. A U.S. deputy marshal went ashore with Master Long and accompanied him until he had paid this sum.[15]

Many revenue captains experienced frustration in combating such lawbreakers when, after the racing cutter outran and boarded a merchant vessel, they found that the ship's captain had just married the white whaler to his female Eskimo companion. More often than not, as the nimble cutter bore down upon the merchant vessel the cuttermen observed the suspect and his native woman dashing toward the wheelhouse to find the captain, who had the power to marry them.

The trials and tribulations of Captain Henderson in one such unsuccessful attempt to apprehend a violator of the law were typical. On 14 July 1907, James A. Tilton, the master of the whaling steamer *Herman* out of San Francisco, came aboard the *Thetis* at Port Clarence. He wanted to know how to obtain permission to carry a native female from the Arctic to Unalaska. He wanted this girl, his own daughter, to attend the school there, which already "contained two other children" of his, "the mothers of whom were all ESKIMO women." When Captain Henderson informed him that he needed a written permit, Tilton promised to apply for one before leaving with her. Two days later William Mogg, the master of the gasoline schooner *Olga* out of San Francisco, came aboard. He explained to the cutter captain his desire to take a native woman and child from Port Clarence to Herschel. "The woman had borne him three children," the schooner master said, and he wanted to take her with him to the *Olga* at Point Barrow. Captain Henderson stated that Mogg would have to marry the woman before a written permit could be issued. Not only did he agree to marry the woman but in addition he "subsequently told people at Teller, Alaska, that such was his intention." The schooner master returned on 19 July and asked the cutter captain to marry them as soon as the sea moderated. Henderson readily agreed to perform the ceremony whenever he desired but warned him "not to take her out of the harbor in the meantime." Knowing that the *Herman*, on which Mogg planned to take passage, would not be able to take on coal and leave before 22 July, the cutter captain sailed to Teller to obtain water for the cutter.[16]

Unbeknownst to Henderson, the *Herman* departed Port Clarence for the Arctic on the afternoon of 21 July, taking Mogg, the native woman, and the child as passengers. By the time the cutter captain learned of these deliberate violations of his instructions and had readied the *Thetis* for pursuit, the *Herman* already had more than six hours' head start. Since her reported destination was some undetermined port on the Siberian coast, Captain Henderson deemed it inadvisable to give chase. He made this decision, he later reported, after consulting with one of his passengers, the federal district attorney, who felt that the master of the *Herman* would marry Mogg and the woman if the cutter overtook them.[17] Fortunately for all concerned, the Reverend S. R. Spriggs, a Presbyterian missionary at Point Barrow, married Mogg and the woman on 15 August. The other masters, apparently fearful that this misconduct by masters of the *Herman* and *Olga* might reflect badly on the integrity of the remaining officers of the whaling fleet, had urged this step upon their fellow whaler. Henderson expressed gratification upon news of this marriage and expressed confidence that the whaling masters would not behave in an illegal manner with native women in the future.

The same trick to thwart the heavy hand of the law was sometimes practiced on land. The governor of Alaska, John G. Brady, informed the secretary of the interior of one such instance that he had observed personally while being transported to Yakutat by the revenue steamer *Rush*. "Five or six white men," he wrote, "who were living with Indian women unmarried, had occasion to waken the missionary early in the morning to get married before we got ashore." In sharp contrast, on another cruise aboard the *Rush* to "the native village of Hoonah to clean that place up," he and the cuttermen had "found two men each having two wives and two women each having two husbands and all living in the upper story of one building. There were other cases of adultery. They had just trials and the convicted ones were punished. This created a healthy tone in that community that has abided."[18]

The officers and enlisted men of the cutters carried out their orders to enforce the laws made by legislators many miles removed from the northern frontier. There is no doubt many of the skippers felt that some of the laws would help the natives of the region. Capt. Calvin L. Hooper, for example, in his reports while in command of the *Corwin* noted that the Inuit "were

entitled to the protection of the American flag," and he took "a personal satisfaction" in curtailing the illegal liquor trade in the Arctic.[19] Captain Healy's
near obsession with stopping the liquor trade is detailed in chapter 3. True,
Captain Hooper may simply have been pursuing what was dubbed "the
white man's burden," and many may say that he simply illustrated a nineteenth-century paternalism toward "barbaric" peoples, but his actions also
indicate a desire to help. Captain Healy's reasons are much more compli-
cated and difficult to fathom. As pointed out in chapters 3 and 11, Healy
suffered from a drinking problem. Did this problem help spur on his drive
to stop the flow of liquor to the natives because he knew the dangers first
hand, or could there have been other reasons? Captain Healy's desire to help
is best shown in his work to introduce reindeer into North America. Further, Healy would at times ask his officers to contribute money to assist the
natives.

The best example of the feelings of the cuttermen is the medical help
given to the villages. The U.S. Revenue Cutter Service, an organization
notorious for counting pennies, did not fund cutter captains for medical care
provided to those in the isolated settlements of the Bering Sea or Arctic
regions. Without orders and completely on their own—and probably breaking a regulation or two—the cutter captains allowed medical care to be given
to those in need. If one reads the Alaskan files in the National Archives, it is
evident that the cuttermen pursued their duties in law enforcement concerning the natives of the Bering Sea and Arctic regions in a professional way.
While there is no clear dividing point in time, it is also evident that by at least
the 1890s the cuttermen had begun to look upon the natives as people, and
would help them in any way they could muster. Captain Hooper went so
far as to write that "in the few instances where trouble has occurred between
Innuits and white men, it appears to have been the fault of the latter."[20] The
early cuttermen have never received the credit due them for their efforts as
seagoing policemen who served the indigenous people of an isolated region.

# ELEVEN

# "A Lot of Wardroom Carping and Complaining"

C apt. Michael A. Healy, U.S. Revenue Cutter Service, is, to paraphrase Winston S. Churchill, a mystery wrapped in an enigma. One writer notes that the story of Captain Healy is an "American tragedy."[1] The ancient Greek priests would have delighted in presenting his story at Delphi. Healy is known for his humane treatment of the natives of the far north. Yet he could order the shelling of an Indian village. From 1874 until 1895 he sailed to the Bering Sea and Arctic regions, commanding the *Bear* for the last nine of those years. The *Bear* and Captain Healy became—for all practical purposes—the Bering Sea Patrol to most people. Healy could also be a hard taskmaster. He tended to give enlisted men more leeway, probably because he had come "up through the hawse pipe"—making the difficult journey from before the mast to officer in the merchant marine. His junior officers, however, soon learned to their consternation why he deserved the sobriquet "Hell Roaring Mike." Fame eluded him because of a flawed personality. Captain Healy also kept to himself the secret of his racial background, and that secret remained concealed until the 1960s. At the helm of the *Bear* in 1895, Healy stood at the pinnacle of his career. The stage was set for the beginning of the "American tragedy."

The 1895 Bering Sea Patrol began no differently than any other. Healy's initial orders for the season called for an investigation of the Shumagin Islands, a short distance from the Aleutian passes leading to the Bering Sea. The *Bear* also, of course, would patrol the Pribilofs in search of illegal sealing operations. Healy's former skipper and mentor, Capt. Calvin L. Hooper,

161

commanded the patrol. Captain Hooper already had received reports of sealing vessels congregating near the Shumagins, waiting for the normal bad weather, which they would use as cover in order to sneak into the prohibited area to harvest a quick, lucrative cargo of illegal pelts.

The *Bear* groped slowly through a thick fog toward her area of operations. At 2:30 P.M. on 6 June, 2d Lt. Howard Emery, navigation officer and then the officer of the deck, spotted a small island off the port bow through a break in the fog. Lieutenant Emery notified Captain Healy of the sighting and informed him that he felt the island resembled Korovin, one of the Shumagins. Healy first ordered slow ahead, and he questioned Emery's identification of the island. When the wind freshened about 5:00 P.M., Healy had the engines stopped and the mainsail set. He then went below to his cabin, leaving 1st Lt. George Daniels, the new officer of the deck, with the conn, but without any specific orders. Although this routine practice has taken place millions of times since sailors have gone to sea, this seemingly banal act became the harbinger of the fall of Capt. Michael A. Healy.[2]

Months later, both Daniels and Emery would testify that Captain Healy showed "the influence of alcohol at the time."[3] The various changes in the *Bear*'s speed over the preceding days had made an accurate dead reckoning fix impossible, Daniels further explained, and had placed the ship "in a dangerous position close to the island in conditions of limited visibility." At the 6 June dinner in the wardroom, Emery expressed his uneasiness over the dangers "of going among the islands in thick fog," while "not knowing the position of the vessel accurately." The other officers in the wardroom echoed similar reservations. First Lt. Albert Buhner, the executive officer, even argued that "the ship should have been put into the bay that afternoon."[4]

Emery again went on watch as the officer of the deck at 8:00 P.M., with the cutter's position doubtful, the skipper below in his cabin, and the only orders being "go slow ahead." In a scene that would seem strange, if not bizarre, to a modern deck officer, Buhner and Daniel joined Emery and began to discuss their concern over the present situation. The fog then lifted. Recognizing Korovin Island, Lieutenant Buhner apparently took over the deck watch for a short period of time and ordered a course change, one paralleling the island and following a deep channel into Stepovik Bay. He next went below to notify Captain Healy of his actions and receive orders for the night. After knocking at the cabin door and receiving no response, the lieutenant went topside to the pilot house and wrote the night orders. According to later testimony, Buhner undertook this action on his "own responsibility," something he had never done before, because "frequently the Captain had spent 24, 48 or even 72 hours straight on deck, and I thought he needed his sleep." Captain Healy came on deck briefly at 11:00 P.M. and issued orders to reduce sail and continue sailing offshore during the night. He made no other changes to the night orders. Lieutenant Emery remembered the captain being unsteady and "very drunk."[5]

At 4:30 A.M. on 7 June, Buhner and Daniels, along with Eng. J. E. Dory, were relaxing in the wardroom over coffee prior to turning in. Suddenly they heard the sound of the captain's service bell summoning his personal steward. The bell rang several more times before they heard Captain Healy leave his cabin and make his way to the area where the stewards slept. He screamed obscenities and cursed them for not answering the bell for over an hour, then returned to his cabin. Daniels later swore that he heard Healy strike one of the Japanese stewards, although he did not actually see the captain strike the man.

The *Bear* spent the next two weeks cruising among the Shumagins. On those rare occasions when Healy appeared on deck, his officers noted his "showing the effects of constant drinking." The executive officer finally decided to confiscate his liquor supply "for the Captain's own good," since the ship's doctor had advised him that Healy's drinking "was injuring him seriously." At this time, naval officers could legally drink aboard ship. Lieutenant Buhner and the ship's carpenter found an unopened case of whiskey and several additional bottles, which they gave to the ship's doctor.[6]

Early August found the *Bear* hove to with the whaling fleet off Icy Cape, above the Arctic Circle, waiting for the ice conditions to improve before pushing on to Pt. Barrow. On 23 August, Healy decided to wait no longer and ordered the cutter south. Much later, at his courts-martial, some of his officers would try to prove that this decision resulted from the captain's craving for liquor, not his knowledge of Arctic navigation. The relations between the officers and the skipper of the *Bear* apparently had degenerated to a dangerous degree, which helps explain what happened next at Unalaska.

The *Bear* came to in Unalaska on 11 September, joining the other vessels participating in the final stages of the 1895 Bering Sea Patrol. As required by naval custom, Captain Healy immediately made his call upon the commander of the patrol, Captain Hooper, aboard the cutter *Rush*. Later, under oath, Hooper admitted recognizing the signs that "Captain Healy had been drinking, but I would not say he was drunk."[7]

Captain Hooper soon received another visitor from the *Bear,* Lt. Chester M. White, who declared his intentions to file charges of misconduct against

Healy. Captain Hooper did not ask for the particulars, but did request the lieutenant not to pursue his formal charges any further. Hooper subsequently informed Healy of the incident by letter, ordering the message to be delivered only "when Healy was sober."

At the time of the *Bear*'s visit, four other U.S. Revenue Cutter Service cutters—the *Corwin, Grant, Perry,* and *Rush*—lay at anchor in Unalaska, as well as a British warship, the HMS *Pheasant.* The officers usually spent this period of time in Unalaska either working or socializing. At one ball ashore, Healy, who had a reputation for intimidating junior officers, so flustered a young officer that he appealed to both his own commanding officer, Capt. D. F. Tozier of the *Perry,* and patrol commander Captain Hooper to prevail upon Healy to cease his harassment. Later, Capt. Frank A. Garforth, RN, commanding the *Pheasant,* invited the U.S. Revenue Cutter Service officers to a wardroom party aboard his cruiser. "A lot of whiskey was going around," Captain Hooper much later recalled, "and I would be surprised that anyone got away sober that evening." When Hooper noticed Healy, the captain already had dozed off in a chair. As the party began breaking up, Healy's deep voice bellowed across the room, "Ross, be a man." Upon hearing his name, 1st Lt. Worth Ross, of the *Grant,* hurried over to the captain. He then suggested farewells were in order and offered to accompany Healy back to the *Bear.* When his offer was summarily rejected, the lieutenant protested, explaining that it had been made "in a friendly spirit."[8]

Healy next turned on Chief Eng. A. L. Broadbent, who had served with him for years, despite the fact that the two—nursing some unknown grudge—had not spoken in a long time. "Broadbent," Healy roared, apparently disoriented either from his nap or drink, "get out of my cabin or I will put you under arrest." Broadbent shot back: "I don't belong to your ship," and walked away. The *Bear*'s captain started to rise from his chair, but then sat down again.

Captain Garforth and 1st Lt. F. M. Dimmock of the *Rush* next tried to convince Healy to leave. Lieutenant Ross again volunteered his services, coaxed Healy on deck, and, with the help of Lieutenant Dimmock, escorted him back to his cutter. The British captain confided to Lieutenant Daniels that if he "had realized Captain Healy was not a gentleman, he would not have invited him."[9]

Two days later, Healy made his way down the pier to see off the *Perry.* One minute Healy was on the pier and the next, according to amazed observers, he was floundering in the bay. Quite naturally, his opponents blamed drunkenness for his fall. Seaman Benjamin Hutton, however, later testified that the captain had inadvertently tripped on something and had been unable to regain his balance. Hauled aboard the *Perry,* the drenched revenue cutter officer admitted in astonishment to having fallen overboard. "So, I perceive, sir," replied 1st Lt. John G. Barry, while Captain Tozier remarked, "Captain, I regret to see you in this condition." Both revenue officers, according to their later statements, believed Healy intoxicated.[10]

Captain Healy spent the next week at the home of Mr. Harvey N. Nice of the Alaska Commercial Company, recuperating from his plunge into the bay. The *Bear*'s surgeon, Dr. Thomas Bodkin, treated him for cuts and bruises.

In the meanwhile, Captain Hooper, the senior U.S. Revenue Cutter Service officer on the West Coast, had been presented with a document entitled "Request for Investigation into the Conduct of Captain Michael A. Healy." It contained the signatures of twenty-five officers. Not too surprisingly, virtually all of the junior officers on the four revenue cutters had put their names to the document, and the first lieutenants had placed their names with those of the junior officers; interestingly enough, however, First Lieutenants Buhner and Dimmock refused to sign. The document alleged seven specifications of misconduct. Six dealt with Captain Healy's failure to conduct himself as a gentleman and his treatment of junior officers, while the seventh dealt with the HMS *Pheasant* incident involving Chief Engineer Broadbent. It is interesting that no mention of the intemperate use of alcohol appeared anywhere. Hooper did not consider this document as official charges against Captain Healy, and he advised the treasury secretary to postpone any action until the *Bear* returned to San Francisco in November, stating that a copy of the document had been forwarded to Healy for his reply.[11]

Upon the *Bear*'s return to home port, Lieutenant Daniels, learning of Captain Hooper's unofficial decision on the seven charges by Lieutenants White and Emery and himself, preferred formal charges against his commanding officer. Service regulations required these charges be routed through the executive officer of the *Bear,* Lieutenant Buhner, for Captain Healy's endorsement prior to transmittal to Washington. When Healy delayed too long, Buhner went to Healy's home, obtained the documents, and mailed them.[12]

Healy finally returned to the *Bear* on 29 November and, finding Lieutenant Daniels ashore, left orders for the lieutenant to report to his cabin immediately upon coming aboard the cutter. Not surprisingly, Daniels felt

"Hell Roaring Mike" might try to provoke him in the privacy of his cabin into striking the captain. The lieutenant stationed Emery and Engineer Officer Dory outside the open door of Healy's cabin. Daniels later swore that Healy called him a liar upon his entrance and spat in his face. Healy countered that he had merely expressed his disgust at his subordinate's incorrect ship log entries by spitting upon the deck in front of his feet. The two witnesses carefully placed by Daniels did not actually observe either Healy or Daniels in the cabin, although they did report hearing no mention of the log. They did hear Healy calling Daniels a liar and the lieutenant's immediate exclamation that the captain had spit upon him. As fate would have it, when Healy left the cutter shortly thereafter, one of the witnesses to the "confrontation," Lieutenant Emery, remained aboard as officer of the deck, the senior duty officer aboard at the time. What happened next may have modern naval officers shaking their heads but, again, with the climate aboard the cutter, perhaps it was only a logical escalation of events.

Emery violated all rules of the military chain of command by firing off a telegram to Assistant Secretary of the Treasury Charles Hamlin. Emery signed the message "1st Lieut. Temporarily in charge," and reported "Captain Healy is intoxicated on board the *Bear* insulting his officers. Immediate action necessary."

Hamlin's reply on 30 November summarily relieved Healy of command pending a board of inquiry to consider the charges against him. The assistant secretary also ordered Emery to file new formal charges.[13]

Hamlin's actions remain inexplicable today. Surely anyone familiar with the military would have been expected to reprimand Emery for his violation of the chain of command, since any recommendation for the removal of Captain Healy should have come from his immediate superior, Captain Hooper. The only rationale put forth by historian Gerald O. Williams is that this senior treasury official had become very weary over a troublemaker who had created a major public relations disaster and needed to be pushed aside. Perhaps Emery already knew that Healy had faced a hearing in 1890 concerning cruelty and drunkenness and felt that it was now time to replace him.[14]

Captain Healy's friends advised him not to contest the charges. "The cloud is very dark and more threatening than I thought," wrote his brother James, now bishop of Portland, Maine.[15] Captain Hooper, his superior officer, mentor, and friend, also advised against fighting the charges. Again, the atmosphere aboard the *Bear* almost predetermined the result: Healy decided to fight. He engaged the services of San Francisco attorney Bradley Henley

The officers and warrant officers of the U.S. Coast Guard cutter *Bear* in 1896 that had so much to do with Capt. Michael A. Healy's fall from grace. *Back row, left to right:* Dr. Bodkin, Engineer Coffin, Lieutenant Daniels, Lieutenant White, Lieutenant Emery, unidentified warrant officers. *Front row, left to right:* Chief Engineer Schwartz, Captain Healy, Engineer Dory, Lieutenant Buhner. Healy shows his age in this photograph.

who immediately sent a letter to Secretary of the Treasury J. G. Carlisle, pointing out that the charges originally had begun with Lieutenant White who, "within the last few days it has been publicly announced . . . resigned from the Service (and incidentally deserted his wife in the process), [which] would seem to indicate that there is an abandonment of the accusation, the existence of which he is mainly responsible for." The reason for White's desertion: He ran off with a chorus girl. Secretary Carlisle, however, refused to bow to the implied threat of adverse publicity resulting from a formal trial.[16]

The San Francisco newspapers began a pretrial frenzy not unlike that of some modern trials. The sympathies of the press in this case rested with the

Arctic veteran and local hero, Captain Healy. Witnesses against him received short shrift.[17]

The Treasury Department announced the members of the courts-martial board: Capt. D. B. Hodgsdon, of the cutter *Fessenden* at Detroit, president of the board; Capt. Louis N. Stoddard, captain of the Port of New York; Capt. W. C. Coulson, on duty with the U.S. Life-Saving Service and a friend of Healy's; 1st Lt. H. H. Rogers, of the cutter *Hartwell* in the Bay area, to be recorder; and chosen with the task of prosecuting officer, 1st Lt. William E. Reynolds, of the *Grant*. Ironically, Reynolds had served under Captain Hooper and First Lieutenant Healy in the *Corwin* in 1881. During that tour of duty Reynolds raised the flag over Wrangell Island to claim it for the United States, and he served as a member of the overland expedition landed in Siberia to search for the missing polar exploring ship *Jeannette*.[18]

Captain Healy realized that his alleged misconduct aboard the British ship could prove extremely damaging. In hope of containing the damage, he wrote Captain Garforth of the *Pheasant*, who replied that "as far as I and my officers are concerned, you did not give any cause whatever for offense." Strangely, Garforth then wrote to Secretary Carlisle about Healy's letter and said: "Captain Healy who I fancy was hardly sober when he came aboard after a time went to sleep in an armchair, and when some officers tried to wake him up, he had an idea he was aboard his own ship, as he ordered one of the officers of the U.S. Revenue Service belonging to another ship to go out of his cabin."[19]

Captain Hodgedon's first act consisted of moving the trial from the cutter *Rush* to the more spacious room 83 of the Appraiser's Building in San Francisco. The preliminaries began on 18 January 1896 with the introduction of documentary exhibits and, at 1:00 P.M. on 23 January, the trial commenced. Captain Healy sat at a long table in front of the room and reportedly exhibited nervousness, when the board entered the room. The trial would be worthy of the pen of Herman Wouk.[20]

The prosecuting officer read the six charges. They included conduct unbecoming an officer and that, on specified occasions, Healy had been intoxicated while on duty in command of the *Bear*, putting at hazard its safety and the accomplishment of its mission. The most serious charge, of course, was hazarding the safety of his vessel. Conviction on such a charge, even today, would result in at least immediate loss of command, if not dismissal from the service. Captain Healy's attorney entered his plea of "Not Guilty" on all accounts. Attorney Henley would later tell the court-martial that this was a "melancholy case, as melancholy as any recorded in the naval or military annals of our country." He feared that conviction would erase the name of Captain Healy from history. Henley proved prophetic.[21]

The prosecution called its first witness. Lieutenant Jones described and provided details on the events aboard the HMS *Pheasant*, the altercation with Chief Engineer Broadbent, and the captain's fall from the dock. Henley's cross-examination revealed that Jones had made several critical and disparaging comments concerning his captain to the officers of the cutter and within hearing of the enlisted men. Jones denied conspiring against his commanding officer but did admit to forming "a common interest early in the cruise" with other officers, and their agreement "to observe incidents that might form a basis on which to initiate some form of official action" against Healy.[22] Interestingly enough, Harvey Nice, in whose home Captain Healy had recuperated after his fall, swore that his guest had not been drunk during his stay. The *Bear*'s surgeon, Dr. Thomas Bodkin, despite pointed cross-examination, steadfastly maintained that the only liquor he knew of Healy's having consumed during the 1895 cruise was the medicinal brandy mixed with quinine prescribed by himself for a severe cold. Later, however, Dr. Bodkin noted that "one drink of any high liquid shows very perceptively on Captain Healy."[23]

Lieutenant Daniels covered the same ground as Jones but refused to admit making derogatory remarks about Healy and denied conspiring against him. Daniels also denied that "his testimony was motivated by any personal malice" toward his captain. Nine officers testified regarding Healy's alleged misbehavior aboard the British warship. When Chief Engineer Broadbent took the stand, however, he testified to having "no recollection whatever of the incident." Later, even a direct order from Assistant Secretary Hamlin to tell all he knew of Healy's drinking failed to shake Broadbent's testimony.[24]

Captain Hooper testified several times during the trial, always attempting to cast Healy in the best light. His responses show that nicely worded evasion is not a modern invention. Here, for example, is his response to a question about the Arctic legend's reputation for insobriety: "That I hardly know, some claim he drinks a good deal, and others claim he does not. I do not know exactly what would constitute a reputation. In the manner of his reputation as a sailor, that is universal." Healy, Hooper continued, "was always considered a strict if not severe commanding officer" who treated his junior officers "always good until this year," when "complaints" began surfacing.

Hooper, in response to a question requesting his opinion of Healy's qualifications as an officer, as well as his diligence, good judgment, courage, and sobriety, responded: "Healy did not lack in any of them, except possibly in sobriety. . . . Captain Healy has occasionally taken a drink—perhaps too much—in days past, ever since I have known him, and at times which he ought not to have done it. Otherwise he is an exceptionally good officer, an able, intelligent, bright, skillful officer." When asked if he had advised Captain Healy to plead guilty to the charges, Captain Hooper said, "As I have stated before, and it is no secret, my advice to him was to acknowledge the fact that he was under the influence those three days in Unalaska."

Capt. D. F. Tozier, of the cutter *Grant,* despite his observations at the time of the captain's fall into the harbor, also equivocated. Was Healy an efficient officer, a strict disciplinarian, abusive to subordinates, and so forth? The *Grant*'s captain explained that Healy was "strict, and perhaps annoying. I cannot explain myself any better than that. He is a hard man to sail with. They [the junior officers] dread to go near him. . . . I have heard a great many complaints of his abusive treatment of officers, and that he would frequently send them to the crow's nest to punish them." At times, Captain Tozier related, Healy would be on deck continuously for seventy-two hours or more at a time: "He works his officers hard, but works hard himself."

The transcripts of the court-martial stored in the National Archives reveal an interesting schism between the young officers of the *Bear* and the grizzled warrant officers and enlisted men. To a man, the warrants and enlisted men denied ever seeing their captain in an intoxicated condition or, for that matter, doing anything wrong. The following, for example, took place when the prosecutor attempted to examine the incident with the Japanese wardroom attendants. Unfortunately for Reynolds, F. Sumii was listed as a "witness for the prosecution":

"Did Captain Healy strike, kick, or ill-treat you, early in the morning of the 7th of June last?"

"I have no remembrance of that. . . ."

"Did Captain Healy use any profane language to you?"

"I have no remembrance of it."

"Did not Captain Healy say to you, 'You damned son-of-a-bitch, get up!' or words to that effect?"

"He did not say that."

Then Henley asked Sumii: "Did Captain Healy treat you kindly always?"

"Captain Healy was very kind to me. And besides, he asked Mr. Hamilton to teach English to me. For that reason, I think the Captain was very kind to me."

The transcript shows that Reynolds gave "notice that [he desired] at a future time to impeach the testimony of this witness as being directly contrary to what he [had told him] on preliminary examination."

The other cabin attendant, T. Ohno, also denied being "struck or illtreated by any officer" of the *Bear*.

William F. Quintall, a quartermaster, when asked if Captain Healy had "been habitually kind and good to his men and officers," replied, "Yes, sir, he has been pretty good, sir." He also denied Healy had placed the ship in danger.

Frederick Arnold, an ordinary seaman, said, "I have always seen him sober since I have been in the ship. . . ."

Lieutenant Buhner, after relentless prodding by Reynolds, reluctantly admitted changing course off the Shumagin Islands without authority, because his captain "had been drinking"; he also conceded that he had confiscated the alcohol in Healy's cabin. The executive officer steadfastly maintained, however, that at no time was Healy so drunk that he could not understand what he was doing. When questioned about Healy's treatment of his officers, Buhner replied that the "Captain is strict, but he is just." As in any ship, he had heard "a lot of wardroom carping and complaining," but he had "just learned to ignore it." Reynolds became so frustrated with Buhner's loyalty to his captain that he resorted to an unprecedented action.

The prosecutor fired off a telegram to Assistant Secretary Hamlin requesting that Hamlin order Buhner to tell the truth about Healy's drinking. Hamlin replied the next day, directly ordering Buhner to "[g]ive [his] testimony without reservation or concealment."[25]

In his next appearance before the court-martial board, the executive officer posed an indignant question about the telegram. "This is an insult," he stated, for "it touches upon my integrity. I demand to know of this honorable body, if it has been in correspondence with the Treasury Department concerning my testimony." Reynolds readily admitted sending a message to Washington after becoming convinced that Buhner had not been forthcoming in his answers.

The San Francisco newspapers jumped on this latest revelation as another example of the department's hostile attitude toward Captain Healy. The newspapers of the Bay area kept their readers fully informed of each day's events. Hamlin "will probably pass finally upon Captain Healy's case," blasted the *San Francisco Chronicle*, and the "chances for the Captain's reinstatement in the service are considered to be very poor." The paper's Washington, D.C., correspondent also reported an unnamed official source at the Treasury Department as saying that Buhner "and one or two others are so anxious to shield Captain Healy that they are endangering their own reputations . . . and that is the reason Asst. Secy. Hamlin wired him as he did." Ominously, the department officially designated Capt. Francis Tuttle the new commanding officer of the *Bear*.[26]

One historian, Gerald O. Williams, finds much in Hamlin's actions. Hamlin, according to Williams, had the trial delayed so that Dr. Benjamin Sharp, a Philadelphia scientist who had accompanied the *Bear* for part of the 1895 cruise, could come to San Francisco to testify against Captain Healy. Under cross-examination the doctor, who has been described as "a supercilious young man,"[27] told of his dislike for the captain who, citing a departmental regulation, had forbidden him to trade with the Eskimos for artifacts or specimens that he had hoped to acquire for the Philadelphia Museum. Sharp did, however, admit that Healy had treated him courteously and had once taken the *Bear* out of its way so the scientist could collect specimens.[28]

Once Reynolds announced that the prosecution had rested, attorney Henley began presenting the defense's case, calling crewmen, whalers, and so forth. All spoke favorably of Healy. Captain Hooper returned to the stand once again to praise Healy's skills. During cross-examination, Reynolds again asked about Healy's sobriety. In his hands, the prosecuting officer had copies of the letters Hooper had written from Unalaska to Captain-Commandant Shoemaker giving details regarding Healy's drinking and his being drunk on duty. Once alerted by an unidentified member of the court-martial board to the existence of these letters, Hamlin not only ordered Captain-Commandant Shoemaker to send copies to Reynolds but also forbade him from warning Captain Hooper. The captain-commandant, however, ignored his superior and wrote to Hooper. Thus, forewarned, attorney Henley rose to object when Hooper's testimony was in jeopardy of being impeached. "We do not contest the issue of Captain Healy's having been intoxicated during that period," he said, before claiming this line of questioning was "improper." To Reynolds's question "You are conceding this issue then?" Henley simply stated, "Yes." Captain Hooper then stepped down without answering.[29]

Capt. Michael A. Healy now took the stand to defend his actions and professional career. With his intoxication at Unalaska already conceded, he needed to challenge only the allegations of mistreating his officers and the more serious charge of endangering his vessel.

"I play no favorites," Captain Healy testified. "I go up there to do my duty and to do right as far as I can, and I expect every officer to do the same. I seldom speak to an officer roughly, unless it is the third time I have to speak. I want to say, though, that when I am in charge of a vessel, I think I always command. I think that I am put there to command, and I do command, and I take all the responsibility and all the risks, and the hardships that my officers would call upon me to take. I do not steer by any man's compass but my own. I do not phrase my words with an 'if you please.' I say 'set the mainsail' or whatever the order may be."

During cross-examination, Reynolds asked Captain Healy only two questions: "Do you always treat your officers justly?"

"Yes."

"Then why are there so many complaints of unjust treatment?"

"I cannot account for it all, I think that I have been too good to them."

In his summation, Henley pleaded with the court-martial board to give the greatest credence to the testimony of the enlisted men, for most had sailed with Captain Healy for more than ten years. The testimony against him, on the other hand, came from junior officers who were personally antagonistic toward the captain because he subjected them to the tough discipline necessitated by the dangerous conditions of the Arctic frontier. In closing, attorney Henley elaborated upon Captain Healy's professional qualifications, strongly suggesting "that no other officer would be capable of replacing him as captain of the BEAR."

Lieutenant Reynolds in his summation to the board brushed off the warrant and enlisted men's statements by remarking that the "testimony of these men is avowedly and unmistakably hostile towards the officers who have complained of Captain Healy's conduct." He went on to say that "the officers who have testified have no motive to deceive, each may have jeopardized his own future career by coming forward as witnesses against their commanding officer." Reynolds did not mention Surgeon Bodkin's echoing testimony or that of Capt. Horatio D. Smith, commanding the cutter *Perry*, who had not only described Captain Healy as "one of the best navigators in the service and most competent commander in the Bering Sea patrol" but who had also denied ever seeing the Arctic pilot drunk on duty, having observed merely an occasional social drink.

The prosecuting officer met the formidable task of dealing head on with Healy's reputation as a great Arctic navigator. Healy possessed excellent professional abilities when sober and "a record of which all are proud," Reynolds admitted, but he wondered, "Might not others have done as well?" As for the argument that Healy could not be replaced, the lieutenant stated: "I am not prepared to accept [that statement.]" Reynolds further hammered at this point.

"Quick judgment should be possessed by those who follow the sea," he reminded the board members. "A brain clouded by alcohol cannot work rapidly, and is incapable of grasping a situation of peril."

The court-martial board adjourned to consider the verdict, which was announced on 5 March 1896. Capt. Michael A. Healy, who at one time had been considered the most popular man in the far north, found himself guilty of all the charges and specifications, and it was recommended that he "be dismissed from the Service." The final action now rested in the hands of Secretary Carlisle. Hamlin confided to his diary that "[s]trenuous efforts were made by friends" of Healy. "Congressmen, Senators, and hundreds of others, among whom was Bishop Healy of Portland, Maine, a brother of Captain Healy, all joined in begging such a reversal."[30] The *San Francisco Call* reported that its sources in Washington, D.C., had confirmed that Hamlin had recommended Healy's dismissal. "There was so much perjury on both sides," confided a board member after the court-martial, "that much of the testimony had to be disregarded in its entirety."[31] On 8 June 1896 the secretary of the treasury finally made his decision known. He ordered "That Captain Michael A. Healy be dropped to the foot of the list of Captains of the Revenue Cutter Service, and that he retain that place hereafter, that he be suspended from rank and command for a term of four years, and that he be publicly reprimanded by reading this order on board all vessels of the Revenue Cutter Service, by the commanding officer of each, at a muster of the commissioned officers, and admonished that if again found guilty of the excessive use of intoxicants during the term of his sentence or hereafter, whether afloat or on shore, he will be summarily dismissed from the service."

Why Secretary Carlisle did not dismiss the revenue captain remains another of the many unanswered questions in the story of Michael A. Healy. All Carlisle had to do was rubber stamp the board's findings, and the blame would have fallen upon some of the senior officers of the Revenue Cutter Service.

The story of Michael A. Healy is one in which things are never as they seem on the surface. There continues today among those few who know the story a debate whether he drank as much as the junior officers claimed and whether he actually put the *Bear* in danger. The evidence that Healy drank is too strong to deny, and, in fact, as time passed, his predilection for alcohol finally overtook him.

The issue of Captain Healy's racial background plays an important part in his story. Historian Gary O. Williams, one the few researchers into Healy's life, feels that, especially on the East Coast, people must have known of the captain's race because of the prominence of his brothers. That may be why Healy never left the West Coast. In the transcripts of the trial in the National Archives there is a reference to an officer calling Healy an "Irish Catholic son of a bitch." With the hostile environment on the *Bear,* if anyone had known of their captain's ancestry there is little doubt that the fact would have been made very clear to the press. Prof. James M. O'Toole asks whether, if someone had known of Healy's race, he would not have used a word that would "have been more hurtful and insulting." In the light of the behavior of the officers on the *Bear* in 1896, Professor O'Toole's further observation should be pondered by all those who study the life of Capt. Michael A. Healy: "People are most truthful and least calculating when they are calling other people names. The absence of racial insult . . . indicates the success with which Captain Healy was able to define himself as white rather than black."[32]

What is important here is that Healy masked his African-American heritage, and for good reason: There is no record of a black commanding any federal ship until at least World War II, and then only briefly. Healy knew that if his background came to light he would lose everything. How this may have worked on his mind is in the realm of the psychologist, but surely it must be offered up as a contributing factor in his drinking problem.[33]

Captain Healy's fate was sealed in 1870. Strangely enough, this came about when someone tried to improve a poor practice. As previously mentioned, prior to 1870 the U.S. Revenue Cutter Service recruited its officers from the merchant marine. The collectors of customs were the ones who made these appointments, and, since the collectors changed each time political power in Washington changed, revenue officers' posts depended upon politics. Then, a lawyer and former politician from Maine who had become a long-time Treasury Department employee, Sumner Increase Kimball, took over the reins of the service. Kimball felt that politics had no place in the service, and he changed the method of appointing new officers. He created a

School of Instruction with a cadet system that eventually evolved into today's U.S. Coast Guard Academy. Thenceforth, younger officers learned the ways of the sea at school instead of through a long apprenticeship. The school also provided a means for the service's future commanders to keep pace with the rapid changes in technology. The move away from political appointments, especially by the collectors of customs, and the fielding of well-educated officers who knew the current technology, were significant benefits of the School of Instruction.

There was, however, another and more subtle side to the effects of this embryo service academy. The young officers graduating from the School of Instruction, like those who graduated from Annapolis and West Point, considered themselves to be officers and gentlemen, and certainly superior to those old-time officers who had come up through the ranks. The service academies have "long been accused of being . . . aristocratic institution[s], which churned out an elitist and privileged class of officers for a nation dedicated to equality, democracy and the common man."[34]

Complicating the situation even further, the service did not have a retirement system. The school-trained and highly ambitious young officers viewed Captain Healy and the other senior officers as the old guard, backward men lacking in the social graces. More important, these uncouth elderly officers hung tenaciously to their positions and ranks, thereby blocking young officers from promotions they felt they richly deserved. Many officers, including junior officers who had not attended the School of Instruction, developed as a result an "us against them" mentality. In retrospect, it is not at all surprising that the younger officers aboard the *Bear* in 1895—Lieutenants Daniels, Emery, and White—signed the charges against Healy. As the tenth most senior captain in the service, the *Bear*'s skipper held up the promotions of those below him and most clearly personified what these new officers so hated about the old guard. Paul H. Johnson, former librarian at the U.S. Coast Guard Academy and one who has studied Healy, feels that if there had been a retirement system in effect there would never have been a trial in San Francisco. Events following the trial seem to confirm Johnson's observation.[35]

Was Captain Healy guilty? Yes—but guilty only of living at a time of great changes in the social mores of this nation, coupled with large changes at sea; he was guilty of not recognizing these changes and adapting to them. Captain Healy is not to be singled out: It is equally doubtful that the U.S. Revenue Cutter Service saw these changes; nor did other senior officers. It was, however, Captain Healy's fate to be the one who was unlucky enough to be in command of the cutter where all the forces of change and social problems were brought together. Added to the already volatile situation, the nature of life in the tight, gritty atmosphere of a small cutter on a long patrol added the necessary spark to cause the explosion that led to a court-martial. Anyone, however, who thought the controversy over the trial of Captain Healy finished was a poor judge of history.

Four years after Healy's court-martial, his sentence served, events again propelled the captain into controversy. Capt. W. C. Coulson, commanding the cutter *McCulloch,* sent an urgent message to headquarters: "Wife very ill; Dr. says I should not leave her. Will Department assign temporary Commander *McCulloch* until return Seattle, last [of] June and grant me temporary leave?" If a screen writer penned a script for a Hollywood rendition of Healy's life, this would be the perfect means of bringing back the captain and restoring his name. In fact, the *McCulloch* sailed from San Francisco on 28 May 1900 with Capt. Michael A. Healy in command.[36]

All seemed to go well. The primary mission of the *McCulloch* that year was to help reprovision the cutter *Nunivak,* which patrolled the Yukon River. On 25 June, Captain Healy brought the cutter to St. Michael. Dr. James Taylor White, the *McCulloch*'s surgeon, and four crewmen were then transferred to the other cutter. "[A]t the request of her husband," Captain Healy allowed Mrs. Ada P. French aboard the *McCulloch* "for passage to Seattle." On the night of 26 June, Healy shaped a course to Nome and after a brief stop, proceeded to Unalaska. The cutter departed for Seattle on 5 July.[37]

On 7 July, with the cutter in midocean, 1st Lt. P. W. Thompson, the executive officer, received an urgent summons from Mrs. French. He found her locked in her room and Captain Healy sitting outside her door. Mrs. French appealed to the lieutenant, "saying that the captain just threatened to take his life and that he was constantly calling her and she feared for her life."[38]

Lieutenant Thompson had officers call in the wardroom piped. To the assembled officers, he outlined what Mrs. French had told him: At five in the morning, Captain Healy had called out to her: "For Christ sake come out for my sake," and he had kept up his calling for at least an hour; he then asked "if [he] could be friends with [her]," but she replied that it was impossible. He continued for at least another hour until Mrs. French asked what he wanted. "I am going to kill myself right now," replied the captain. Following this episode, Mrs. French expressed a preference for staying on deck rather than "remaining in the cabin," and she was transferred to the wardroom.

Lieutenant Thompson later stated that Captain Healy was in "a state of intoxication." He called another meeting of the officers and discussed whether Healy should be relieved of command. The executive officer entered the following in the *McCulloch*'s log: "It was finally decided that as long as . . . [Healy] did nothing to jeopardize the safety of the vessel or her personnel, no drastic measures should be resorted to."

The next evening, 8 July, Captain Healy came on deck. He saw Mrs. French, turned to her, said, "Good-bye, Madame," put both of his legs over the rail, and prepared to leap into the sea. Second Asst. Eng. J. J. Bryan, who happened to be topside, managed to grab the captain and wrestled with him, calling for help. Bryan managed to subdue Healy, who was taken to his cabin. Thompson had officers call piped again, this time in the captain's cabin. Over a half-century before Herman Wouk's fictional *Caine Mutiny* appeared in bookstores, the executive officer of the cutter *McCulloch* took the highly unusual and seldom attempted act of removing a ship's captain while at sea. The executive officer later entered in the cutter's log that, in Healy's presence, he had decided that "Healy's mental condition, brought on by intemperance, was such to render him a desperate and dangerous man, that he was manifestly determined to take his own life, and that his further remaining in command would imperil the lives of those on board as well as jeopardize the safety of the vessel. . . . [For] these reasons, we the . . . commissioned officers of this vessel, for the best interests of all concerned, do hereby declare it necessary to relieve Capt. M. A. Healy RCS of the command of the Revenue Steamer *McCulloch* and to restrict him in confinement, under guard, until the Department is communicated with." At an all hands muster in the evening, the cutter's enlisted men officially learned of the situation and Lieutenant Thompson's assumption of command.

Two days after Lieutenant Thompson made his log entry about Captain Healy, the captain leaped from his bunk, raced past his unsuspecting guard, Seaman C. W. Strickham, and attempted to throw himself off the *McCulloch*'s stern. Strickham, although startled, moved fast enough to grab Healy before he could jump. Lieutenant Thompson then ordered Healy's door locked and the key kept by a guard. Half an hour later, Seaman Strickham yelled for an officer. He reported that "Captain Healy had gotten something from his pantry and hidden it under his bunk." A search revealed glass hidden at the foot of the captain's bunk. Thompson ordered a lattice be placed over the pantry door. Healy made two further attempts on his life that same day, one time slightly slashing his wrists.

On 12 July, only a day from Port Townsend, northwest of Seattle, Washington, Healy again attempted suicide, this time nearly succeeding. The captain had hidden a watch crystal with which he had slashed his left forearm, which "was bleeding profusely" when discovered. It took four large men to restrain Healy while his wound received attention.

When the *McCulloch* dropped anchor at Port Townsend, Lieutenant Thompson went ashore to arrange for Healy's transfer to the Marine Service Hospital. The lieutenant then took the cutter to Seattle and telegraphed headquarters about Healy's condition. A Seattle newspaper soon learned the story, and, under the headline "Revenue Cutter Commander a Raving Maniac," informed readers that there was "little hope that he will recover his reason." The *Seattle Post-Intelligencer,* however, wrote that the officers of the cutter "refused point blank to be interviewed concerning the insanity of Capt. Healy."[39]

At Port Townsend, Surg. C. H. Gardner of the Marine Hospital charged Healy with insanity. On 14 July a special session of the superior court of Jefferson County, the county in which Port Townsend is located, convened at the hospital to examine the charge. The physicians found that Healy had "had many attacks of insomnia, lasting a week or more" and caused by "mental worry" during the preceding four years of his exile. The doctors went on to report that Healy's "intemperate use of liquors, within the last two weeks," had caused his suicidal "mania."[40]

On 15 July, Healy was transferred to the Western Washington Hospital for the Insane at Fort Steilacoom. The *Seattle Post-Intelligencer* reported that although the captain's doctors "do not think there is any chance of the unfortunate man recovering his mind, his many friends here are hopeful that his derangement is only temporary, and that under the scientific treatment he will soon be well again." Interestingly enough, by September 1900, with the notation "recovered" on his medical chart, Captain Healy returned to his home in San Francisco and reported this fact to headquarters.[41]

Yet again, questions arise. According to the terms of Healy's 1896 court-martial, "if again found guilty of excessive use of intoxicants . . . , whether ashore or afloat, he will be summarily dismissed from the service." Instead the captain found himself on waiting orders for three months. None of the participants in the *McCulloch* affair ever journeyed to Washington to speak on the matter—even though Lieutenant Thompson offered to come to Washington—nor did anyone from the Treasury Department ask for an explanation. Historian Gary C. Stein, the only researcher to make an in-depth examination of the affair, makes the interesting observation that all of the "statements and all of the correspondence relating to this episode of Healy's career have been removed from the files of the Revenue-Cutter Service. The story of the affair can only be pieced together from the *McCulloch*'s log of the 1900 cruise and the brief abstracts of incoming correspondence in the letter books of the Revenue-Cutter Service."[42]

Amazingly enough, after the *McCulloch* affair, Captain Healy held several temporary commands in San Francisco and, even more interestingly, the service restored him to his original position on the captain's list on 11 January 1902. In the spring of the same year, he received command of the *Thetis* and again sailed northward. He commanded the same cutter in 1903 and was reprimanded "for using indecent language in the presence of his officers and crew."

By then, the U.S. Revenue Cutter Service had a retirement system, and "Hell Roaring Mike" was retired because of age. He died of heart failure in San Francisco less than a year later on 30 August 1904.[43]

Thus ended the life of one of the best Arctic navigators of the nineteenth century. He remains an enigma today, for unanswered questions still abound. Why was Healy not dismissed in 1900? Why are there no materials in the records of the service about the 1900 incident? Why was he restored to his original position on the captain's list?

Some tentative answers have been proposed: His brothers used political influence to restore the captain to his position on the list; his brothers used political influence to keep the 1900 incident hushed up; and, most interestingly, the U.S. Revenue Cutter Service knew that Healy was an African-American and wanted nothing messy to arise that might bring out this fact. There is not a whisper in any records of this period, however, to indicate that anyone in the service knew of his heritage. In fact, it was not until the late 1960s and early 1970s that Captain Healy's heritage became known in the U.S. Coast Guard. Political influence by his brothers may have had something to do with the 1896 trial, but Bishop Healy died in Portland in August 1900, and Father Patrick Healy spent much of the time thereafter putting his brother's affairs in order. Father Patrick, moreover, was very ill at this time, and he would die in 1910 in Washington, D.C.[44] Healy's life has spawned many questions, rumors, and stories. One of the best of the apocryphal stories deals with Healy's race and testifies as to how well he kept his background hidden. In the 1930s a Hollywood film production company wished to make a film about Healy's life and asked his daughter-in-law for permission to examine his four-volume diary. She, apparently reading it for the first time, learned that her husband's grandmother had been a slave and—in shock—destroyed it.[45]

There may be questions and controversy surrounding the revenue captain, but one fact remains: Capt. Michael A. Healy was one of this country's great Arctic navigators, an enigmatic man who still has not received the place in history he deserves. In 1998 the U.S. Coast Guard launched a new polar icebreaker. The name chosen for the cutter: Michael A. Healy. It seems fitting that the name of Michael A. Healy will again be seen in the waters of the far north.[46]

# Epilogue

By 1914 the routines and duties of the U.S. Revenue Cutter Service were well established. When the service joined with the U.S. Life-Saving Service and the U.S. Coast Guard came into being, the work continued as before, the only difference being the name of the organization. In 1918, for example, the *Unalga* became the first cutter to visit the Bristol Bay region of Alaska following the mass deaths caused by the great influenza epidemic. U.S. Coast Guardsmen went ashore, even in the face of possible death, to help villagers.[1]

The only major break in patrol routine came during World War II. Robert Erwin Johnson has detailed the work of the cutter *Haida* from July 1941 to March of 1943. Prior to Pearl Harbor, Johnson's description of his first Bering Sea Patrol is remarkably similar to those of the U.S. Revenue Cutter Service years. For example, the *Haida*'s small boat put ashore at Port Clarence to obtain fresh water, something that is in the logs of the *Bear* and other earlier cutters. Once the conflict began, the cutter found herself as a convoy escort in the far north. After hostilities ended, the cutters took up where they had left off.[2]

The Judicial Cruises, described in chapter 3, continued into the early 1950s. The junior author of this book sailed in the cutter *Northwind* (WAGB-282) on the Bering Sea Patrols and Arctic Operations of 1961 and 1962. The cutter visited villages from the Aleutian Islands to as far north as Point Barrow. At each settlement, a U.S. Public Health doctor and dentist as well as medical technicians from the cutter went ashore. At one point during the Bering Sea Patrol, U.S. Coast Guardsmen assisted a scientist in conducting oceanographic operations, and then the *Northwind* returned to visiting villages. Arctic Operations consisted largely of scientific undertakings.

Vice Adm. Joseph E. Stika, recalling in 1975 his experiences on the Bering Sea Patrol of 1914, spoke of going ashore to shoot caribou. In 1962 some crew members of the *Northwind* also went hunting. Admiral Stika remarked about the poor quality of the food during the 1914 patrol and, in 1962, U.S. Coast Guardsmen could be heard mumbling about the "chow."[3] The only difference between the patrols of the nineteenth and early twentieth centuries and those of the 1960s is that the equipment and living conditions improved greatly, although many on the *Northwind* have said that living aboard a cutter built during World War II could hardly be called comfortable. Technology, however, eventually caught up with the cutters sailing the Bering Sea. Many villages could now be reached much more quickly by small, light aircraft, and communications of course made quantum leaps forward. The U.S. Coast Guard officially announced the end of the Bering Sea Patrol on 4 September 1964. The term "Bering Sea Patrol," according to the rationale given, was "not sufficiently descriptive of the modern Patrol's many law enforcement and conservation tasks." Accordingly, the service announced a new name—the Alaska Patrol. This, in effect, put an official end to ninety-seven years of work.[4] Cutters still make trips to the Bering Sea, but most of the work is now centered on fishery enforcement and SAR in connection with fishing vessels.

The work of all the cuttermen in the Bering Sea and Arctic Ocean and, indeed, in all of Alaska, has been largely forgotten by historians and those who chronicle the maritime world. As pointed out elsewhere, the U.S. Coast Guard itself has done very little to perpetuate the memory of the Bering Sea Patrol. To be sure, there have been attempts at shedding some light upon the patrol. For example, the U.S. Coast Guard Cutter *Storis* (WMEC-38), a fifty-five-year Arctic veteran of both Greenland and Alaska, has performed community outreach with outlying Alaskan villages in the spirit of the Bering Sea Patrol. In 1995, for example, the *Storis* visited the Pribilof Islands, bringing with her a dentist, an eye doctor, and two chaplains. While the people of St. Paul were receiving medical and spiritual assistance, crew members helped in community rebuilding, cleaning, and painting.[5]

In the 1980s, Native Pride of Unalaska restored the graves of cuttermen, including the grave of Seaman C. C. Mauethrop. But most of these efforts, while commendable, remain strictly local, or at least within the Seventeenth

Coast Guard District (Alaska), not being sponsored more widely by the service. The U.S. Coast Guard last published a history of the Bering Sea Patrol in 1942, unfortunately as an internal publication.[6] All of this helps to explain why the people who sailed the Bering Sea and contributed so much to Alaskan and maritime history have been forgotten.

Perhaps the old cuttermen would prefer to be remembered only among sailors. Admiral Stika, when asked if he felt that duty on the Bering Sea Patrol was special, replied that "everybody was sort of proud of having gone through Bering Sea Patrol. . . . We wanted to be as good as the next fellow, as experienced as the rest of them."[7] There seemed to be pride in being a sailor in those northern waters. Perhaps a bit of doggerel best sums up the feelings of the cuttermen, and is as good a way as any to remember them:

*Full many a sailor points with pride*
*To cruises o'er the ocean wide;*
*But they cannot compare to me,*
*For I have sailed the Bering Sea.*

*What though you've weathered the fiercest gales,*
*And every ocean you have sailed;*
*You cannot salty sailor be,*
*Until you've sailed the Bering Sea.*[8]

# Notes

**CHAPTER 1. ALASKA AND THE U.S. REVENUE CUTTER SERVICE**

1. Gwen L. Killey, "Opening the Door to Alaska: The Cruises of the Revenue Cutter *Thomas Corwin*," *Naval History Magazine,* 2, no. 4 (fall 1988): 24; Stephen H. Evans, *The United States Coast Guard, 1790–1915: A Definitive History (With a Postscript, 1915–1950)* (Annapolis, Md.: Naval Institute Press, 1949), 112.

2. William R. Hunt, *Arctic Passage: The Turbulent History of the Land and People of the Bering Sea* (New York: Charles Scribner's Sons, 1975), 340.

3. Quoted in Evans, *U.S. Coast Guard,* 121.

4. The original ten boats—small, speedy, and highly maneuverable sailing vessels—were called cutters, a term adopted from the British. The U.S. Revenue Cutter Service continued using this name even after its craft could no longer technically be called cutters, as does the U.S. Coast Guard (USCG) today.

5. Capt.-Comdt. Horatio Davis Smith, U.S. Revenue Cutter Service (USRCS), *Early History of the United States Revenue Marine Service (or United States Revenue Cutter Service, 1790–1849.* Edited by Rear Admiral Elliot Snow, U.S. Navy (USN) Retired (Washington, D.C.: Naval Historical Foundation, 1932), 2. The fact that the U.S. Navy was not formed until 1798 makes the U.S. Coast Guard, a direct descendant of the U.S. Revenue Cutter Service, the oldest continuous federal seagoing service of the United States.

6. Ibid., 2, 9.

7. The best single study of the U.S. Coast Guard's antecedents is Evans, *U.S. Coast Guard.* The more detailed, lengthier, and documented histories by Irving H. King, *George Washington's Coast Guard: Origins of the U.S. Revenue Cutter Service, 1789–1801* (Annapolis, Md.: Naval Institute Press, 1978), and his *Coast Guard*

*under Sail: The Revenue Cutter Service, 1789–1865* (Annapolis, Md.: Naval Institute Press, 1989), contain valuable information.

8. Dennis L. Noble, *Gulf Coast and Western Rivers: A Brief History of U.S. Coast Guard Operations* (Washington, D.C.: U.S. Coast Guard Headquarters, 1989), 5.

9. The U.S. Revenue Cutter Service, U.S. Lighthouse Service (USLHS) and lifesaving stations were all within the Treasury Department until 1903, when the USLHS was transferred to the Department of Commerce and Labor.

10. A heated debate still rages today over the invention of the lifecar, or surfcar. One side claims that Joseph Francis should have credit for the invention. For a discussion on the device and the debate, see Robert F. Bennett, *Surfboats, Rockets, and Carronades* (Washington, D.C.: GPO, 1976), 46–53; and Dennis L. Noble, *That Others Might Live: The U.S. Life-Saving Service, 1878–1915* (Annapolis, Md.: U.S. Naval Institute Press, 1994), 113–17.

11. Evans, *U.S. Coast Guard*, 61.

12. Unless otherwise noted, all material on the Yakima Indian War is found in Truman R. Strobridge and Dennis L. Noble, "Cuttermen and Indians: Early Coast Guardsmen and the Yakima Indian War," *United States Coast Guard Academy Alumni Association Bulletin* 45, no. 2 (March/April 1983): 30–37.

13. *Army and Navy Journal*, 26 November 1864, 218.

14. Florence Kern, *The United States Revenue Cutters in the Civil War* (Washington, D.C.: GPO, 1988), 3–5.

15. James Phinney Baxter III, *The Introduction of the Ironclad Warship* (Cambridge: Harvard University Press, 1933), 217.

16. U.S. Navy Department, *Official Records of the Union and Confederate Navies in the War of the Rebellion*, series I, vol. 7 (Washington, D.C.: GPO, 1898), 369.

17. For an excellent account of the revenue steamer *Shubrick*'s role as the flagship of the expedition and later existence as a lighthouse tender, see Richard D. White, "Saga of the Side-Wheel Steamer *Shubrick:* Pioneer Lighthouse Tender of the Pacific Coast," *The American Neptune* 36 (spring 1976): 45–53.

18. James Alton James, *The First Scientific Exploration of Russian America and the Purchase of Alaska* (Evanston, Ill., and Chicago: Northwestern University, 1942), 45, 137–38.

19. Historical Section, Public Information Division, USCG Headquarters, *The Coast Guard at War: Alaska* (Washington, D.C.: USCG Headquarters, 15 February 1946), 19.

20. Evans, *U.S. Coast Guard*, 90–96.

21. U.S. Revenue Cutter Service, *The United States Revenue Cutter Service in the War with Spain, 1898* (Washington, D.C.: GPO, 1899).

22. Evans, *U.S. Coast Guard*, 161. See also Robert Erwin Johnson, *Guardians of the Sea: History of the United States Coast Guard, 1915 to the Present* (Annapolis, Md.: Naval Institute Press, 1987), 18–31; and Noble, *That Others Might Live*, 147–56.

23. Gerald O. Williams, *The Bering Sea Dispute: A Monograph on the Maritime History of Alaska* (Eugene, Ore.: Alaska Maritime Publications, 1984), 7.

24. Samuel Flagg Bemis, *A Diplomatic History of the United States* (New York: Holt, Rinehart and Winston, 1967), 413.

25. Fredericka Martin, *The Hunting of the Silver Fleece* (New York: Greenberg, 1946), 30.

26. Jeanne Van Nostrand, "The Seals Are About Gone," *American Heritage* (June 1963): 12–14.

27. Ibid., 14, 16.

28. Williams, *Bering Sea Dispute*, 7–10.

29. A hand-written and undated history of the U.S. Revenue Cutter Service on stationery of the U.S. Treasury Department, 3-4, in the Alaska File of the Revenue-Cutter Service, 1867–1914, Microcopy No. M641, Microfilm Roll 19, Records of the U.S. Coast Guard, Record Group (RG26), National Archives and Records Administration (NARA). The history seems to be from the U.S. Revenue Cutter Service to the State Department.

30. Ibid., 6.

31. Table entitled "Seizures by Vessels of the Revenue Cutter Service in Bering Sea—Years 1884–1911." Ibid., n.p.

32. Charles S. Campbell, Jr., "The Anglo-American Crisis in the Bering Sea, 1890–1891," *Mississippi Valley Historical Review* 47 (December 1961): 393–94. For a detailed study of the fur seal controversy, see James Thomas Gay, *American Fur Seal Diplomacy: The Alaskan Fur Seal Controversy* (New York: Peter Lang, 1987).

33. Ibid., 396–97.

34. Ibid., 404–5.

35. Unless otherwise noted, all material on negotiations is from ibid., 405–14.

36. Van Nostrand, "The Seals Are About Gone," 78.

37. Quoted in ibid., 79.

38. Ibid., 80.

CHAPTER 2. CUTTERMEN OF THE NORTH

1. Smith, *Early History of the U.S. Revenue Marine Service*, 36.

2. Commissions Revenue Cutter Service 1812–1844, RG26, NARA; A. J. Gordon Kane to E. P. Bertholf, 27 November 1916, File "020 1910–1922 General," RG26, NARA; Smith, *Early History of U.S. Revenue Marine Service*, 35–37; Thomas H. S. Hammersly, *General Register of the United States Navy and Marine Corps for One Hundred Years (1782–1882)* (Washington, D.C.: GPO, 1882), 362.

3. U.S. Coast Guard, *Record of Movements: Vessels of the United States Coast Guard, 1790–December 31, 1933,* 2 vols. (Washington, D.C.: U.S. Coast Guard, [1935?]), 507.

4. Commissions Revenue Cutters 1812–1844, RG26, NARA.

5. "Statement of Captain William A. Howard's History in the USRC Service, 1829–1870," n.d., William A. Howard file, RG26, NARA. Some of the accusations in this anonymous statement, when checked against the official records, proved to be patently false; others are echoed in "Charges against Revenue Cutter Officers," n.d., Captain Alex V. Frazer file, RG26, NARA. Any one of Howard's fellow officers, however, might well have had enough professional jealousy to destroy his reputation. Conversation, Dennis L. Noble and Teresa F. Matchette, National Archives, 15 June 1979; Walter C. Capron, *The U.S. Coast Guard* (New York: Franklin Watts, 1965), 14.

6. USCG, *Record of Movements,* 513; K. Jack Bauer, *Surfboats and Horse Marines: U.S. Naval Operations in the Mexican War, 1846–1848* (Annapolis, Md.: Naval Institute Press, 1969), 23–25.

7. A. J. Gordon Kane to E. P. Bertholf, 27 November 1916, File "020 1910–1922 General," RG26, NARA. For mention of Howard in official dispatches, see U.S. Navy Department, *Index to U.S. War of the Rebellion: A Compilation of the Official Records of the Union and Confederate Armies,* 128 vols. (Washington, D.C.: GPO, 1880–1901).

8. "Howard's History," RG26, NARA.

9. The honor of being the first cutter to ply Alaskan waters belongs to the *Shubrick.* Commanded by Charles M. Scammon, U.S. Revenue Cutter Service, this cutter acted as the flagship for the six-vessel Western Union expedition in 1865 to lay a telegraph cable to Siberia. See Evans, *U.S. Coast Guard,* 106–7; Truman R. Strobridge, "Early Lake Captains, Revenue Cutters, and Politics," *Inland Seas: Quarterly Journal of the Great Lakes Historical Society* 29 (1973): 247; A. J. Gordon Kane to E. P. Bertholf, 27 November 1916, File "020 1910–1920 General," RG26, NARA.

10. "Scrapbook, U.S. Revenue Cutter Service, Alaska," n.d., p. 95, RG26, NARA; see the annual U.S. Revenue Cutter Service registers of officers and vessels of the service (Washington, D.C.: GPO, 1886–1901); Evans, *U.S. Coast Guard,* 115–17.

11. Robley D. Evans, *A Sailor's Log: Recollections of Forty Years of Naval Life* (New York: Appleton, 1901), 327, 328.

12. U.S. Revenue Cutter Service, *The United States Revenue Cutter Service in the War with Spain, 1898,* 13; Truman R. Strobridge and Dennis L. Noble, "North in the Spring, South in the Fall," *Alaska Journal* 8 (1976): 61; U.S. Revenue Cutter Service, *Register of Officers and Vessels . . . July 1, 1900* (Washington, D.C.: GPO, 1900), 6–7; Register of U.S. Revenue Cutter Service Officers, 1790–1914 (service records), vol. 7: 17, 51, RG26, NARA.

13. Irving Crump, *Our United States Coast Guard Academy* (New York: Dodd, Mead, 1961), 102; Evans, *U.S. Coast Guard,* 94–95.

14. John F. Murphy, "Cutter Captain: The Life and Times of John C. Cantwell," (Ph.D. dissertation, University of Connecticut, 1968), 1, 6–8; Register of USRCS Officers, 1790–1914 (service records), vol. 3: 220, RG26, NARA.

15. Murphy, "Cutter Captain," 12.

16. Ibid., 76.

17. Ibid., 77.

18. Ibid., 103–4.

19. Ibid., 201–3; Dennis L. Noble, *Historical Register U.S. Revenue Cutter Service Officers: 1790–1914* (Washington, D.C.: U.S. Coast Guard, 1990), 10; Register of USRCS Officers, 1790–1914 (service records), vol. 6: 68. For a complete description of the *Nunivak*'s work, see 1st Lt. J. C. Cantwell, *Report of the Operations of the U.S. Revenue Steamer "Nunivak" on the Yukon River Station, Alaska, 1899–1901* (Washington, D.C.: GPO, 1902).

20. J. W. White to F. A. Nelson, Collector of Customs, Port Townsend, WT, Letter Book A, RG26, NARA.

21. Completed questionnaire of F. S. Sandel, 1977, in author's files. Unless otherwise noted, this document is the source for the following biographical information on Sandel and the quoted statements about the everyday life of the enlisted men on the U.S. Revenue Cutter Service's Bering Sea Patrol.

22. J. Brown to H. D. Smith, 5 July 1896, M641, Roll 6, RG26, NARA.

23. Quoted in John Muir, *The Cruise of the* Corwin: *Journal of the Arctic Expedition of 1881 in Search of DeLong and the Jeannette* (Boston: Houghton Mifflin Company, 1917), xxiv.

24. Aled Eames, Lewis Lloyd, Bryn Parry, eds., *Letters from America: Captain David Evans of Talsarnau, 1817–1895* (Denbigh, Wales: Gwynedd Archives, 1975), 67–68.

CHAPTER 3. "HELL ROARING MIKE"

1. This ubiquitous quotation probably first appeared in Evans, *U. S. Coast Guard*, 121.

2. John Bockstoce, "The Arctic Whaling Disaster of 1897," *Prologue: The Journal of the National Archives* (Spring 1977): 29.

3. Capt. M. A. Healy, *Report of the Cruise of the Revenue Marine Steamer* Corwin *in the Arctic Ocean in the Year 1884* (Washington, D.C.: GPO, 1889), 22–23.

4. Register of USRCS Officers, 1790–1914 (service records), vol. 2: 82–123, RG26, NARA.

5. As of 1998, no one has published a biography of Healy. Gerald O. Williams's voluminous "Michael J. [*sic*] Healy and the Alaska Maritime Frontier, 1880–1902," an unpublished master's thesis (University of Oregon, 1987) is the only in-depth scholarly work done on the man.

6. Albert J. Foley, *Bishop Healy: Beloved Outcaste* (New York: Farrar, Straus and Young, 1954), 2–8.

7. Ibid., 11–16.

8. Williams, "Michael Healy," 33–37.

9. Ibid., 36–38.

10. Ibid., 38, 40–43; M. Healy to Capt. Stephen Cornell, USN, 18 January 1865, Applicant File, RG26, NARA.

11. Williams, "Michael Healy," 43–44.

12. Ibid., 111.

13. Ibid., 88–89.

14. "Taking its name from Kootznahoo, a place near the Sitka garrison where it was manufactured in quantities, the native liquor 'kootzenoo,' or 'hoochenoo' (hence 'hootch')." Evans, *U.S. Coast Guard,* 107.

15. Capt. M. A. Healy to Secretary of the Treasury (SECTREAS), 29 June 1892, Alaska File, Letters (Ltrs.) Received by the U.S. Revenue Cutter Service (USRCS), 1869–1910, RG26, NARA.

16. Williams, "Michael Healy," 267.

17. Capt. M. A. Healy to SECTREAS, 7 October 1893, Alaska File, Ltrs. Received by the USRCS, 1869–1910, RG26, NARA.

18. U.S. Congress, "Joint Resolution Commending Captain Michael A. Healy, U.S. Revenue Marine," H.R. 2507, 48th Cong., 2d Sess., 19 January 1885; *San Francisco Chronicle,* 7 September 1888, and 14 December 1889; "Memorial to Secretary of the Treasury," 2 December 1889, Alaska File, RG26.

19. Williams, "Captain Healy," 307.

20. Mrs. M. B. Eden, WCTU, to SECTREAS, 29 January 1890, in "Case of Captain Michael A. Healy," RG26, NARA.

21. Murphy, "Cutter Captain," 45–46.

22. "Case of Captain Michael A. Healy (1890)," 210–11, RG26, NARA.

23. Capt. M. A. Healy to Capt.-Cmdt. L. G. Shepard, 28 April 1890, Alaska File, Ltrs. Received by the USRCS, 1869–1910, RG26, NARA.

24. Quoted in Evans, *U.S. Coast Guard,* 119.

25. Quoted in Williams, "Michael Healy," 382.

26. Dr. Jackson and Capt. Healy noted that the Alaska Commercial Company supposedly brought reindeer into the Aleutian Islands in 1880. Murphy, "Cutter Captain," 50–52; Williams, "Michael Healy," 376–77, 411n.

27. Sheldon Jackson, *Preliminary Report to W. T. Harris, Commissioner of Education, Department of Interior, on the Introduction of Reindeer into Alaska, November 12, 1890* (Washington, D.C.: GPO, 1892).

28. Sheldon Jackson, "Exploring for Reindeer in Siberia: Being the Journal of the Cruise of the U.S. Revenue Steamer Bear," *Journal of the Presbyterian Historical Society* 31, no. 2 (April 1953): 100.

29. Of all the activities of the U.S. Revenue Cutter Service in Alaska, the story of the importation of reindeer has probably received the most attention. The genesis of the idea, as mentioned, is given to many. One of the prevailing accounts, and one given in the past by one of the authors, actually has the idea for the project originating when Jackson and Healy visited the starving natives of King Island. This

apparently comes from a garbled rendition of the first reindeer-buying expedition. The *Bear,* already with the first reindeer on her decks, stopped at King Island and observed the condition of the natives. As is related later in the narrative, Healy dealt with the issue in the only manner he could. The cutter then proceeded on to Indian Point and purchased twelve additional animals. No doubt Jackson and Healy discussed the starvation at King Island after their departure. This is apparently the basis for the one version of the introduction of reindeer into Alaska.

30. Sheldon Jackson to W. T. Harris, commissioner of education, 26 August 1892, quoted in Williams, "Michael Healy," 398.

31. Evans, *U.S. Coast Guard,* 133.

32. The Lapp herders, brought to Alaska in 1898, "were subsequently to stake the richest gold mine claims at Nome a year later." Williams, "Michael Healy," 415n.

33. Ibid., 29.

34. Capt. M. A. Healy to the wardroom officers of the *Bear,* 1 September 1891, quoted in ibid., 394–95.

CHAPTER 4. THE INDOMITABLE *THETIS*

1. Steward B. Nelson, *Oceanographic Ships Fore and Aft* (Washington, D.C.: Office of the Oceanographer of the Navy, 1971), 77; telephone conversation Dennis L. Noble and John Riley, U.S. Navy Historical Center, Ships' Histories, Washington, D.C., 18 August 1976.

2. Farley Mowat, *The Polar Passion* (Boston: Little, Brown, 1967), 161–62; James E. Caswell, *Arctic Frontiers: United States Exploration in the Far North* (Norman: University of Oklahoma Press, 1956), 96–106.

3. Quoted in Caswell, *Arctic Frontiers,* 111–12.

4. Ibid., 113; Mowat, *Polar Passion,* 189, 195–96.

5. A. P. Swineford, *Annual Report of the Governor of Alaska to the Secretary of the Interior for the Fiscal Year 1888,* dated Sitka, Alaska, 1 October 1888.

6. U.S. Coast Guard, *Records of Movements,* 39.

7. Sheldon Jackson, *Ninth Annual Report on Introduction of Domestic Reindeer into Alaska 1899* (Washington, D.C.: GPO, 1900), 131.

8. Log Book of the U.S. Revenue Cutter *Thetis* from 27 May to 30 September 1899, RG26, NARA.

9. Ibid., 10 July 1899.

10. Ibid., 11 July 1899.

11. Ibid., 12 July 1899.

12. Ibid., 13–14 July 1899.

13. Ibid., 15 July 1899.

14. Ibid., 19 July 1899.

15. Ibid., 29 July 1899.

16. Ibid., 23 August 1899.

17. Ibid., 20 July 1899.

18. Ibid., 23 July 1899.

19. Ibid., 28 July 1899.

20. Ibid., 24 July 1899.

21. First Lt. A. Buhner to SECTREAS, 2 October 1899, M641, Roll 8, RG26, NARA.

22. U.S. Coast Guard, *Record of Movements*, 39.

23. First Lt. Buhner to SECTREAS, 2 October 1899, M641, Roll 8, RG26, NARA.

24. U.S. Coast Guard, *Record of Movements*, 39.

25. Ibid., 39–42.

26. U.S. Revenue-Cutter Service, *Annual Report of the U.S. Revenue-Cutter Service for the Fiscal Year Ended June 30, 1912* (Washington, D.C.: GPO, 1913), 88.

27. "The Last Bowhead," an unpublished manuscript in the papers of Rear Admiral James F. Hottel, USCG, U.S. Coast Guard Academy Library, New London, Conn.

28. Captain Michael A. Healy to SECTREAS, 16 July 1902, M641, Roll 9, RG26, NARA.

29. Hottel, "Bowhead," n.p.

30. Ibid., n.p.

31. Captain O. C. Hamlet to SECTREAS, 11 September 1906. A reproduced copy is located in the files of the historian of the U.S. Coast Guard, U.S. Headquarters, Washington, D.C.

32. Ibid.

33. U.S. Coast Guard, *Record of Movements*, 40.

34. USRCS, *Annual Report of the U.S. Revenue-Cutter Service for the Fiscal Year Ended June 30, 1913* (Washington, D.C.: GPO, 1913), 96.

35. "*Thetis*, Honolulu, 1912 [*sic*]," *U.S. Coast Guard Magazine* 4, no. 9 (August 1930): 14.

36. U.S. Revenue Cutter Service, *Annual Report 1913*, 79.

37. U.S. Coast Guard, *Record of Movements*, 42.

38. E. Maunder, Merchant Tailor of St. Johns, Newfoundland, to Captain S. F. Gray, USCG, Chief, Public Affairs Division, 19 September 1950, located in the files of the historian of the U.S. Coast Guard, U.S. Coast Guard Headquarters, Washington, D.C.

39. Ibid.

40. Nelson, *Oceanographic Ships*, 71.

CHAPTER 5. EXPLORING UNCHARTED REGIONS

1. SECTREAS to Capt. W. H. Howard, 4 June 1867, in House Ex. Doc. 177, 40th Cong., 2d Sess., 1868.

2. Capt. W. H. Howard to SECTREAS, 17 August 1867, in ibid.

3. Capt. W. H. Howard to SECTREAS, September 1867, First Report, in ibid.

4. Ibid.

5. First Lt. D. B. Hodgsdon, to Capt. W. A. Howard, 11 September 1867, in ibid.

6. Capt. W. A. Howard to SECTREAS, n.d., Final Report, in ibid.

7. Ibid.; Robert L. Reynold, "Seward's Wise Folly," *American Heritage* 12, no. 1 (December 1960): 108; Byron L. Reed, "The Contributions of the Coast Guard to the Development of Alaska," U.S. Naval Institute *Proceedings* 55, no. 315 (May 1929): 407–8.

8. William Gouverneur Morris, Special Agent of the Treasury Department, to SEC-TREAS, Report on Alaska, 25 November 1878, in Senate Ex. Doc. 59, 45th Cong., 3d Sess., 1879.

9. Quoted in Evans, *U.S. Coast Guard,* 111–12.

10. Leonard F. Guttridge, *Icebound: The* Jeannette *Expedition's Quest for the North Pole* (Annapolis, Md.: Naval Institute Press, 1986), 165; Killey, "Opening the Door to Alaska," 24.

11. Muir, *Cruise of the* Corwin, 44.

12. E. W. Nelson, "Birds of Bering Sea and the Arctic Ocean," 56a, in *Cruise of the Revenue-Steamer* Corwin *in Alaska and the N.W. Arctic Ocean,* House Ex. Doc. 429, 47th Cong., 2d Sess., 1883.

13. I. C. Rosse, "Medical and Anthropological Notes on Alaska," 11–12, in ibid.

14. Muir, *Cruise of the* Corwin, 150.

15. Ibid., 153.

16. Ibid., 155; *National Geographic Magazine,* November 1916, 425.

17. Muir, *Cruise of the* Corwin, 167.

18. John Muir, "Botanical Notes on Alaska," 52–53, in *Cruise of the Revenue-Steamer* Corwin *in Alaska and the N.W. Arctic Ocean,* House Ex. Doc. 429, 47th Cong., 2d. Sess., 1883. The United States did not follow up on Captain Hooper's action by officially recognizing its ownership of this desolate Arctic island, nor did it challenge the Russian czar's later claim of sovereignty. Jonathan M. Nielson, *Armed Forces on a Northern Frontier: The Military in Alaska's History, 1867–1987* (Westport, Conn.: Greenwood Press, 1988), 33–34.

19. Muir, *Cruise of the* Corwin, 220–22.

20. Caswell, *Arctic Frontiers,* 76–82.

CHAPTER 6. LT. JOHN C. CANTWELL, EXPLORER

1. Caswell, *Arctic Frontiers,* 195–99; Morgan B. Sherwood, *Exploration of Alaska 1865–1900* (New Haven: Yale University Press, 1965), 124–31; Evans, *U.S. Coast Guard,* 124–25.

2. Healy, *Cruise of the* Corwin *in 1884,* 49.

3. Evans, *U.S. Coast Guard,* 125.

4. Letter (Ltr.), SECTREAS to Speaker of House of Representatives, 28 February 1885, in Healy, *Cruise of the* Corwin *in 1884,* 3.

5. Third Lt. J. C. Cantwell, "Exploration of the Kowak River, Alaska," in ibid., 54ff.

This work is the source for all citations from Cantwell's first-hand account of his Kowak River expedition, unless otherwise indicated.

6. Ltr. of Transmittal, Capt. M. A. Healy to SECTREAS, 10 November 1884, in ibid., 5.

7. Third Lt. J. C. Cantwell, "Descriptions of Bogoslov Island and the New Volcano in Bering Sea," in ibid., 39–41.

8. Sherwood, *Exploration of Alaska*, 126–27; Caswell, *Arctic Frontiers*, 198–99; Evans, *U.S. Coast Guard*, 126.

9. Capt. M. A. Healy, *Report of the Cruise of the Revenue Marine Steamer* Corwin *in the Arctic Ocean in the Year 1885* (Washington, D.C.: GPO, 1887), 6.

10. Charles H. Townsend, "Notes on the Natural History and Ethnology of Northern Alaska," in ibid., 83, 85–97.

11. Third Lt. John C. Cantwell, "A Narrative Account of the Exploration of the Kowak River, Alaska, 1885," in ibid., 25.

12. Ibid., 34.

13. Ibid., 37ff.

14. Caswell, *Arctic Frontiers*, 198–201; Sherwood, *Exploration of Alaska*, 129–32.

15. Third Lt. Cantwell, "A Narrative Account of the Exploration of the Kowak River, Alaska, 1885," in Healy, *Cruise of the* Corwin *in 1885,* 46.

16. Second Asst. Eng. S. B. McLenegan, "Exploration of the Nhistak River, Alaska," in ibid., 58, 53–76.

17. Healy, *Cruise of the* Corwin *in 1885,* 12.

18. Quoted in Sherwood, *Exploration of Alaska*, 129.

19. Caswell, *Arctic Frontiers*, 215.

20. Ltrs., Capt. M. A. Healy, Commanding *Bear,* to SECTREAS and Capt.-Commandant Leonard G. Shepard, 9 June 1891, both in M641, Roll 2, RG26, NARA; Sherwood, *Exploration of Alaska*, 80.

21. Cantwell, Nunivak *on the Yukon River Station, Alaska, 1899–1901,* 52.

22. Third Lt. Eugene Blake, Jr., "Reconnaissance of the Dall River-Koyukuk Trail, Alaska," in ibid., 250ff.

23. Cantwell, Nunivak *on the Yukon River Station, Alaska, 1899–1901,* 61ff.

24. Second Lt. B. H. Camden, "Reconnaissance of the Koyukuk River, Alaska," in ibid., 239–48.

25. Sherwood, *Exploration of Alaska*, 1–14.

## CHAPTER 7. THE SMITHSONIAN'S NAVY

1. SECTREAS to Capt. W. H. Howard, 4 June 1867, in House Ex. Doc. 177, 40th Cong., 2d Sess., 1868.

2. Healy, *Cruise of the* Corwin *in 1884,* 8.

3. Capt. M. A. Healy, *Bear,* to SECTREAS, 15 October 1885, M641, Roll 1, RG26, NARA.

4. Secretary of the Smithsonian Institution to SECTREAS, 24 April 1899, M641, Roll 8, RG26, NARA.

5. Asst. SECTREAS to Capt. J. F. Wild, *Bear,* Dutch Harbor, Alaska, 11 August 1903, M641, Roll 10, RG26, NARA.

6. Asst. Secretary of the Smithsonian, to Asst. SECTREAS, 18 April 1904, and to Capt. C. F. Shoemaker, Chief, Division of USRCS, 29 July 1904, both in M641, Roll 10, RG26, NARA.

7. Secretary of the Smithsonian Institution to SECTREAS, 7 February 1906, M641, Roll 10, RG26, NARA.

8. Secretary of the Smithsonian Institution to the SECTREAS, 26 February 1906; SECTREAS to Secretary of the Smithsonian Institution, 9 February 1906; both in M641, Roll 10, RG26, NARA.

9. Henry G. Bryant, President, Geographic Society of Philadelphia, to Asst. SEC-TREAS, 17 April 1900, and USRCS written comments on it, M641, Roll 8, RG26, NARA.

10. First Lt. B. H. Camden, to Capt. H. B. Rogers, commanding *McCulloch,* 16 October 1907, forwarding Report on the Bogoslof Island; Ltrs. Received by R.C.S., American Museum of Natural History (18 October 1907), Geographical Society of the Pacific (12 November 1907), Massachusetts Institute of Technology (19 November 1907), and National Geographic Society (23 November 1907); all in M641, Roll 12, RG26, NARA.

11. Prof. Joseph Schafer, University of Oregon, to SECTREAS, 17 May 1905; Senator C. W. Fulton to SECTREAS, 22 May 1905; SECTREAS to Senator C. W. Fulton, 25 May 1905; all in M641, Roll 10, RG26, NARA.

12. Capt. W. H. Roberts, commanding *Perry,* to SECTREAS, 6 July 1905, M641, Roll 10, RG26, NARA.

13. Cantwell, Nunivak *on the Yukon River Station, Alaska, 1899–1901,* 259.

14. Capt. A. J. Henderson, commanding *Thetis,* to SECTREAS, 11 July 1908, forwarding Report on Northern Cruise 9 June–11 July 1908, M641, Roll 12, RG26, NARA.

15. Postmaster General to SECTREAS, 23 July 1909; Inspector in Charge, Post Office Department, Spokane, Washington, 13 July 1909; Acting SECTREAS to Postmaster General, 27 July 1909; Acting SECTREAS to USRCS Captains Commanding the Bering Sea Patrol Fleet and the *Thetis,* 27 July 1909; all in M641, Roll 13, RG26, NARA.

16. Census Office, Alaska Division, to Superintendent of Census, 14 April 1890; Superintendent of Census to SECTREAS, 22 April 1890, with handwritten "Approv'd" on its file, Roll 1; Director of Census to SECTREAS, 18 April & 2 May 1899, Roll 8; M641, RG26, NARA.

17. Capt. A. J. Henderson, commanding *Thetis,* to SECTREAS, 11 July 1908, forwarding Report on Northern Cruise 9 June–11 July 1908, Roll 12; Capt. Calvin

L. Hooper, commanding Bering Sea Fleet, to Capt. M. L. Philips, Commanding *Wolcott,* 27 June 1896, Roll 6; Acting SECTREAS to Capt. O. C. Hamlet, commanding *Bear,* and Bishop P. T. Rowe, Sitka, Alaska, 27 May 1905, Roll 10; all in M641, RG26, NA.

18. Capt. M. A. Healy, commanding *Bear,* to SECTREAS, 5 September 1888, and 9 June 1893, M641, Roll 1 and 3, respectively, RG26, NARA.

19. Capt. W. C. Coulson, commanding *McCulloch,* to SECTREAS, 28 August 1903; Senate Committee on Territories to Capt. W. C. Coulson, 27 August 1903; and Senator N. P. Dillingham to SECTREAS, 30 September 1903; all in M641, Roll 9, RG26, NARA.

20. Chairman, Representative Committee on Industrial Arts and Expositions to SECTREAS, 3 April and his reply of 6 April 1905; Chairman to SECTREAS, 12 April and his reply of 15 April 1905; all in M641, Roll 10, RG26, NARA.

21. Commanding Officer (C.O.), *Grant,* to SECTREAS, 22 July 1899, Roll 8; Senior Captain F. M. Munger, Commanding Bering Sea Patrol, forwarding Report of Asst. Surg. Robert Olesen, U.S. Public Health and Marine Hospital Service (PH & MHS), of Conditions Existing in the Aleut Village in Akutan Harbor, to SECTREAS, 21 July 1908, Roll 12; both in M641, respectively, RG26, NARA.

22. USRCS Chief to Alice Sandford, Women's National Relief Association, 18 May 1905, and her reply a day later; C.O., *Manning,* to SECTREAS, September 1905; all in M641, Roll 10, RG26, NARA.

23. Capt. W. C. Coulson, commanding *McCulloch,* to SECTREAS, 24 December 1900, Roll 9; Morris Marcus, L. Foster & Co., San Francisco, California, to USRCS Chief, 1 June 1905, Roll 10; both in M641, RG 26, NARA.

24. Capt. O. C. Hamlet, commanding *Bear,* to USRCS Chief, 25 March 1906; Henry Koenig, Point Hope, Alaska, to SECTREAS, 6 December 1905; USRCS Chief to Capt. O. C. Hamlet, 21 March 1906; all in M641, Roll 10, RG26, NARA.

25. Interior Secretary to Attorney General, 12 May 1899; Telegram, Governor of Alaska to Interior Secretary, 5 May 1899; Attorney General to SECTREAS, 13 May 1899, with a USRCS handwritten notation on it; all in M641, Roll 8, RG26, NARA.

26. Judge M. C. Brown of the District of Alaska to Attorney General, 16 February 1901; Attorney General to SECTREAS, 7 & 15 March, with a USRCS handwritten notation on the latter one; both in M641, Roll 9, RG26, NARA.

27. U.S. Commissioner, Colville District, Alaska, to USRCS Chief, 8 December 1903, and his reply of 25 February 1904; C.O., *McCulloch,* to SECTREAS, 24 December 1900; all in M641, Roll 9, RG26, NARA.

28. C.O., *Thetis,* to SECTREAS, 24 September 1907, Roll 12; C.O., *Rush,* to Commander Bering Sea Fleet, 5 June 1905, Roll 13; Acting SECTREAS to Secretary of Commerce and Labor, 22 July 1909, Roll 18; Commander Bering Sea Fleet to SECTREAS, 26 August 1909, Roll 13; all in M641, RG26, NARA.

29. Acting SECTREAS to Secretary of Interior, 27 April 1897, Roll 15; Secretary of the Interior to SECTREAS, 22 March 1900, Roll 8; both in M641, RG26, NARA.

30. C.O., *Thetis,* to SECTREAS, 19 August 1903, Roll 9; Bureau of Education to Secretary of Interior, 29 March 1905, Roll 10; Acting SECTREAS to Secretary of Interior, 10 May 1905, Roll 10; all in M641, RG26, NARA.

31. First Asst. Secretary of Interior to SECTREAS, 20 May 1909, and his reply of 22 May 1909, Roll 13; Acting SECTREAS to Secretary of Interior, 10 May 1904, Roll 10; SECTREAS to Secretary of Interior, 30 June 1906, Roll 10; C.O., *Thetis,* to SECTREAS, 2 September 1909, Roll 13; all in M641, RG26, NARA.

32. C.O., *Bear,* to Mr. L. M. Stevenson, School Teacher, Point Barrow, Alaska, 30 July 1893, Roll 3; 3d Lt. C. M. White, to C.O., *Bear,* 18 July 1893, Roll 3; Commander Bering Sea Fleet to SECTREAS, 30 September 1909. Roll 13; all in M641, RG26, NARA.

33. USRCS Chief to C.O., *McCulloch,* and Washington State Member of Congress., House of Representatives, to SECTREAS, both 16 June 1906, M641, Roll 10, RG26, NARA.

34. Secretary of Agriculture to SECTREAS, 26 March 1901, Roll 9; C. C. Georgeson, Special Agent in Charge, Alaska Experiment Stations, to Acting USRCS Chief, 1 May 1900, and C.O., *Perry,* to SECTREAS, 31 October 1899, Roll 8; both in M641, RG26, NARA.

35. Acting Commissioner, Bureau of Fisheries, to Asst. Deputy of Commerce and Labor, 28 April 1906, Roll 10; SECTREAS to Secretary of Commerce and Labor, 17 May 1906, Roll 10; Capt. W. V. E. Jacobs, commanding *Manning,* to SECTREAS, 13 May & 3 June 1909, Roll 13; all in M641, RG26, NARA.

36. Secretary, Department of Commerce and Labor, to SECTREAS, 1 May 1905; M641, Roll 10, RG26, NARA.

37. SECTREAS to President, 16 May 1905, with handwritten comments "Approved May 16th 1905 T. Roosevelt"; Capt. W. H. Roberts, commanding *Perry,* to SECTREAS, 6 September 1905, forwarding Report on Seal & Salmon Fisheries of Alaska; M641, Roll 10, RG26, NARA.

38. Capt. F. Tuttle, commanding *Perry,* to SECTREAS, 24 August 1903, M641, Roll 9, RG26, NARA.

39. War Department to SECTREAS, 11 May 1899, Roll 8; Corps of Engineers, Portland, Oregon, to Light-House Board, 4 May 1906, Roll 10; Asst. SECTREAS to C.O., *Thetis,* 5 May 1906, Roll 10; Supervising Inspector General, Steamboat-Inspection Service, to SECTREAS, 28 March & to USRCS Chief, 1 April 1899, Roll 8; Capt. W. F. Kilmore, commanding *Perry,* to SECTREAS, 21 October 1899, Roll 8; SECTREAS to Interior Secretary, 29 May 1906, Roll 10; all in M641, RG26, NARA.

40. Cantwell, Nunivak *on Yukon River Station, 1899–1901,* 86–87.

41. LeRoy Pelletier to USRCS Chief, 19 November 1902; USRCS Chief's reply to Pelletier, 24 November 1902; M641, Roll 9, RG26, NARA.

42. Director, American Museum of Natural History to Capt. A. J. Henderson, commanding *Thetis,* 22 January 1909; Capt. A. J. Henderson to SECTREAS, 3 February 1909; Acting SECTREAS to Director, American Museum of Natural History, 15 February 1909; M641, Roll 13, RG26, NARA.

43. Capt. A. J. Henderson, commanding *Thetis,* to SECTREAS, 2 November 1907, M641, Roll 12, RG26, NARA.

44. E. deK. Leffingwell, Anglo-American Polar Expedition, Flaxman Island, Alaska, to Superintendent of the U.S. Coast and Geodetic Survey (C&GS), 16 August 1907, M641, Roll 12, RG26, NARA.

45. Superintendent, U.S. C&GS, to USRCS Chief, 8 November 1907, M641, Roll 12, RG26, NARA.

46. RCS Chief to Superintendent, U.S. C&GS, 16 November 1907; Superintendent, U.S. C&GS, to USRCS Chief, 18 March and 21 April 1908; M641, Roll 12, RG26, NARA.

47. USRCS Chief to Mr. Leffingwell, The Quadrangle Club, Chicago, 23 February 1909, M641, Roll 13, RG26, NARA.

48. Consulate of Norway & Sweden to U.S. Collector of Customs, San Francisco, 10 March 1905; SECTREAS to U.S. Collector of Customs, San Francisco, 27 March 1905; Capt. W. H. Roberts, commanding *Perry,* to SECTREAS, 4 September 1905, forwarding 1905 Cruise Rpt. of the *Perry;* M641, Roll 10, RG26, NARA.

49. Acting Secretary, Interior Department, 22 October 1908; Acting SECTREAS to Secretary, Interior Department, 27 October 1908; V. Jochelson to SECTREAS, 31 January 1909; M641, Roll 13, RG26, NARA.

50. Hunt, *Arctic Passages,* 340.

CHAPTER 8. THROUGH ICE AND HOWLING GALE

1. Irving H. King, *The Coast Guard Expands 1865–1915: New Roles, New Frontiers* (Annapolis, Md.: Naval Institute Press, 1996), is the latest to tell this story. Dorothy Jean Ray, *The Eskimos of Bering Strait, 1650–1898* (Seattle: University of Washington Press, 1975), is the first to question the necessity of the importation of reindeer and of the overland expedition; it should be examined by anyone wishing to look at the whole story.

2. Capt. George E. Bailey, U.S. Revenue Marine (USRM), *Report upon Alaska and Its People* (Washington, D.C.: GPO, 1880)· 18.

3. Information on the sled expedition may be found in 1st Lt. W. J. Herring, to Capt. C. L. Hooper, commanding *Corwin* at sea in Arctic Ocean, 30 June 1881, submitting Report on the Preparations for the Expedition by Dog Sledges along the Siberian Coast, M641: Roll 2, RG26, NARA; Muir, *Cruise of the* Corwin, 47–49.

4. Muir, *Cruise of the* Corwin, 92–98.

5. *Ibid.,* 67–69, 72, 73, 144, 145, 184–86.

6. Healy, *Cruise of the* Corwin *in 1884,* 8, 9.

7. *Ibid.*, 13.

8. *Ibid.*, 14, 15.

9. Capt. M. A. Healy, commanding *Bear*, to SECTREAS, 5 September 1888, M641, Roll 1, RG26, NARA.

10. Masters of Wrecked Schooner *Jane Grey* and Barks *Young Phoenix, Fleetwing*, and *Mary & Susan* to SECTREAS, 5 September 1888, M641, Roll 1, RG26, NARA.

11. "List of vessels lost in the Bering Sea, summer of 1900," compiled by 2d Lt. William E. H. Lee of the *Manning*, San Francisco, California, 24 December 1900, M641, Roll 9, RG26, NARA.

12. Capt. W. C. Coulson, commanding *McCulloch*, to SECTREAS, 24 December 1900, forwarding 1900 Bering Sea Cruise Report, M641, Roll 9, RG26, NARA.

13. Capt. M. A. Healy, commanding *Thetis*, to SECTREAS, 16 July 1902, forwarding Report of Search for Missing Steamers *Portland* and *Jeanie*, M641, Roll 19, RG26, NARA.

14. Capt. W. C. Coulson, commanding *McCulloch*, to SECTREAS, 22 July 1903, forwarding Report on Rescue of Boat Crew of Japanese Sealing Schooner *"Sifu Maru,"* M641, Roll 9, RG26, NARA.

15. Capt. M. A. Healy, commanding *Thetis*, to SECTREAS, 12 September 1903, reporting progress on the annual 1903 Northern Cruise, M641 Roll 9, RG26, NARA.

16. Capt. F. M. Munger, commanding Bering Sea Patrol, to SECTREAS, 15 September 1907, confirming his telegram of same date concerning the *Thetis, McCulloch*, and shipwrecked persons, M641, Roll 12, RG26, NARA.

17. Capt. F. M. Munger, commanding Bering Sea Patrol Fleet, to SECTREAS, 22 November 1907, submitting Report of Operations for the 1907 Season; Capt. A. J. Henderson, commanding *Thetis*, to SECTREAS, 24 September 1907, forwarding Synopsis of Work Performed by *Thetis* from 23 July to 15 September 1907; both M641, Roll 12, RG26, NARA.

18. Capt. A. J. Henderson, commanding *Thetis*, to SECTREAS, 23 November 1908, forwarding Northern Cruise Report, 11 July to 18 November 1908, M641, Roll 12, RG26, NARA.

19. Capt. A. J. Henderson, commanding *Thetis*, to SECTREAS, 11 July 1908, forwarding Northern Cruise Report, 9 June to 11 July 1908, M641, Roll 12, RG26, NARA.

20. Capt. A. J. Henderson, commanding *Thetis*, to SECTREAS, 12 November 1909, forwarding Report of 1909 Cruise in Northern Waters, M641, Roll 13, RG26, NARA.

CHAPTER 9. DOCTORS, NATIVES, AND CUTTERS

1. Evans, *U.S. Coast Guard*, 192; King, *U.S. Coast Guard Expands*, 152.

2. Granted the few published cruise reports of the revenue cutters in the last century often

contained lengthy, detailed reports of the ship's surgeon, such as the well-written 1881 report for the *Corwin*, but they were printed about a hundred years ago. The few surviving copies are extremely hard to find apart from the Library of Congress.

3. Asst. Surg. Robert White, U.S. Marine Hospital Service (USMHS), "Notes on the Physical Conditions of the Inhabitants of Alaska," in Capt. George W. Bailey, U.S. Revenue Marine (USRM), *Report upon Alaska and Its People* (Washington, D.C.: GPO, 1880), 41–49.

4. Healy, *Cruise of the* Corwin *in 1885,* 5ff.

5. Capt. M. A. Healy to SECTREAS, 15 October 1885, M641, Roll l, RG26, NARA.

6. Healy, *Cruise of the* Corwin *in 1885,* 11ff.

7. Ibid., 17.

8. Fleet Surg. Gardiner P. Pond, USRCS, to Capt. C. L. Hooper, Commanding Bering Sea Fleet, 17 September 1897, forwarding his 1897 Report for Hospital at Dutch Harbor, M641, Roll 7, RG26, NARA.

9. Capt. C. L. Hooper, Commanding Bering Sea Fleet, to SECTREAS, 18 September 1887, M641, Roll 7, RG 26, NARA.

10. Bailey, *Report upon Alaska and Its People,* 24.

11. Capt. A. J. Henderson to SECTREAS, 12 November 1909, M641, Roll 13, RG26, NARA.

12. Surg. R. N. Hawley, USRCS, to 1st Lt. D. H. Jarvis, commanding Bear, 11 November 1899, forwarding his Report of Medical and Surgical Cases—Arctic Cruise 1899, M641, Roll 8, RG26, NARA.

13. Surg. James T. White, USRCS, to Capt. M. A. Healy, commanding *McCulloch,* 26 June 1900, forwarding his Report of Health and Sanitation, M641, Roll 9, RG26, NARA.

14. Cantwell, Nunivak *on the Yukon River Station, 1899–1901,* 10.

15. Surg. James T. White, USRCS, "Report of the Medical Officer of the U.S. Steamer *Nunivak,* Yukon River, Alaska," in ibid., 258ff.

16. Ibid., 271.

17. Ibid., 274.

18. Capt. Charles C. Fengar and Surg. Howson W. Cole, Jr., USRCS, to SECTREAS, 31 December 1903, forwarding the Medical Report of the Rush from 13 July 1903 to 1 January 1904, M641, Roll 9, RG26, NARA.

19. Surg. Henry Horn, USRCS, to SECTREAS, 2 November 1904, forwarding his Medical and Surgical Report of the U.S. Revenue Steamer *McCulloch* from 30 June to 2 November 1904, M641, Roll 10, RG26, NARA.

CHAPTER 10. LAW ENFORCERS OR HUMANITARIANS?

1. Evans, *U.S. Coast Guard,* 106; Nelson, *Armed Forces on a Northern Frontier,* 3,4, 10–14; Claus-M. Naske, *A History of Alaska Statehood* (Lanham, Md.: University

Press of America, 1985), 1–13; Claus-M. Naske and Herman E. Slotnick, *Alaska, A History of the 49th State* (Norman: University of Oklahoma Press, 1987): 63–99.

2. Capt. J. M. Selden, commanding *Wolcott,* to SECTREAS, 3 March 1879, M-641, Roll l, RG 26, NARA; Truman R. Strobridge and Bernard C. Nalty, "When the Navy Ruled Alaska," *Navy, The Magazine of Sea Power* 10, no. 1 (January 1967): 20–21, 37–38; Morgan B. Sherwood, "Ardent Spirits: Hooch and the Osprey Affair at Sitka," *Journal of the West* 4, no. 3 (July 1965): 301–44; Nielson, *Armed Forces on a Northern Frontier,* 29–34.

3. Melody Webb, *The Last Frontier* (Albuquerque: University of New Mexico Press, 1985), 3, 123–41, 154, 248; Naske and Slotnick, *Alaska,* 86, 87, 92, 94–96.

4. Bailey, USRM, *Report upon Alaska and Its People,* 3–5, passim.

5. Ibid., 26.

6. Capt. W. H. Howard, SECTREAS, 17 August 1867, in House Ex. Doc. 177, 40th Cong., 2d Sess., 1867; Nielson, *Armed Forces on a Northern Frontier,* 14–16.

7. King, *The Coast Guard Expands,* 28; Roland L. De Lorme, "Liquor Smuggling in Alaska, 1867–1899," *Pacific Northwest Quarterly* 66, no. 4 (October 1975): 145–52; Williams, "Michael Healy," 228–31.

8. Nora and William Kelly, *The Royal Canadian Mounted Police: A Century of History 1873–1973* (Edmonton, Alb.: Hurtig, 1973): 20–22, 53–70; Major James P. Tate, USAF, ed., *The American Military on the Frontier: The Proceedings of the 7th Military History Symposium, U.S. Air Force Academy, 30 September–l October 1976* (Washington, D.C.: Office of Air Force History and USAF Academy, 1978), 15, 17, 18, 35, 48, 49, 57.

9. Wm. Gouverneur Morris, Collector, Custom House, Sitka, Alaska, to SECTREAS, 9 November 1882, M641, Roll l, RG26, NARA; Nielson, *Armed Forces on a Northern Frontier,* 32–34; Williams, "Michael Healy," 100–107.

10. Capt. A. J. Henderson, commanding *Thetis,* to SECTREAS, 5 October 1907, M641, Roll 12, RG26, NARA.

11. H. R. Thornton, American Missionary Association, New York, to SECTREAS, 15 January 1892, M641, Roll 2, RG26, NARA; Theodore C. Hinckley, "Publicist of the Forgotten Frontier," *Journal of the West* 4, no. 1 (January 1965): 27–40.

12. The *Nome Semi-Weekly Nugget,* August 10, 1904, p. 2.

13. First Lt. M. A. Healy, commanding *Rush,* to SECTREAS, 14 September 1881, M641, Roll 1, RG26, NARA.

14. Capt. O. C. Hamlet, commanding *Thetis,* to SECTREAS, 14 November 1904, M641, Roll 10, RG26, NARA.

15. Capt. A. J. Henderson, commanding *Thetis,* to SECTREAS, 23 November 1908, M641, Roll 12, RG26, NARA; Williams, "Michael Healy," 210–13, 241, 242; Capt. Stanley V. Parker, USCG, compiler, *Alaska Commissioners' Manual for the use of Coast Guard Officers acting as U.S. Commissioners* (San Francisco, Calif.: U.S.

Coast Guard, 1937); Mr. Edward J. Knapp, Former Alaskan Missionary, *Memorandum: Notes on Certain Features of the Eskimo Problem in Alaska* (New York: 1907), being a twenty-eight-page, uncopyrighted pamphlet; U.S. Coast Guard, *Records of Movements*, 40; Commodore Byron L. Reed, USCG (Ret.), "The Contribution of the Coast Guard to the Development of Alaska," U.S. Naval Institute *Proceedings* 55, no. 315 (May 1929): 410.

16. Capt. J. A. Henderson, commanding *Thetis*, to Collector of Customs, San Francisco, California, 27 July 1907, M641, Roll 12, RG26, NARA.

17. Capt. J. A. Henderson, commanding *Thetis*, to SECTREAS, 15 September 1907, M641, Roll 12, RG26, NARA.

18. John G. Brady, Governor of Alaska, to Secretary of the Interior, 22 November 1905, M641, Roll 10, RG26, NARA.

19. Quoted in, Evans, *U.S. Coast Guard*, 111–12.

20. Ibid., 120.

CHAPTER 11. "A LOT OF WARDROOM CARPING AND COMPLAINING"

1. Paul H. Johnson, "Portrait of Captain Michael A. Healy, Part III," *U.S. Coast Guard Academy Alumni Bulletin* 41, no. 3 (May–June 1979): 30.

2. Williams, "Michael Healy," 4–6.

3. Charges Against RCS Officers, Seamen and Vessels, Legal Cases, ca. 1830–1896. General Court, Capt. M. A. Healy, 1896, Box 10, RG26, NARA, hereinafter, "General Court, Healy."

4. Ibid.

5. Ibid.; Williams, "Michael Healy," 6–7.

6. Williams, "Michael Healy," 7–9.

7. Ibid., 9–13; "General Court, Healy."

8. "General Court, Healy."

9. Ibid.

10. Ibid.

11. Williams, "Michael Healy," 20–21.

12. Ibid., 419–20.

13. Ibid.

14. Ibid., 418.

15. Ibid., 428.

16. Ibid., 421–22; quoted in ibid., 426–27.

17. Ibid., 424–25.

18. Ibid., 432.

19. Lt. Cdr. Frank A. Garforth, Royal Navy, to Healy, 25 November 1895; Healy to SECTREAS, 2 December 1895, enclosing letter of Garforth; Garforth to Carlisle, 12 December 1895, RG26, NARA.

20. Williams, "Michael Healy," 433.

21. Quoted in Mary and Albert Cocke, "Hell Roaring Mike: A Fall from Grace in the Frozen North," *Smithsonian* 13, no. 11 (February 1983): 119.

22. Unless otherwise noted, all quotes concerning the trial are in "General Court, Healy."

23. Coxe and Coxe, "Hell Roaring Mike," 132.

24. Williams, "Michael Healy," 443.

25. Lt. L. T. Reynolds to SECTREAS, 26 January 1896; Hamlin to Buhner, 30 January 1896; RG26, NARA.

26. *San Francisco Chronicle,* 14 February 1896.

27. Williams, "Michael Healy," 134.

28. Ibid., 443.

29. "General Court, Healy"; Williams, "Michael Healy," 444–45.

30. Charles S. Hamlin Papers, Diary, Manuscript Collections, Library of Congress, Washington, D.C., 245–46.

31. Quoted in Williams, "Michael Healy," 430.

32. James M. O'Toole, "Racial Identity and the Case of Captain Michael Healy, USRCS," *Prologue: Quarterly of the National Archives and Records Service* 29, no. 3 (fall 1997): 199.

33. Bishop James Healy's biographer, Father Albert S. Foley, notes that James at first concealed his African-American heritage, then seemed to try to advance in the church without hiding it but doing nothing to call attention to it. It appears that most of his parishioners knew of his heritage, but Bishop James "did discourage research into his life and his background. To a young man who wished to write his biography, he wrote stiffly that all he wished to be published about himself had already appeared in Appleton's *Cyclopedia of Biography.* There his mother is described as a scion of an aristocratic Southern family, which no doubt was literally true. With reason, James shunted off all inquiries about the family background by saying that his mother was from Santo Domingo (a not too unlikely surmise), or that she was from an old Virginia family. At all costs, he was concerned with drawing a veil over the slave background, keeping it as a family secret even from his younger brothers and sisters." Foley, *Bishop Healy: Beloved Outcaste,* 109, 217–18.

34. Truman R. Strobridge, "West Point, Thayer & Partridge," *Military Review* 49, no. 10 (October 1989): 85.

35. Johnson, "Portrait of Captain Michael A. Healy, Part III," 29.

36. Coulson to SECTREAS, 25 May 1900; Healy to SECTREAS, 28 May 1900, Letters Received by the U.S. Revenue Cutter Service, Box 90, RG26, NARA.

37. Quoted in Gary C. Stein, "A Desperate and Dangerous Man: Captain Michael A. Healy's Arctic Cruise of 1900," *The Alaska Journal* 15, no. 2 (spring 1985): 40.

38. All material on the happenings aboard the *McCulloch,* unless otherwise noted, is found in "Log of USS *McCulloch,* May 28–December 23, 1900," RG26, NARA.

39. Quoted in Stein, "A Desperate and Dangerous Man," 43.

40. Physicians Certificate. Healy Case. Jefferson County Probate No. 241, Jefferson County, Courthouse, Port Townsend, Washington.
41. Stein, "A Desperate and Dangerous Man," 44.
42. Ibid.
43. Michael's immediate family all died within eight years of his passing. Mary Healy died in 1907 and son Fred in 1912. Material on deaths of family obtained from gravestones. U.S. Revenue Cutter Service Register of Officers, vol. 3 (1886–1901), 20; vol. 4 (1895–1905), 37.
44. Foley, *Bishop Healy: Beloved Outcaste,* 237, 240–42.
45. Johnson, "Portrait of Captain Michael A. Healy, Part III," 30.
46. At the launching, something went wrong with the side launch and a large wave showered many people with water, mud, and debris. There were some injuries. A few superstitious sailors noted that Healy may have tried to get even for his treatment. It seems that the name Healy is once again causing officials problems.

EPILOGUE

1. The best source for the work of the *Unalga* is the reports of Capt. F. G. Dodge in "Report of Operations of *Unalga* during Influenza Epidemic," RG26, NARA.
2. Robert Erwin Johnson, *Bering Sea Escort: Life Aboard a Coast Guard Cutter in World War II* (Annapolis, Md.: Naval Institute Press, 1992), see esp. 13–34.
3. Dennis L. Noble, *Recollections of Vice Admiral J. E. Stika, U.S. Coast Guard, Retired: On The Revenue Cutter Service and Bering Sea Patrol* (Washington, D.C.: U.S. Coast Guard Headquarters, 1975): 40–41.
4. Press Release 59-64, 4 September 1964, p. 1, in Historical Files, U.S. Coast Guard Headquarters.
5. USCGC *Storis* (WMEC-38) News Releases 01-97 and 04-97, 20 February 1997, and 27 May 1997, provided Dennis L. Noble by BMC Richard Belise, U.S. Coast Guard Cutter *Storis.*
6. U.S. Coast Guard, *Bering Sea Patrol* (Washington: Research and Statistics Section, Operations Division, U.S. Coast Guard, 1942).
7. Noble, *Vice Admiral J. E. Stika,* 40.
8. Officers of the Bering Sea Patrol, *Below Zero: Songs and Verses from Bering and the Arctic* (New London, Conn.: U.S. Coast Guard Academy Alumni Association, 1939): 6–7.

# Selected Bibliography

ARCHIVAL MATERIAL

Library of Congress, Washington, D.C., Manuscript Collections
    Papers of Charles S. Hamlin
Presbyterian Historical Society, Philadelphia, Pa.
    Sheldon Jackson Scrapbooks
U.S. Coast Guard Academy Library, New London, Conn.
    Papers of Rear Admiral James F. Hottel, U.S. Coast Guard Headquarters
Historian of the U.S. Coast Guard, Washington, D.C.
    Alaska Files
    Bering Sea Patrol Files
    Biography Files
    Cutter Files
U.S. National Archives and Records Administration, Washington, D.C. All materials
    cited are in Record Group 26, Records of the U.S. Coast Guard
    Alex V. Frazer File
    Alaska File, Microfilm M641, Rolls 1–19.
    Applicant File
    Case of Captain Michael A. Healy (1890)
    Charges against RCS Officers, Seamen and Vessels, Legal Cases, ca. 1830–96.
        General Court, Capt. M. A. Healy, 1896.
    Commissions Revenue Cutter Officers, 1812–44
    General File, U.S. Revenue Cutter Service, 1910–22
    Letter Books
    Log Books of various U.S. Revenue Cutter Service Cutters

Scrapbook, U.S. Revenue Cutter Service, Alaska
U.S. Revenue Cutter Service Register of Officers (Service records)
William A. Howard File

BOOKS, ARTICLES, AND MISCELLANEOUS

Bailey, George E. *Report upon Alaska and Its People.* Washington, D.C.: GPO, 1880.

Bailey, Thomas A. "The North Pacific Sealing Convention of 1911." *Pacific Historical Review* 4, no. 1 (1935): 1–14.

Bauer, K. Jack. *Surfboats and Horse Marines: U.S. Naval Operations in the Mexican War, 1846–1848.* Annapolis, Md.: Naval Institute Press, 1969.

Baxter, James Phinney, III. *The Introduction of the Ironclad Warship.* Cambridge: Harvard University Press, 1933.

Bemis, Samuel Flagg. *A Diplomatic History of the United States.* New York: Holt, Rinehart and Winston, 1967.

Bockstoce, John. "The Arctic Whaling Disaster of 1897." *Prologue:* The *Journal of the National Archives* (spring 1977): 27–42.

Browning, Robert M. "The Lasting Injury: The Revenue Marine's First Steam Cutters." *American Neptune* (winter 1992): 25–37.

Campbell, Charles S., Jr. "The Anglo-American Crisis in the Bering Sea, 1890–1891." *Mississippi Valley Historical Review* 47 (December 1961): 393–414.

Canney, Donald L. *U.S. Coast Guard and Revenue Cutters, 1790–1935.* Annapolis, Md.: Naval Institute Press, 1995.

Cantwell, J[ohn] C. *Report of the Operations of the U.S. Revenue Cutter Steamer "Nunivak" on the Yukon River Station, Alaska, 1899–1901.* Washington, D.C.: GPO, 1902.

Capron, Walter C. *The U.S. Coast Guard.* New York: Franklin Watts, 1965.

Caswell, John Edwards. *Arctic Frontiers: United States Explorations in the Far North.* Norman: University of Oklahoma Press, 1956.

Cocke, Mary and Albert. "Hell Roaring Mike: A Fall from Grace in the Frozen North." *Smithsonian* 13, no. 1 (February 1983): 119–37.

Completed Questionnaire F. S. Sandel. 1977. In author's files.

Eames, Aled, Lewis Lloyd, and Bryn Parry, eds. *Letters from America: Captain David Evans of Talsarnau.* Denbigh, Wales: Gwynedd Archives Service, 1975.

Evans, Robley D. *A Sailor's Log: Recollections of Forty Years of Naval Life.* New York: Appleton, 1901.

Evans, Stephen H. *The United States Coast Guard, 1790–1915: A Definitive History (with a Postscript. 1915–1949).* Annapolis, Md.: Naval Institute Press, 1949.

Foley, Albert J. *Bishop Healy: Beloved Outcaste.* New York: Farrar, Straus, and Young, 1954.

Gay, James Thomas. *American Fur Seal Diplomacy: The Alaskan Fur Seal Controversy.* New York: Peter Lang, 1987.

Guttridge, Leonard F. *Icebound: The* Jeannette *Expedition's Quest for the North Pole.* Annapolis, Md.: Naval Institute Press, 1986.

Hammersly, Thomas H. *General Register of the United States Navy and Marine Corps for One Hundred Years (1782–1882)*. Washington, D.C.: GPO, 1882.

Healy, Michael A. *Report of the Cruise of the Revenue Steamer* Corwin *in the Arctic Ocean in the Year 1884*. Washington, D.C.: GPO, 1889.

——. *Report of the Cruise of the Revenue Steamer* Corwin *in the Arctic Ocean in the Year 1885*. Washington, D.C.: GPO, 1887.

Hinckley, Theodore C. "Punitive Action at Angoon." *Alaskan Sportsman* 39 (January 1963): 8–9, 43–45.

——. "Rustlers of the North Pacific." *Journal of the West* 2, no. 1 (January 1963): 22–30.

Hooper, Calvin L. *Report of the Cruise of the Revenue Steamer* Corwin *in the Arctic Ocean, 1880*. Washington, D.C.: GPO, 1881.

——. *Report of the Cruise of the Revenue Steamer* Corwin *in the Arctic Ocean, 1881*. Washington, D.C.: GPO, 1882.

Hunt, William R. *Arctic Passage: The Turbulent History of the Land and People of the Bering Sea*. New York: Charles Scribner's Sons, 1975.

Jackson, Sheldon. "Exploring for Reindeer in Siberia: Being the Journal of the Cruise of the U.S. Revenue Steamer *Bear.*" *Journal of the Presbyterian Society* 31, no. 1 (March 1953): 1–112.

——. *Preliminary Report to W.T. Harris, Commissioner of Education, Department of the Interior, on the Introduction of Reindeer into Alaska, November 12, 1890*. Washington, D.C.: GPO, 1892.

James, James Alton. *The First Scientific Exploration of Russian America and the Purchase of Alaska*. Evanston, Ill., and Chicago: Northwestern University, 1942.

Johnson, Paul H. "Portrait of Captain Michael A. Healy, Part III." *U.S. Coast Guard Academy Alumni Bulletin* 41, no. 3 (May–June 1979): 3–30.

Johnson, Robert Erwin. *Bering Sea Escort: Life Aboard a Coast Guard Cutter in World War II*. Annapolis, Md.: Naval Institute Press, 1992.

——. *Guardians of the Sea: History of the United States Coast Guard, 1915 to the Present*. Annapolis, Md.: Naval Institute Press, 1987.

Kern, Florence. *The United States Revenue Cutters in the Civil War*. Washington, D.C.: GPO, 1988.

Killey, Gwen L. "Opening the Door to Alaska: The Cruises of the Revenue Cutter *Thomas Corwin.*" *Naval History Magazine* 2, no. 4 (fall 1988): 23–27.

King, Irving H. *The Coast Guard Expands, 1865–1915: New Roles, New Frontiers*. Annapolis, Md.: Naval Institute Press, 1996.

——. *The Coast Guard under Sail: The Revenue Cutter Service, 1789–1865*. Annapolis, Md.: Naval Institute Press, 1989.

——. *George Washington's Coast Guard: Origins of the U.S. Revenue Cutter Service, 1789–1801*. Annapolis, Md.: Naval Institute Press, 1978.

Martin, Fredericka. *The Hunting of the Silver Fleece*. New York: Greenberg, 1946.

Mowat, Farley. *The Polar Passion*. Boston: Little, Brown, 1967.

Muir, John. *The Cruise of the* Corwin: *Journal of the Arctic Expedition of 1881 in Search of DeLong and the* Jeannette. Boston: Houghton Mifflin Company, 1917.

Murphy, John F. "Cutter Captain: The Life and Times of John C. Cantwell." Ph.D. diss., University of Connecticut, 1968.

Naval Historical Foundation. *The Incredible Overland Rescue*. Washington, D.C.: Naval Historical Foundation, 1968.

Nelson, Jonathan M. *Armed Forces on a Northern Frontier: The Military in Alaska's History, 1867–1987*. Westport, Conn.: Greenwood Press, 1988.

Nelson, Steward B. *Oceanographic Ships Fore and Aft*. Washington, D.C.: Office of the Oceanographer of the Navy, 1971.

Noble, Dennis L. "Fog, Reindeer, and the Bering Sea Patrol, 1867–1964." In *The Sea in Alaska's Past: First Conference Proceedings*, 112–54. Anchorage, Alaska: Office of History and Archaeology, 1979.

——. *Gulf Coast and Western Rivers: A Brief History of Coast Guard Operations*. Washington, D.C.: U.S. Coast Guard Headquarters, 1989.

———. *Historical Register U.S. Revenue Cutter Service Officers: 1790–1914*. Washington, D.C.: U.S. Coast Guard, 1990.

——. *Recollections of Vice Admiral J. E. Stika, U.S. Coast Guard, Retired: On The Revenue Cutter Service and Bering Sea Patrol*. Washington, D.C.: U.S. Coast Guard Headquarters, 1975.

——. *That Others Might Live: The U.S. Life-Saving Service, 1878–1915*. Annapolis, Md.: Naval Institute Press, 1994.

Noble, Dennis L., and Truman R. Strobridge. "The Arctic Adventures of the *Thetis*." *Arctic: Journal of the Arctic Institute of North America* 30, no. 1 (March 1977): 2–12.

——. "Early Cuttermen in Alaskan Waters." *Pacific Northwest Quarterly* 48, no. 3 (July 1987): 74–82.

——. "U.S. Revenue Cutter *Tahoma:* Pride of the Bering Sea Patrol." *Explorer's Journal: Official Quarterly Journal of the Explorers Club* 57, no. 1 (March 1979): 10–14.

Officers of the Bering Sea Patrol. *Below Zero: Songs and Verses from Bering Sea and the Arctic*. New London, Conn.: U.S. Coast Guard Academy Alumni Association, 1939.

Orth, David J. *Dictionary of Alaska Place Names*. Washington, D.C.: GPO, 1967.

O'Toole, James M. "Racial Identity and the Case of Captain Michael Healy, USRCS." *Prologue: Quarterly of the National Archives and Records Service* 29, no. 3 (fall 1997): 190–201.

Ransom, M. A., and Eloise Kathenne Engle. *Sea of the Bear: Journal of a Voyage to Alaska and the Arctic, 1921*. Annapolis, Md.: Naval Institute Press, 1964.

Ray, Dorothy Jean. *The Eskimos of Bering Strait, 1650–1898*. Seattle: University of Washington Press, 1975.

Reed, Byron L. "The Contributions of the Coast Guard to the Development of Alaska." *U.S. Naval Institute Proceedings* 55, no. 315 (May 1929): 406–10.

Reynold, Robert L. "Seward's Wise Folly." *American Heritage* 12, no. 1 (December 1960): 44–47, 103–8.

Shepard, Isabel S. "In Olden Days." *U.S. Coast Guard Magazine* 2, no. 10 (August 1929): 3–4, 42–44.

Shepard, Isabel S. *The Cruise of the U.S. Steamer "Rush" in Behring Sea: Summer of 1889.* San Francisco: Bancroft Company, 1889.

Sherwood, Morgan B. *Exploration of Alaska, 1865–1900.* New Haven: Yale University Press, 1965.

Smith, Horatio Davis. *Early History of the United States Revenue Marine Service (or United States Revenue Cutter Service) 1790–1849.* Washington, D.C.: Naval Historical Foundation, 1932.

Stein, Gary C. "A Desperate and Dangerous Man: Captain Michael A. Healy's Arctic Cruise of 1900." *Alaska Journal* 15, no. 2 (spring 1985): 39–45.

Strobridge, Truman R. "Early Lake Captains, Revenue Cutters, and Politics." *Inland Seas: Quarterly Journal of the Great Lakes Historical Society* 29, no. 1 (winter 1973): 240–48.

——. "West Point, Thayer & Partridge." *Military Review* 69, no. 10 (October 1989): 78–86.

Strobridge, Truman R., and Dennis L. Noble. "Cuttermen and Indians: Early Coast Guardsmen and the Yakima Indian War." *U.S. Coast Guard Academy Alumni Association Bulletin* 45, no. 2 (March/April 1983): 30–37.

——. "North in the Spring, South in the Fall." *Alaska Journal* 8, no. 1 (winter 1976): 60–69.

——. "The *Perry* Takes a Poacher." In *The Alaska Journal: A 1981 Collection,* edited by Virginia McKinney, 35–38. Anchorage: Alaska Northwest Publishing Company, 1981.

——. "Polar Icebreakers of the United States Coast Guard." *Polar Record: Journal of the Scott Polar Research Institute* 18, no. 115 (January 1977): 351–60.

"*Thetis,* Honolulu, 1912 [*sic*]." *U.S. Coast Guard Magazine* 4, no. 9 (August 1930): 14.

U.S. Coast Guard. *Bering Sea Patrol.* Washington, D.C.: Research and Statistics Section, Operations Division, U.S. Coast Guard, 1942.

——. *The Coast Guard at War: Alaska.* Washington, D.C.: U.S. Coast Guard Headquarters, 1946.

——. *Record of Movements: Vessels of the United States Coast Guard, 1790–December 31, 1933,* 2 vols. Washington, D.C.: U.S. Coast Guard, [1935?].

U.S. Revenue Cutter Service. *The United States Revenue Cutter Service in the War with Spain.* Washington, D.C.: GPO, 1899.

Van Nostrand, Jeanne. "The Seals Are About Gone." *American Heritage* (June 1963): 10–17, 78–80.

White, Richard D. "Saga of the Side-Wheel Steamer *Shubrick:* Pioneer Lighthouse Tender of the Pacific Coast." *American Neptune* 36 (spring 1976): 45–53.

Williams, Gerald O. *The Bering Sea Dispute: A Monograph on the Maritime History of Alaska*. Eugene, Ore.: Alaska Maritime Publications, 1984.

——. "Michael J. [*sic*] Healy and the Alaska Maritime Frontier, 1880–1902." Master's thesis, University of Oregon, 1987.

NEWSPAPERS

*San Francisco Chronicle*
*Seattle Times*

# Index

# ABOUT THE AUTHORS

A native of Sault Sainte Marie, Michigan, Truman R. Strobridge served in the merchant marine and the U.S. Army Air Forces. He holds degrees in geography and history and has taught at the University of Alaska. He worked as an archivist and historian in the federal government for more than thirty years and has held positions with the Army, National Archives, Marine Corps, Joint Chiefs of Staff, and unified combatant commands in Alaska, Europe, and the Pacific. He was the Coast Guard historian from 1970 to 1976 and is the author of nearly one hundred articles and two books.

Dennis L. Noble entered the U.S. Coast Guard in 1957 and retired as a senior chief marine science technician in 1978. Sea duty took him to the Arctic six times, including two Bering Sea Patrols, and to the Antarctic twice. Since his retirement he has earned a Ph.D. in U.S. history from Purdue University and has worked as a park ranger, a U.S. Army historian, and a prison and public librarian. Now a resident of Sequim, Washington, he is the author of *Lighthouses and Keepers: The U.S. Lighthouse Service and Its Legacy* and *That Others Might Live: The U.S. Life-Saving Service, 1878–1915*, both published by the Naval Institute Press.